AND THEN
THERE WERE NONE

By   E. M. HAZELL

TABLE OF CONTENTS

FORWARD iii
DEDICATION iv
MANNHEIM 1
THE VILLAGE 7
THE THIRD REICH 10
THE CLAY DIGS, PART I 19
CHILDREN OF THE RING 24
G6.13-16 29
A VERY SPECIAL GIFT 31
KRISTALL NACHT 36
EXCURSIONS OF THE MIND 41
DISASTER 54
A DISPUTE AMONG NATIONS 64
A WOMAN'S DUTY 71
CHEMICAL WARFARE 76
APPETITES 82
AIR WARFARE 87
STALINGRAD 94
ASSASSINATION ATTEMPT 107
OLD HEIDELBERG 118
RAVAGED CITY 123
SAILOR 132
BRUCHSAL 138
AMICABLE COEXISTENCE 143
CHRISTMAS, 1943 148
FRANZISKA'S PLACE 153
GRANDMOTHER 156
ALSATIANS AND AUDITIONS 162
RUSSIA 167
LAKE CONSTANCE 173
DEATH AD INFINITUM 179
STUTTGART 183

i

REQUIEM 195
NO-MAN'S-LAND 204
JUDAS 212
SOLDIER/WORKER 218
THE ENEMY 226
APOCALYPSE 231
THE CLAY DIGS, PART II 240
DEATH THROES 248
SURRENDER 253
MOROCCANS 260
SENTIMENTAL JOURNEY 270
AUSCHWITZ 275
EMIGRANT-AUSWANDERER 283
DENAZIFICATION 286
WARBRIDE 291
OUTCAST 297
HOMECOMING 302

FOREWARD BY ALVA LEE HAZELL, JR.

And Then There Were None was written by my mother, Elsa Hazell, when she was in her late 50's. She had a photographic memory for details and events. In this biography she recounts events leading up to, and including, the eventual decline of Hitler. She recalls with vivid detail some of the horrific events that shaped her view of the world, and her search for a better life. She never discussed any of the following events and horrors of war with any of her family until she wrote this piece of history. After we had become young adults we were made aware of that part of her life that had remained private and personal for so many years. As you read *And Then There Were None,* know that there is nothing in it that is fictionalized. It takes you on a journey through the mind, heart, and eyes of a young adult as she finds herself in the middle of a war torn country filled with scared and hungry people. The politics of bigotry and fear, along with the anger of a nation, became the fuel that ignited a fire that scorched a continent. E. M. Hazell speaks of this in a clear and concise method as she recalls her life in this book.

Her second book, *Finding America: The Junior Chronicles*, is a sequel to *And Then There Were None.*

DEDICATION BY AUTHOR

This book is dedicated to the fifty-seven million men, women, and children, mostly Europeans, who fell victim to World War II. This book is also written in defense of those Germans who had no voice in the creation of the Third Reich, but are still blamed for the genocide of SIX million Jews. And while no words can adequately describe the cruelty to all life forms that is part of warfare, it will give my children and my children's children a real perspective of what it meant to exist, endure and survive Hitler's Third Reich and World War II.

While the political climate of that time was determined by men, it would be the widows, the orphans and the maimed survivors who would carry the burden of reconstruction, and endure subsistence levels of existence in silent desperation in order to return their ravaged world to cultural and economic normalcy.

Wars are often justified by a male oriented minority. They are led by Kings, Emperors, and Presidents or as in this case, the Fuehrer. They are patriarchal in nature, by definition male, and apparently without qualms about shedding innocent blood. Most of them are quick to justify the WAR. World War I was justified by the assassination of a Crown Prince at Sarajevo. World War II was justified by the unfairness of the Treaty of Versailles, caused by World War I.

As is the case in most wars, there are winners and losers. As usual, the loser pays tribute, now known as "Reparation," to the winner. In the case of "Reparation" for World War I, the Versailles Treaty saddled Germany with a burden it simply could not bear. A majority of world leaders understood that and made an attempt at changing the staggering sum that was imposed on Germany. England did not wish to change the terms of the treaty. It needed the money Germany paid in reparation in order to pay the debt it had incurred to the USA. France did not wish to change the terms of the treaty because it now had access to the Saar, the Ruhr, Alsace Lorraine, and the Rhineland, in short it controlled and cashed in on all of Germany's vital natural resources. There were also the Sudeten and the grain and oil rich areas that fell to the Eastern Nations. Germany also lost its colonies in Africa. The Emperor was forced to abdicate and an autocratically oriented nation was left sans leadership, in abject poverty and unable to care for its own.

For a Hitler, not even German by birth, but charismatic by nature, those conditions made a rise to power not only plausible, but also possible. He offered a political philosophy referred to as National Socialism. To many a German that was the preferred choice over what was in the offering, namely communism.

Hitler was not alone in seeing this type of opportunity. The Junker class, knights and lower nobility that could trace its line clear through the middle ages, the people who traded the sword and the shield for a factory and machines that made ammunition. All those people, who had been deprived of accessing international wealth, saw a way and means for making money again.

The promise of "Prosperity" lulled the conscience to sleep and united a starving multitude behind the Fuehrer. "Deutschland Erwache!" Roared the beast and the beast roared back: "Ein Volk Ein Reich Ein Fuehrer!" It was so easy for Hitler to tell Germany to wake up, and so easy for the people to respond with one nation, one realm and one leader. Germans, after all, had been born and bred to autocracy.

Those were the conditions when I was born. I was born on December 15th, 1926 at Frankfurt. But I was raised in Mannheim. My poor mother bore a double burden. She came from a small village that traced its origin back to 720 A.D. when the first peasant in that village was sold lock, stock, and barrel to the Catholic Monastery at Lorsch. Twelve hundred years of uninterrupted Catholicism left the village submitting as a whole to Catholic precepts. In order for marriage to occur, there had to be a Catholic female and a Catholic male. My birth father was not a Catholic male. My mother was forced to leave the village and I was born in Frankfurt.

My cousin Anneliese had been born a week earlier. But she was born to a Catholic mother and a catholic father, a man, damaged by World War I. He had a head wound, and was therefore socially excused for his brutality to his family. But Anneliese had a family.

I was given to foster parentage, Frau Martin at first, somewhere in Mannheim and Frau and Herr Roth shortly after that. Frau Roth told me frequently how they came to have me. She said they almost passed me by because I appeared to have been in the early stages of malnutrition. But as she debated I offered her my only possession, a boiled potato. She said I did it with a smile and with eyes that were so blue and lashes that were so black, she simply could not resist.

That was how the city of Mannheim and I embarked on a similar course that would leave us both devastated when the Third Reich collapsed on top of us.

Mannheim had not wanted Hitler. Mannheim had voted with 60% of its people against National Socialism. Mannheim did not want the "NATIONAL SOZIALISTISCHE DEUTSCHE ARBEITER PARTEI." But as the nation went, so was the city forced to go.

I had absolutely no idea what politics was, what philosophies were. I had just learned how to walk. I had been persuaded to walk on a little garden path, from one person to another. I was not walking for the persons; I was walking because at the end of that little walk there was a wonderful, heavenly, chocolate praline. And even at that early age, chocolate commanded my immediate and undivided attention.

Herr and Frau Roth lived at 64 Friedrich Ebert Strasse in a comfortable apartment on the second floor. The apartment building was old. The stairs were hewn of red granite and years of constant use had left little indentations on the individual stair steps. The banister was made of wrought iron. In the wintertime it provided me with those chief, cheap thrills, to stick my tongue against cold metal. That came to a sudden halt when my tongue got stuck one day and I was unable to get it loose. I screamed like a banshee, received assistance from Mama Roth and some applied psychology across my posterior. I learned early in life that NO was a definite NO, and could have painful consequences.

I really don't know if my mother voted for Hitler or not. I have my doubts. I do know that my mother and the man she married, who became my father, had friends who were Jewish. My mother did marry a Catholic eventually. She was not fond of the church, although she did attend Mass on Sunday. She disliked most priests on the basis that they were priests and I think that had something to do with what happened in the village. She did have me baptized the day after I was born. She blessed me with three names, Elsa Elisabeth Margarethe. She did that because traditions within the clan demanded that female children born into the clan, carry the name of St. Elisabeth and St. Margarethe.

It could be said that from the point of birth I was provided with ample portions of tradition. There were Catholic Traditions; there were Family Traditions; there were Clan Traditions, and later on those written and unwritten laws and traditions of the Third Reich. There were always those traditions that governed proper behavior according to Mama Roth. Those were the important laws and traditions of my childhood. They governed "feeling good" and "feeling bad."

MANNHEIM

Mannheim and I certainly had commonalties. The city, surviving that First World War, was poor, and so were its people and I was a small part of its common poor. I was a small, common, poor person.

Mannheim, rich in art and culture nonetheless, shared its wealth with the poorest of the poor. It had the National Theater, the Rosengarten, where concerts were held, The Augusta Anlage, the Water Tower and its fountains, the park along the Rhine, the Sternwarte, a wonderful old observatory with rickety circular stairs that went up to a small room with a circular marble table and a telescope. There was the Zeughaus with its stone lions, a marvelous museum, the Castle and the old churches. There were free concerts at the Marktplatz; there was the Kaserne across from Friedrich Ebert Strasse 64 the forest at Kaefertal and the little ZOO at the Karl Stern.

Mannheim, I understand, is the only city whose streets do not have names but are based on the letters of the alphabet. At the heart of the city was the castle. The wall that once encircled the city would come down and by the time I became a "Mannemer," the wall was known as Ring Street. The big main thoroughfare going from south to north was the Planken and the one going from west to east, the Breite Strasse. It was from the Breite Strasse that the blocks extended in an orderly fashion. From the castle on the north side running west to east were the blocks A through K. On the south side from the castle to the Neckar River were the letters L through U. As the boundary on south and north was the Ring Strasse, so the boundary from west to east were the Rhine River on the west side and the Neckar River on the East

1

Side. There were streets on the other side of the Neckar River. On the West Side of the Rhine River, connected by a large bridge, lay the Sister City Ludwigshafen. Ludwigshafen was off limits to me. I really never knew why, unless it was always thought to be territorially French. Ludwigshafen and Mannheim were considered to be the major civic hub of the Kurpfalz, the Palatinate. Strangely enough, the city, named after its founding clan, the family Mannin, had been sold to the Monastery Lorsch, lock, stock, and peasants at the same time as the village where my mother came from.

The similarity ended there. Two rivers cradled that little parcel of land, donated to the monastery for the benefit of the souls of the clan Mannin. It would serve as a fortress against any enemy. Long after the Middle Ages rolled across the often hotly contested territory, the Kurfuerst, the Prince Elect, developed the settlement into a city, complete with castle and moat, to serve as a center where art, philosophy and music could develop freely. Mannheim gained the reputation of being free from prejudice and open to all religions, to all philosophy, to all creative endeavors across the land. Schiller worked there, so did Mozart, Goethe, Wagner, Schubert, Schumann, and many more.

Because of its size and its close proximity to Rhine and Neckar river, the city quickly developed into one of the largest inland harbors in Europe. Prior to World War II, the city counted 300,000 inhabitants. When the war was over, there would be only 100,000 left.

I was not considered a "waschecht" (safe to be laundered) child of the city during my early childhood days, The Friedrich Ebert Strasse was to the east across the Neckar. It was a part of the city that lay beyond the Keep, outside the Ring. At the end of that street was the "Festwiese," the Common Greens, a place where May Day Festivals took place and in October, the "October Fest," the traditional Thanksgiving for a good harvest.

At the southern end of the Greens were the sheep enclosures. The city still owned a flock of sheep that was pastured on the banks of the Rhine and the Neckar. In the early evening hours, when the shepherd returned with his flock, the people who had small garden plots on the outskirts of the city, followed him to collect those priceless droppings. Sheep manure was a highly valued natural resource that was free for the taking.

Mannheim had its own conglomerate of satellite communities. There was Kaefertal, Sandhofen, Feudenheim, and Neckarau just to mention a few. Kaefertal always fascinated me. I knew that a beetle was a Kaefer and a Tal was a valley. Was the village named because of beetles that lived there? Or was it named because of a valley full of beetles that once existed there? No one ever told me. In an autocratic society children are to be seen and not heard. Certainly they did not merit having their childish little questions answered. "Warum Darum Basta" was the answer as a rule. That translated into "Why? Because! And that's it!!!"

Near Kaefertal was the Kaefertaler Wald, a forest we visited on those frequent walking tours that Herr and Frau Roth and their friends took. It was out early on a sunny morning and endless walking till we reached the timber. But the trees swallowed us up and the sunlight disappeared. The fragrance of moss and humus rich soil seemed intoxicating. And there were

3

those wonderful little brown May Beetles that appeared in early May. I loved to place them on the tip of my finger, watch them pump up those little air sacks on their white abdomen, spread those delicate feelers and take off into the wind. May Beetles, Mama Roth said, swim through the air on pillows of air. It was hard to understand but it was a concept that was pleasant to the mind.

I suppose my education started long before I entered the age of reason. Herr and Frau Roth used to watch the street below from the balcony of their second floor apartment. They placed me on a pillow between them and they taught me words. It was mainly words that were written on the sides of the passing streetcars. It was Chlorodont and not Schlorodont and I learned to pronounce properly. Chlorodont was toothpaste, they said, but not all toothpaste was Chlorodont. I struggled with that for a while but then considered that that was just one more of those things you couldn't ask about.

The Third Reich and the age of reason hit me at about the same time. Not that I understood what it was all about. It was just that there had been an election and the grown up people voted and a man by the name of Hitler became the leader of our nation. Herr Roth had voted. Frau Roth had voted. Neither one of them had voted for Hitler. Herr Roth had grumbled something about Hitler making voting obsolete. We read from the newspaper the next morning that 60% of the city had voted against Hitler. Herr Roth was terribly unhappy. But I was barred from the discussion that ensued. I was sent to bed.

The following morning there was a MARCH, a demonstration in the street below. I watched from that balcony in the second floor apartment, as a river of

4

angry men exploded down below, poured through the street, fists rose skyward in a salute I did not know. Herr Roth said they were Communists. They were not happy with Hitler. Beyond that he said nothing. I sort of trembled in fear. I had never seen so many angry men marching down the street with voices hoarse from shouting and fists raised to the sky.

Herr Roth picked me up, carried me inside and closed the balcony. After that we went to the kitchen and played "Mensch Aergere Dich Nicht," something akin to Parcheesi. The game that I knew as "Don't Get Mad Man" was another means the Roths had of teaching me arithmetic before I began school. I had to be careful to count properly and to move the proper amount of spaces. We played a lot of games like that and although I did not know it, I was taught to think, to make logical choices and to play fair.

It was before I entered school that I was also introduced to the rest of my family. So, now I understood that "family" for me was different from other children's families. I had a Mama and a Papa. But I also had a Mutti who came to visit me frequently. No one explained that to me. But I was happy nonetheless when she came one day and told me that we were going on a trip by train to see my Grandmother. No one explained to me what a "Grandmother" was. And a train, Mama Roth told me, was just a little bigger and a little noisier that a streetcar. I was so excited, I bounced up and down on the bed and hit my head against a sharp part of the bed frame and bled profusely. That almost put an end to the entire adventure. After that, when I was told to calm down, I did so immediately for fear of consequences. I was lucky. The bleeding stopped. There was apparently no concussion and I was told I could go, providing I behaved "well." I knew what behave-well meant. I could sit in a chair and play with my fingers.

THE VILLAGE

We took the train to the village Neibsheim, where
my mother was born. There I was introduced to all of
my cousins. There was Heinz and Anneliese. I loved
Anneliese. I hated Heinz. Heinz was always right
when I wanted to be right. Heinz was allowed to fight,
but I was forbidden to fight. Then there were the
cousins once removed. Those were the children of our
mothers' cousins. Franzl and Karl were the sons of
Uncle Johann's wife's brother. Edmund was the son
of the farmer across from Uncle Johann's farmstead.
He was nice and polite and fun to talk to. His sister
Agnes was a little shy. Lioba, Friedel, and their little
brother Wolfgang were from the lower village. They
were the grandchildren of our Grandmother's brother.
I learned a lot about relationships and how people
talked different and dressed different. I was so
impressed with our Grandmother. She was
Grandmother to all the cousins. Most of all I found
out what a Grandmother was. She was tall, almost like
a tree. She had a small smile and hair like white frost
or snowflakes. I thought it was white but Karl, being
so much older than I, at least by three years, said it
was silver. I had not formed concepts of silver and
gold. I had not formed concepts of rich and poor. But
all my cousins had formed concepts. I was from the
city and they were country cousins. And that was how
it remained, always.

In looking back, what amazes me was the amount
of learning that was expected of me. Now that I am
adult I have true respect and admiration for the mental
energy of a three-year-old, or a four year old who
must learn what comes close to being a foreign

language without a text book before the child learns to read.

Anneliese and Ida and Lioba and Friedel and the girl from the farm behind my uncle's farm we sort of became a little group. And we stayed in that little group all through the growing years. We were put together in the summer time. We were a little like the goose herd's flock. The goose herd came around in the morning, blew his horn and gathered the geese and the ducks at a small pond on the outskirts of the village. There they congregated in a locked enclosure till nightfall when the goose herd opened the gate and all the geese trotted home in little groups of four and five. The mean one was always the gander, my cousin Karl told me. And when I asked him what the others were he said: "Stupid." That was my introduction to male chauvinism.

We all stayed at the village in the summertime. Our mothers were there to help bring in the harvest, and we were there to learn from our grandmother how to grow up being useful females.

I wasn't interested as much in that as I was interested in all those huge animals. The cows fascinated me. I had seen draft horses pulling the flat wagons on the Friedrich Ebert Strasse. But these were cows and they always chewed. Uncle Johann said they chewed their cud. And when I asked him why, he said because they had four stomachs. I had a belly button on my stomach. Did that mean the cow had four belly buttons? My Uncle Johann laughed and answered my questions. I learned a lot from him.

The first two weeks were a little like heaven. I could run wild and free and there were flowers and plants and things and animals and the air smelled deliciously of fresh straw, of fresh milk and of wood

8

smoke in the evenings when the fires were lit and supper was cooked. When Uncle Johann milked the cows, we lined up with our mugs and he squirted milk from the cows' udder into our mugs. Our mugs always had a crest of foam that was a little like whipped cream. We loved it.

Two weeks were wonderful. But we always stayed six weeks and by the time the third week rolled around, I had been in trouble more than I had really cared to be. I missed Mama Roth; I missed Mannheim. I missed the smells of the city. I missed streetcars and the people and the noises.

I usually became very quiet and unwilling to do things by the time we'd stayed four weeks. During the fifth week even the cows and the chickens had lost their charm. I was homesick for Mannheim.

The ride back on the train was always longer than the ride from the city. Anticipation made me restless. By the time we got off the train and had walked within a block of Mama Roth's apartment house, I was running. I was blissfully happy. I was home. I was after all, a child of the city.

THE THIRD REICH

I entered the first grade in 1933. Hitler took his place as Fuehrer of the German people and the Third Reich came into existence. It's not easy to explain to a six-year old what the Third Reich was and what a Fuehrer was and why there wasn't a Kaiser anymore and why so many men wore brown uniforms.

In school we practiced reading and writing. I did not get a passing grade for "Handwriting". I couldn't manage the ink without "Kleckse," those nasty little round globules that always rested between the letters or on top of them.

The school I attended for the first three years of my academic career was named "WOHLGELEGEN." It was an unusual name for a school. Roughly translated, it meant "WELL PLACED." It was not named after a person, a place, or a thing. It was named for a situation. Papa Roth explained that to me when I asked him about that name. After all, no one had ever told me what a "WOHLGELEGEN" was. A lesson learned early in life was that few people are ever congenially disposed toward lengthy explanations. Nor was lengthy explanations part of the public school curriculum. The way a child learns is to spot the opportunity when a question can be asked and will be answered. But Papa was in the mood to answer that question that day.

The school was well placed. To the west, not far away was the Neckar River. To the north of the school the streetcar had a big stopping place that offered lots of food for the inquiring mind. Adjacent to the east was a large sinkhole. It was the size of a city block and all grass. In the spring I could pick clover blossoms and dandelion heads. I made floral arrangements and sometimes a little root and a little dirt came with them. I placed my little creations on the side altar of the St. Boniface Church. If the debris on the pristine altar cloth annoyed the man in the black dress, he never said so. He always smiled at me in passing.

Once a girl got into a fight with a boy at the bottom of the hole. Eventually a good-sized crowd of onlookers, mostly kids, formed a ring around them. The girl never said a word. She just hit him, again and again till he tried to escape. He'd get halfway up the steep side of the sinkhole when she came after him and brought him down again. That went on for quite some time. The boy was bleeding profusely from the nose and a cut on his lip. An adult finally went down and broke up the fight. I ran all the way home. I did not like to fight physically. I was afraid of the girl. The thought of her coming after me almost became a recurring nightmare.

I told Mama Roth about the fight. She said that I was not to watch something like that. Only trash behaved this way. But she did not explain to me how "trash" related to "human female," as in this case. So "trash" became another concept to be filed away for future reference.

I also told Mama Roth about the church and the flowers. She smiled and told me that I was a "Catholic." She said she was "evangelish," apparently that meant that I was a Catholic and she wasn't. She didn't go into details with that either. But she did take me to that Catholic Church. I liked the singing and I liked the candles and lots and lots of flowers on the altar. I loved the statues. They seemed so life-like, mute beings from a different time and a different place. No explanations there either. I loved the

11

incense and the fragrance that pervaded every corner of that place. I did not like the larger than life crucifix above the altar. There was no doubt that the human figure hanging there was suffering. That was not explained for a long time.

There were other ways when Mama Roth was an expert at clearing up situations. When I became afraid of a shadow on the kitchen wall, she handed me a wooden spoon and told me to beat the hell out of that shadow creature. That took care of the fear. She taught me how to confront my fear, but never told me about hell. When she wasn't in the mood to answer she just told me that I was too young to understand.

There were times when she had disagreements with Papa Roth. Those were the times when she kept me close to her. He'd shout and threaten and she'd tell him that he frightened me. He'd look at me and stop and go away. Soon you could hear him in the other room, singing: "Zu Mantua in Banden, Andreas Hofer war."

Apparently, Andreas Hofer was a folk hero in Mantua, somewhere in Tyrol. It was a song about betrayal and bleeding hearts. It always made me think of the crucifix and the man hanging there. The Hofer mystery took over fifty years to clear up.

Papa Roth was not the only one to teach by singing. At school we learned about different kinds of lifetime occupations. There was the farmer who plowed the fields and the washwomen who did the laundry and the doctor who made the sick well. There were songs about the men who put the big horses in harness before the flat wagons. What all the songs always stated was that a person worked hard and earned an honest wage. To be "fleissig," to be diligent, hard working, and honest, that was the goal that must be attained.

Other things were taught with songs as well. When the flag of Baden came down and the "Hakenkreuz" went up, we sang those songs of how we owed allegiance to that flag, to our land, and to our people. We also learned by song that there were people who died for that flag and that they marched with us in spirit.

There were other songs and other places and other seasons, but now more than ever, the Third Reich became a part of all things. I began to realize that when Mama Roth took me to a Christmas Celebration. There were a lot of people gathered. There were speeches about this being the holiest of nights but that the holiest of nights was dedicated to motherhood and sacrifice. Then there was a speech by "THE FUEHRER." Once again the situation became frightening. All the people who listened on the radio and all the people, who actually were present where Hitler was, they all shouted. Hitler was almost hoarse and I don't know if it was then or some other occasion that he made the statement: "Vor mir kommt Deutschland und mit mir kommt Deutschland und hinter mir kommt auch noch Deutschland." I suddenly understood that all that shouting about Deutschland was about all the Germans who represented Germany, the Germans who were there before him, those who were with him and those who came after him. When you are a small child, stuck in a big crowd, and there is a person who miraculously talks to you without being there, and he talks about an even bigger crowd, that is scary.

I held on to Mama Roth who placed her hand on my shoulder. Soon the speech was over, the people quieted down and we were asked to come up front to receive our Christmas gift. Some one handed me a doll.

"Take it," Mama Roth whispered and I knew it was a command. I did not want the doll. I would have preferred the stick horse they gave to the boy next to me. But I took the doll, curtsied and said "Danke."

Always take a gift graciously, never mind who gives it, Mama Roth told me. Besides that, little girls always were supposed to play with dolls. Little girls definitely did not play with stick horses. As young as I was, it seemed to me that there was an awful lot of things boys were allowed to do simply because they were boys. The boys had all the fun and the girls had all the work. Mama Roth told me to forget about that. It was the Christmas season and there would be something wonderful at home that night.

It was Christmas Eve. Mama Roth always made a cheesecake. And the Christ Child had delivered the toy that Papa Roth had made for me. It was a miniature grocery store. There was a little balance scale to weigh things on. Papa Roth showed me the markings on the little weights that measured grams. I had no trouble learning that there were 500 grams to one pound. There were little tiny tins of all kinds of food supplies. And there were little tiny cakes made from cookies and well decorated. I stood in front of that little store, almost afraid to touch it, afraid it would go away. I loved it, I played with it. I did not want to eat; I just wanted to stay with my wonderful store. Papa Roth lit the Christmas tree with wax candles. We sang our Christmas song, and this time it was a song about a silent night somewhere far away and a young couple who cradled their first born. There was the warmth of the room, the glow of the candles, the smell of good food and the fragrance of pine needles and candle wax.

If we celebrated Christmas, we also celebrated New Year's Day. It was a nighttime celebration. I was excluded from that in my early years. But Mama and Papa Roth always awakened me at the moment the old year left and the New Year arrived. The three of us stood out in the cold, on the little balcony, and listened to the church bells ring. Mannheim had many churches. Most of them were either Lutheran or Catholic. Mannheim also had two synagogues but Mama and Papa told me that the people who attended there did not celebrate the new year at the same time we did. They did not tell me why and by now I knew when it was a good time to ask and a good time to be silent. This was a good time to be silent.

Although some things changed, life resumed after the holidays, at the usual pace. At school we were getting free milk and bread, compliments of the Third Reich. I did not mind. I was always hungry. An occasional "Ausflug," a trip, a small adventure, broke the monotony of five-days-eight-hours of school. Our teacher was our leader and we followed him in proper order like the geese followed the gander in the village. And we sang. Hali Halo became a theme song for us. Hali Halo and we saw ourselves wandering through the world. Hali Halo had no meaning. It was merely an expression. But I liked that new expression and I Hali-Haloed all through the apartment until Mama Roth told me to put a cork in it.

Sometimes we went to the Rhine and our teacher told us legends of dwarfs and spirits and the Lorelei. He also told us about the French who sometimes claimed the river as their own. But it would always be "Father Rhine" to us. Other times we would go to the old Sternwarte, the observatory. He led us up those rickety stairs and showed us the round table and the marvelous gadget that projected a picture on the table. We could see the streets and the houses down below. At night, he said, we could see the stars above. Once we observed as a woman accidentally knocked a milk container off the window ledge and hit a passer-by squarely on the head. I laughed but I could not tell the teacher what I was laughing at. He thought I was poking fun at him behind his back. I was severely chastised for that.

My teacher did not hold high hopes for me. He said I was a dreamer. I watched the clouds and saw in them giants tossing stones at each other. My teacher said the clouds were inconsequential, knowing arithmetic was important. I disagreed in silence. Time and Life would prove him right, at least about arithmetic.

I liked the trips to the Neckar River. I liked standing on that bridge and looking into the distance where the vague outline of the small mountains at Heidelberg was barely distinguishable.

Mutti made more frequent visits. She brought along a handsome man and Mama Roth told me that he was going to be her husband and my "Vati." Once they came and took me out for a Sunday excursion. We went to the Schlosspark, the small park area behind the castle. We fed the squirrels and he explained to me that those little, red, ear-tasseled squirrels were different from others and that they were rare. He told me many things. He told me how the Rhine River came from huge mountains to the south and how the river ran all the way to the sea. And that was why there were so many ships. He told me things and he answered my questions no matter

16

what they were. I loved him for that. He was patient, quiet and kind.

Summertime always belonged to the village. In the summertime the clan gathered and helped to bring in the harvest. By 1936, I had a new father, and he came along to the village. He was to be addressed as "Vati." He was to be respected and he certainly was handsome. I thought he was beautiful, but I was quickly made to understand that persons of the opposite sex were not beautiful, they were handsome. The fact that he owned a camera made him "wealthy" by any standard of the village children.

Vati took my only picture of that motley crew of cousins in the village. I was first in line, holding up a slip of paper so that every one knew that the first person in that picture was "I."

Karl had grown a bit taller and was insufferably chauvinistic. Franzl was still small. He was smaller than I was. He remedied that situation by creeping up on me from behind and bombarding me with dry cow turds. I suddenly remembered the girl in the sinkhole and I could see myself being just like her. Fingernails extended, I went after Franzl. Franzl screamed and ran and I followed in hot pursuit. It was Uncle Johann who interfered. He swept me up in his arms and held me in the air and looked at me with those blue-green eyes and said: "That's not a smart way to win a battle."

There was an intense conference and Uncle Johann listened carefully to my tale of woe. After I finished, he bent down to me from his imperial heights and he smiled. And where did the girls and the women sit when we took the wagon to the hay field, he asked. There was that unwritten law again. Women sat down below at the side of the wagon. Men and

17

boys sat up front, they drove and gave commands to the draft animals; boys sat in front because they were boys. Karl and Franzl both considered themselves superior to the girls and assumed they were going to be up front. When the wagon was ready my uncle silently held out the whip and pointed. Franzl was to sit down below with Aunt Martha and Anneliese. So was Karl. Uncle Johann placed me up front next to him. "Don't you think that works better than a few claw marks across his face?" he inquired with a smile.

Down below I could see Franzl's ears turning red. The team, the wagon and the crew slowly lumbered out of the farmyard. The sun was bright and the sky was blue and Uncle Johann delivered his lecture about doing battle not with the heart, but with the mind.

THE CLAY DIGS, PART I

That summer proved to be interesting. Friedl, Lioba, Wolfgang, Anneliese, and I played a lot in the old clay digs. The village didn't work the clay digs anymore and so we were left to ourselves with some of the treasures we found. It was the little boy Wolfgang, who played with those funny looking stone sticks. The more we looked at them, the more we realized they were bones. Anneliese got scared and ran. Lioba wasn't inclined to stay there either. Friedl whispered something about "Ghosts." But I was curious. Ghosts and bones are in cemeteries. We were in the clay digs. I wanted to know a little more and Vati was the best person to ask. He listened very quietly and agreed to come to the clay digs with us. Uncle Johann, whose curiosity was piqued, thought it could be old cattle bones. He could not take time out. He had a field of wheat down, ready to be harvested. Vati, Anneliese and I were the only ones to go. Anneliese was my sidekick. Wherever I was, she was.

The old clay dig looked so silent and so peaceful in the early morning sun. It did not take Vati long to understand what we had been playing with. Those were bones, he said. But those were old bones, very old people's bones. Anneliese was clinging to my arm. Nothing to be afraid of, he said. But he insisted that we not return to that place. On the way back Vati told us of an ancient people who lived there long before the place became a village. Those people, he said, were known as the Celts.

Years later, the village printed a book about the ancient heritage. Among those prehistoric finds they mentioned were the ancient burial sites in the clay pits.

After that adventure in the clay pits, Uncle Johann felt that it was necessary for us to be productive, rather than chase around old mines and other places. We were told that we must go with Grandmother to take "Vesper" to the crew in the field. It was the same old thing again. The boys got to do the fun things with the cattle and the wagon. We had to go with Grandmother to carry food. Once we got there, we had to help load. Karl was old enough to take the wagon in. Uncle Johann, Grandmother, Mutti, and I walked home in the evening sunlight. The day was over when the church bell rang at six. We all stopped. Grandmother knelt, Uncle Johann cuffed his cap and the rest of us bowed our heads while we recited the "Angelus, Der Engel des Herrn…" When I asked my Uncle why, he just said that it was always that way. At six in the evening the village church bell would ring and people would stop where ever they were, bow their heads, and recite the Angelus. The prayer was an essential part of daily living for the people in the village. "Lutherans too?" I asked. Uncle Johann's eyes turned cloudburst gray and his lips tightened grimly. "There are no Lutherans", he said.

The expression on his face was a clear indication that the conversation was terminated. Martin Luther may have been dead for centuries, but the controversy he created certainly wasn't; not then and not now.

Hell could freeze over before the first Catholic in that village would acknowledge the first Protestant.

Something that always remained the same was that after two or three weeks of village life I became homesick. I was tired of crowing roosters and cackling hens and scolding aunts and overbearing male cousins.

That year it was decided that after summer vacation I was to leave Papa and Mama Roth and came to live with Mutti and Vati. It was a quiet thing that was done quietly without fanfare and without lengthy farewells. It was not explained to me why I now lived at S.1.7. I was not allowed to visit the Roths and I was not allowed to take my toys. I had a new bed and my old clothes and that was all. Mutti was not very talkative. She suggested that I write for the fun of it. For playthings I had her red beads that snapped apart and could be put together. Vati brought me books.

No other children my age lived there. There was a photographer's studio up stairs and a beauty salon down stairs. S.1. was on the Breite Strasse. There were few living quarters and many shops. Not very far away was the Market Place. Adjacent to that was the St. Sebastian Catholic Church and part of that building was the old Rathaus or city hall. Three times a week the people from the surrounding villages came and sold their produce. On other days the pigeons ruled that domain. There was a seed store adjacent to the Market Place on G.1. Vati sometimes bought me bird feed there and we spend the time feeding the pigeons. The birds were quite tame. All you had to do was hold out a hand full of seeds and the birds landed on your hand and your arms eager to be fed.

There was, of course, the presence of the Third Reich. The event was called a "Fackel Zug," essentially a torchlight parade. Vati and Mutti insisted that we watch from the window. They said it would be safer than on the street down below.

I don't know what the occasion was; I do know that you could feel the vibrations long before the parade arrived. Again it was a startling almost frightening thing to observe. As far as I was concerned, there must have been thousands of men, all in uniform, brown uniforms with buckles that caught the light from the torches. There was always a band up front and there was always singing. "Wir sind heut und morgen, alles was die Zeit erschafft – -"

Those were the songs about whom we were and what we were and how we had to work hard to be worthy of the future. Songs that made me think of the work that was waiting for me. Songs that told me that I had to be "Fleissig," diligent, hard working to be worth my keep.

It was in 1936 that Hitler introduced troops to the Rhineland. The Rhineland had been considered a demilitarized zone. But Hitler had stated that the Rhine must not be a border for Germany. The Rhine belonged to Germany. Germany had a right to have troops in the Rhineland. If the treaty at Locarno forbade troops in the Rhineland, the treaty was a crime against all Germans. And now we saw other uniforms.

They came, a seemingly endless parade of soldiers and weapons and horses. I liked the horses. I loved the horses. Horses brought tears to my eyes, tears of joy I guess. Then came the wagons that were closed. There was a fine white dust on them. When I asked Vati, he said: "That's lime."

I had no idea what lime was. He explained to me slowly that lime was spread over the bodies of the dead in order to hasten the process of decomposition. My mind's eye reviewed the parade again.

There were the proud men in uniform, the prancing horses and there was the lime to be sprinkled on their bodies, after they and the horses had died in battle. And then those tears became tears of sorrow, especially for the horses. Vati took me away.

I don't believe I was prepared to discuss with Vati what I had felt in my heart. It was an awesome mixture of sadness and fear. And yet, there seemed to be nothing to be afraid about.

CHILDREN OF THE RING

When I came to live with Vati and Mutti, I
became a full-fledged child of the city. I now
belonged to Mannheim, and Mannheim belonged to
me. I did not have other children to play with, since
none lived there. We lived at S.1.7, in the heart of the
city. I enjoyed the pungent aroma of coffee roasting at
Coffee House Haag, the pastries in the Konditorei one
block away, and the Nordsee Fish Market just around
the corner. Fresh produce came to the Market Place at
G1. Sometimes there was the smell of spring rains on
the cobble-stoned streets, sometimes the smell of soot
and coal from the train depot.

The city was alive with sights and sounds and I
loved every moment of it. The only sadness I felt, was
not to be allowed to visit Mama Roth. Nor was I
allowed to ask why we could not visit where I had
lived so long.

Children of the Ring, of the Inner City, went to
school at U1. That school was bigger than
Wohlgelegen, but it was closer to the Neckar River.
School days were long. School days began with the
Flag Raising Ceremony every morning. The flag went
up and we stood and saluted with outstretched arms,
singing the National Anthem and the Horst Wessel
Lied. I did not know who Horst Wessel was, but I
would not have dared to admit my ignorance. I knew
it had to do something with the S.A., the men in
brown shirts who died for us so that we could enjoy a
better standard of living. The S.A., it was said, made
the Third Reich possible. The Third Reich gave us
enough bread to eat, jobs to earn money, a roof over
our heads, a free education and milk and bread at
lunchtime, free of charge. That was why we saluted

the flag and sang the Horst Wessel Lied, who ever Horst Wessel was.

For some of us it was a long time to hold that right arm extended like that.

The only big thrill about standing there every morning in the enclosed schoolyard for half an hour, was that we could see the boys at that time. Boys were educated on separate but joint premises. Apparently the Third Reich believed in sexually segregated education. We were curious about the boys. We were also curious why they were educated in a separate part of school. Were they being taught the same things we were taught? Or was there something we missed out on simply because we were not MALE. The boys, however, had little curiosity about us. They treated us as though we were some sort of communicable disease. When I asked Vati about it, he said that was so because we lived in a patriarchal society. It was the kind of government where the men made all the decisions and the women were basically caretakers. They took care of things and people. I was indignant. Why couldn't a person give orders regardless of sex? And why couldn't a person be a caretaker regardless of sex? "What you're really saying is that if I were a boy I would be better?" I shouted. He told me to calm down and he swore that he would have as much admiration, love, and respect for me if I were a boy. But he had to admit that in a patriarchy women were often referred to as the second sex. And were there any other societies around the world? Vati said there were a few. As a matter of fact, he said, there was an island near Greece where a matriarchy existed. Women ran the government; they owned the land and the eldest daughter inherited from the mother. I kind of wished I had been born there. I was, after all, first born. Vati said I was too young to make that choice. He said I lacked experience. And then he terminated that conversation and said we needed to plan an outing.

Mutti and Vati did not go on long outings to the Kaefertaler Wald the way Mama and Papa Roth did. Mutti did not like long outings. But Vati enjoyed bicycle riding. And he taught me to ride a bicycle. He taught me how to concentrate on the road ahead. The first time he let go of the saddle and I was on my own, I shifted concentration from the road ahead to two elderly ladies strolling toward us. It may have been pride of accomplishment. I wanted them to look at me and so I looked at them and rode straight toward them. They screamed and I tumbled. Vati apologized, picked me up, put me right back on the bicycle, "Never mind the people, keep your mind and your eyes on the road." I did just that.

He took me to Heidelberg. We went up the mountain, past the castle. The granite walls glowed softly in the sunlight and white fogs lifted from the coniferous forest down below. The air was fresh. The forest was breathing out what my lungs loved to breathe in. Vati told me that Napoleon had sacked the castle. He said it was done because of a military strategy called "Scorched Earth." Vati knew so much and I so very little. Words that he used and I did not know; I would later research in the Lexicon.

Vati enjoyed gliding down the mountainside on that bicycle. He passed pretty well everything and everyone on the way down. That worked out well until I accidentally stuck my foot in the spokes of the rear wheel. My foot was hurt but not much. Vati's pride was hurt, but true to his way of thinking, we picked ourselves off the side of the mountain, got on the bike and finished the tour and arrived home before dark. It would have been a twenty-five-mile hike. No matter what, no matter all the aching bones, it was the kind of adventure I enjoyed.

With Vati came a new set of grandparents. There was no doubt in my mind that Mutti did not get along with her mother-in-law. That grandmother was a lot like Aunt Anna. She always tattled and nothing ever suited her just right. If the lady was a prophet of doom, her husband was a pleasure to be with. He showed up one snowy winter day at our apartment with a sled. It startled Mutti. But he wanted to take me sledding and I wanted to go. Mutti was not a person to venture out. She preferred the safety of her four walls. In my mind I saw hills and snow and trees and the castle in the background. She finally consented. She gave us two hours, but we sort of stretched it to three.

here was nothing old about this old man. We climbed the hills just to fly down in minutes. My ears were red. My nose was red. I didn't feel the cold. It was just one more hill up to go one more hill down. He explained to me how steering works, how you throw your weight one way to go the other. We took several runs together before he allowed me to solo. And that first run down on my own with no one to guide me, that was an absolute natural high.

When he said it was time to go home I had to go just one more time. The kids on that hill were strangers when we met. But soon we were calling each other by name. Snowballs were flying. Grandfather finally took the sled away from me and said: "We'll have to go home now." He did not say we were late. Mutti and Vati met us. "Late" was not permissible at our house.

Grandfather apologized and Mutti tried to point out that she worried. "It's a big city" she said.

"It's Mannheim," he answered, as if that was self-explanatory.

Mannheim was virtually crime free. Mannheim offered art and beauty and freedom of thought and the children of the city gathered as one out there behind the castle on that hill.

"When your Vati was four, I took him to see the Crown Prince when he came to visit."

"Did he become the Kaiser?" I asked.

Mutti stopped the conversation. She said it was late. Grandfather apologized and I hugged him good-bye. Mutti frowned on that. She came from a clan that did not express affection in public.

"You courtesy and shake hands," she said.

While Mutti did not approve of this grandfather and grandmother, she liked Vati's brother Konrad. Konrad was attractive, a little younger than Vati. Konrad had eyes that smiled, sort of. The only time I saw his eyes not smiling was when he had to join the army of the Third Reich.

Uncle Konrad played the Zither. He came in the evenings and then it was singing and music time. My mother loved folk music and Uncle Konrad played it very well. Sometimes Grandfather and Grandmother came. Grandfather showed me how to dance the Schuhplattler, a Bavarian dance. Vati's family came from Bavaria. Bavarian music, Bavarian Beer, and the Schuhplattler sort of went together.

By Christmas 1936 we were in a new apartment. We were at G6.13-16, compliments of the Third Reich. The apartment complex had several apartment houses, connected with entrance to a common court within. Each apartment had four stories. Our apartment was parterre to the right. Mutti absolutely beamed. She was very happy. She had a new home, new furniture, new family, and new friends. The Fishangs lived in the apartment above us. They had a five-year-old child named Ursula. Although there was a difference in our age, we became good friends.

The couple across from us was named Hoelle and not one of Mutti's favorite couples. Both of them were politically active. He was Block Leiter, in charge of the apartment complex. But I liked them. They had books. They had my favorite books. They had a complete collection of Karl May's Adventure stories. I simply lived in those books. There were stories and adventure with American Indians, with Indian Rajahs, with African treasure hunters. There simply was no end to the worlds those books opened to me. Now there was warmth and color and joy in my life.

For Christmas of 1936 Uncle Konrad gave me a "POESIE" book. It was a little like a memory book. All the people you liked and all the people who cared for you were to write a small poem on a page. I treasured that book. And where nothing survived during that dreadful period of air raids, the book survived. The book is still with me, although so many who wrote in it are no longer alive, but fell victim to the war.

Christmas was quickly followed by a New Year's Celebration. Mutti was an excellent cook. Besides wonderful food and melt-in-your-mouth Christmas cookies, there was glow-wine, made with spices and oranges and lemons and hot tea and sweet red wine. And as the bells heralded in the new year, we stood under starlit skies and listened. I remembered that balcony of my early youth, but it was not wise to talk about it.

We saw the Hindenburg on its way to the North. It was strange to see that huge, cigar-shaped balloon hanging in the sky. It took almost thirty minutes crossing the city. Vati said it was a balloon, a big balloon filled with a gas that was lighter than air. Vati took the opportunity to teach me what air can and can not do. That's how I learned about the importance of oxygen. Of course Grandfather had to share and he gave me a lesson on gravity. He swung a bucket one third full of water in circular fashion over his head. He was fine until he accidentally made contact with the ceiling and dumped the water on himself and over Mutti's polished floor.

"There is no fool like an old fool," his wife grumbled. I thought it was great, but I was not permitted to experiment. I had to admit that there was a difference in grandparents. This one was the epitome of youth and scientific curiosity. Grandmother at the village would have no part of that. "God didn't mean for man to fly. If he did, he would have planted trees up there to tie onto," was her comment on airplanes.

A VERY SPECIAL GIFT

In 1937 on the 20th of April, the youth of Germany became a gift to Hitler. Joining the organization became compulsory. My parents did not purchase my uniform at the appropriate store. Our seamstress made my uniform. The Leather Knot, known as the "Knoten," had to be earned first and then purchased from the leader of the troop. Running the 100-meter dash in 13 seconds, completing the 3-meter broad jump successfully, and throwing the javelin 26 meters earned the "Knoten." Being familiar with Hitler's philosophy and accomplishments was also required. Proof of purchase of Hitler's "MEIN KAMPF" was suggested. Hitler authored the book with Rudolf Hess during his incarceration at Landsberg.

My parents told me that this book would not hold my interest and therefore was not purchased. Vati explained that a book existed for the pleasure of reading, not for status, or for any other reason. He made me promise not to repeat that conversation. Uncle Konrad had taught me the importance of keeping my word. I wondered why the conversation had to be kept silent. I kept my promise.

I earned the "Knoten" purely on the basis that I had a good memory for all the details in Hitler's life.

Until my leader in a specific ceremony handed me the "Knoten," I used a matchbox to fasten the black kerchief around my neck. I kind of thought that we all looked just a little like personified May Beetles. We wore those black kerchiefs over white blouses and we wore black skirts and brown jackets. When I expressed that opinion to my leader she told me that I looked exactly the way a German girl should look; in uniform and with those dark-blond braids and those blue eyes. The braids I was forced to wear because my maternal grandmother thought cutting one's hair was immoral and against the teaching of the Catholic Church. "An de Haar rumpflanzt, in the Hoell rumtanzt," she'd say. (Mess around with your hair, dance around in hell.) When, she wanted to know, was I going to receive First Communion.

Mutti bowed to the wishes of her mother and that is why I received First Communion and the "Knoten," simultaneously, during my eleventh year.

Sometimes it was difficult to tell exactly what philosophy dominated my life; was it political, or was it religious.

Mass on Sunday was compulsory at our house. Sometimes it was spectacular. Sometimes, during the early days of the Third Reich, the S.A. attended Mass. An entire unit replete with breast-shielded flag-bearer and flag attended. Sometimes there were processions around the entire city. Each of its numerous Catholic Churches participated and the seemingly endless snake made up of human beings made its way through the city, chanting and singing. Little girls wore their First Communion Dress and had their hair garlanded. Boys wore suits.

Of course there were also times when the Hitler Youth marched through the streets, singing, and most definitely in step. Our "Leader" saw to that. There was discipline whether it was the church or the state. There was always discipline. There was discipline at home as well. And I was told at an early age that if I disciplined myself, no one else would have to do that.

All in all, it was a well-controlled childhood. Those years of being ten, eleven and twelve were spent in church processions, Hitler Youth marches, standing on street corners, in uniform, and rattling the tin can for donations. The church collected money at mass and the Third Reich collected money on street corners. The common objective was always the "less fortunate."

There was a gradual change in 1937. At school we were taught a lot about victorious Battles of victorious Germans. I am certain there was not a German of that time span who was not well informed about the battle against the Romans in the forest of Teutoburg. In science, the theory of "Natural Auslese," (Natural Selection) was readily applied to the concept of "War." And the thought of war as nature's way to insure the survival of the fittest became a daily injunction.

The soldiers, who marched through the streets, carried weapons. Vati was very stern about guns.

"Remember always, a gun is to kill. It has no other purpose."

When I asked the Priest about the taking of life, he just shrugged his shoulders and said it was sometimes necessary. When I pointed out that one of the ten commandments stated specifically that "Thou shalt not kill," he replied that in that case I had better stop eating meat, because in order for me to have a Sunday roast, an animal would have to he killed.

When I asked the H.J. leader at the next meeting, she laughed and said I was unduly concerned. There would be no war. And even if there was a war, our soldiers were superior to those of other nations. They were well trained and well equipped, none would die. She smiled and patted me on the head and said: "Who told you such nonsense?"

"No one," I said. But I thought about the pictures in the history book, pictures of dying men and dying horses.

Mutti and I discussed it a little. It was clear that she did not want to talk about war. When I told her about my conversation with the leader of my Hitler Youth Group, she insisted on discussing it with Vati first. Vati had the perfect solution. He planned another outing.

This outing was different. This outing introduced me to the world of the performing arts. I became a small part of the group of performers at the National Theater. Vati knew Herr Wagner, who was then stage attendant. I was a little old to start ballet, but I became part of children's choir as well.

Backstage was a world of make-believe. If there was a need for a street urchin in an opera, I could be in it. I could be an extra for a crowd scene. I could have a walk-on part in a stage play. It really didn't matter to me how insignificant the part, as long as I could be on stage.

On stage was also a perfect excuse for not attending the Hitler Youth meetings. And those meeting became more of a dread than a pleasure. We sang a lot of songs at the meetings. But most of the songs dealt with winning the world. I was not interested in winning the world.

At school we learned all about the atrocities inflicted on Germans who lived beyond the boundaries of the Third Reich. Germans were also fleeing from the French in the Saar and the Ruhr, we were told. Germans were abused in Alsace Lorraine. To the east there were the Sudeten.

Now we were being taught a theory invented by the Fuehrer. The Fuehrer said it would become necessary for the borders in the east to be extended because Germany needed Lebensraum. Germans needed room for living. It was time to take back all the places the Versailles Treaty had taken from the Germans.

At home all discussions about Hitler, about "Lebenraum," about Himmler, Goehring, Goebbels, and Hess were forbidden. These things were not be discussed in front of children.

"Why are they taught at school when we can't talk about them at home?" I wanted to know. That question was not answered.

KRISTALL NACHT

Then came the infamous "Kristall Nacht." Vati took me to school that following morning. We went past the Synagogue, or what was left of it. In front of the building was a smoldering pile of rubbish, mostly books with partly burned pages. Around it all was the S.A. I wanted to reach down for one of the books. My father's hand restrained me. He led me away as quickly as possible.

By the time we reached the Kaufhaus Corner, Vati whispered I was not to pay attention. That was more easily said than done. All the display windows had been smashed. People were helping themselves to all the goods on display. People were stealing while the S.A. stood espalier and watched silently.

By the time we reached the St. Sebastian Church I found it impossible to go on without being answered. I struggled against his firm grip. He propelled me into the church. We were seated in the back pew and he began to talk.

"This is an act committed against the Jews", he said.

"Why?" I wanted to know.

"It will probably be explained to you at school," he replied.

He was right. There was a lengthy lecture about the Jews that day. The teacher said that the Jews had been cheating the Germans out of their money and their belongings. Jews were accused of doing things to little girls much too terrible to discuss. What had happened, the teacher said, was that the people rose up against the Jews. The S.A., he said, was there to protect the Jews from the wrath of the people. I raised my hand. He called on me.

"But why burn the books?"

"What books? There were no books burned!" he answered. When I insisted that I saw books, he roared at me.

"God alone knows what you think you've seen. No one in this nation burns books. And that is that!"

My lips quivered and I knew I was going to cry. I turned away. Something inside of me cringed at the sight of violence and the sound of anger.

At lunchtime I was unable to eat and in the early afternoon I was physically ill. My mother was summoned. She came and took me home. She asked me what was wrong and I would not talk.

I was put to bed and given Chamomile Tea.

When Vati came home, he brought me a book. It was a book about a princess in far away India who had been married to a man who insisted that she tell him an interesting tale every night. If she failed to keep his interest, she would be beheaded. I really wasn't certain that I could get into that type or reading at that point in time.

"Read about some one else's problems and your problems will go away!" Vati said. Just to humor him, I started to read. I don't know when he slipped in and took the book away and turned out the light. But I had embarked on the journey through One thousand and One Nights.

At the National Theater we rehearsed for The Nutcracker Ballet. I was in my element. I was a mouse. That was all right because we would also rehearse "Aide" and there I would be a slave, a little black slave.

At school we were told of the new programs Hitler was creating for Germany. There would be the Four-Year-Plan. Crops would be grown in a scientific way, with fields allowed to lay barren for a year in order to produce more. It was hoped that with this kind of agriculture Germany would become independent of other nations. In other words, Germany would become self-sufficient. Hitler also wanted new factories to produce what he called the "Volkswagen." This would be a car that everyone could afford. Near the outskirts of town new small houses went up, called one-family dwellings. Families with many children would have access to these houses. We were told that Hitler thought of the large family as the wealth of the nation. Hitler also used a program that would place financial responsibility for any child beyond four children on the Third Reich. In other words all children after the fourth child were state supported.

Since every family would be able to own a car, Hitler initiated the "Autobahn." At Mannheim the Autobahn would come to the Ring by the Rosengarten. It would be difficult to tell where the Autobahn began and the Augusta Anlage ended.

The infamous Kristall Nacht was now deeply buried in my subconscious mind. There were so many other things. The idea of owning a car, for one, was intoxicating. I had my doubts that we would ever own a one-family house at the outskirts of town. After all this time of living as a family, there was still just the three of us. But the apartment was comfortable and as Hitler promised, there was now enough food for all of us.

G.6.13 was vis-à-vis from the Ghetto. When I asked Vati what a Ghetto was, he explained that it was a housing complex for persons of the Jewish Persuasion. Ursel Mueller was my girlfriend and she lived in G.7. But Vati replied that a lot of people lived in G.7 who were not Jewish. And how could you tell one from the other? I wanted to know. Vati very carefully explained that the Jewish people were required to wear a yellow star on their clothing to identify them. When I asked him why he said that they were considered enemies of the Third Reich. At that point of the conversation Mutti interrupted and sent me on an errand. They were still talking when I left and it had something to do with "-it's not safe to talk in front of her." I could not imagine what was not safe and why it wasn't safe. But I knew by now, from experience that there would be no more questions answered about enemies of the Third Reich. And since no one would explain to me the workings of the Ghetto, I decided to experiment on my own. There were quite a few small stores in G.7. I found out that I could enter any given house of the complex from the street adjacent to H.7., and walk right through and exit in the small alley inside the complex. It didn't take me long to realize that all of the houses in the complex opened in this way to the center alley. It was the only block that I knew that was designed in this way. The only person to answer that question was the priest at St. Sebastian. The priest had a wonderful library and I used to borrow books from him. He said the complex had been designed this way on purpose. During times of persecution, the Jews could escape by leaving through the inner alley. But the priest would not discuss persecutions with me. I knew from my religious instructions that the Christians had been persecuted by the Romans. The priest pointed out that persecutions of this kind were no longer necessary. He said that since all people in the city were registered with the police department, it was easy to apprehend anyone and simply arrest them at home.

Beyond that, the priest would not say anything. I did ask Vati: "Is it true that all people in the city are registered with the police department?"

"Yes." And that was all. After that, Vati said we were due for another outing. I knew by then that this was his way of derailing my one-track mind.

EXCURSIONS OF THE MIND

This excursion was not as far as Heidelberg. We
went to the Public Library. Roughly eight blocks from
home, it was a place where the known yesterdays and
the presumed tomorrows could be had for the taking.
Books, by now, and to my way of thinking, were
exquisite excursions into someone else's mind. From
now on whatever book Vati did not purchase and Frau
Hoelle did not own I borrowed from the Public
Library.

One of the first big books I carted home was a
complete account of Mythology, all myths from all
the people on earth, so the title claimed.

"Fairy Tales," Mutti said.

"Not always," Vati countered. Some so-called
fairy tales or myths were based on facts. I was
particularly interested in those huge, fire-breathing
dragons. Vati said there were still dragons. They were
known as the Komodo Dragons, named after the
island of Komodo where they still existed. Mutti
quickly discouraged that remark but Vati insisted. He
was once again in his element. He said that most
civilizations had myths about dragons and that could
well be because once there were huge sauropods
known as "Dinosaurs."

I listened intently as he told me of the Jurassic
Period in the life of the earth and of large lizards
roaming the land, lizards bigger than a house. I didn't
tell him, but the idea of having a dinosaur for a pet
crept readily into my mind. Imagine, having a pet as
big as a building.

In that book I found the origins of many opera
plots. The Nordic Myths and the ballad of Siegfried
especially captivated me. Wagner had used those

legends as a basis for the Ring Cycle. Vati said there was a possibility of Siegfried having been a real person. Hildebrandt, who made reference to Etzel, had written the story. Etzel was better known as Attila the Hun, and that one I could find in the history books.

My teacher took a dim view of my intellectual diet. He said with all the fantasies in my brain there was no room for real facts. And real facts were what history was all about. We would now learn how the Third Reich had increased in size, thanks to the ingenuity of the Fuehrer. Now we drew maps of Germany prior to the Third Reich. Now, only a few years later, Alsace Lorraine was included in the Reich. So were the Ruhr, the Saar, and the Rhineland. And in the East the Sudeten would once again be German, as well as the Polish Corridor and the free city of Danzig. Latvia and Lithuania would be part of the Reich as well and so would be the Memel. What that meant was that Germans, rein-rassig, pure of blood, were once again part of the German Nation and so was the land on which they existed.

I liked drawing and became an expert at making maps. That pleased the teacher. I liked writing, and particularly liked writing my own fairy tales, the stuff that came from hours of research and grew in my own mind. The teacher liked that as well. I liked science, especially the kind of science that dealt with animals. The teacher had no complaint about that.

The priest who came to the school and taught for an hour per day taught religion. I liked religion. I enjoyed all the historical background as well as the Biblical Version of Adam and Eve. I only got in trouble once when I wanted to know if Adam and Eve were Jewish or German. But the school, just like the

Hitler Youth, became increasingly restrictive. Gone was the freedom of expression and here was the boredom of learning by repetition. My own little world grew smaller as the Third Reich grew larger. I wanted to be free to go where I wanted to go and to do what I wanted to do. And there was simply not enough of that freedom.

Mutti often did not permit enough time to go to the library. The only way out was to run to the library and to lie about having gone to the library.

Mutti did not permit visits to Mama and Papa Roth. I learned to run there too and to lie about having been there.

Soon I was embarked on a career of deceit.

"Dental appointment," I told the teacher and I was out the door, ahead of me freedom and a visit to Mama.

"Knee Injury," I told the teacher. I was out of the building and the day was mine.

"Sickness in the family." It was so easy to shorten the week from six days to three or four.

Then there was the day of reckoning. I told the teacher that Aunt Martha had been run over by the hay wagon and we had to go to the village. Unfortunately my mother and my teacher met at the Farmer's Market that Saturday and my teacher inquired about my aunt. That put an end to my career. Vati believed in applied psychology. He applied that punishment to my tail end. Mutti added three weeks of restriction and all of my friends were now off limits. Sitting was painful for quite some time. I attended school regularly after that. I also had to attend the H.J. meetings. The most painful restriction was not being able to attend rehearsals at the National Theater. Because I could not attend rehearsal, I was dropped from that particular performance. I was furious about that and wanted to know if I was the only one who lied and was it that every one else always told the truth? Mutti shot me a warning glance. The lie was bad enough, talking back was even worse.

Vati relented and took me to a movie. We went to see "Cathargo's Fall." Again, history and fantasy came together and there on the screen was Hannibal's excursion into Italy, Scipio's triumph, and consequently Roman Victory. What I recall most from that movie was Hannibal's elephants and the lady who drank poison who choose death rather than life as a prisoner.

Although I did not skip school again, I still tried for more personal freedom. If I had to go to Tante Toni at the Werderstrasse, what was to keep me from taking the long way home? And taking the long way home allowed me to pass the Tennis Platz. I enjoyed watching the people play Tennis. But the Tennis court was gone. Instead there was a gaping hole. I kept asking around until some one told me that the Third Reich was building a "Bunker" . Of course I did not know what a bunker was. But I could not resist asking when I came home.

"What's a Bunker?"

Vati studied the situation.

BUNKER

"Why do you want to know?"

"Because they're building one."

"Where?"

"Where the Tennis Court used to be."

That slipped out carelessly. I was caught in a lie again. I was ready for 'punishment'. Oddly enough,

44

'punishment' never came. My parents just looked at each other. Vati suggested another 'outing'.

This time we went to the Luisen Park. It was a quiet park with tall trees, bright flowers and a small pond that was home to some goldfish, ducks and, swans. Vati proposed we'd go to the Planetarium. I was in favor of that. But first we would talk about "Bunkers." Once again I was pledged to silence. Again I was cautioned that I must never reveal in public what was discussed in private. It was plain that if I wanted to know about "Bunkers," I had to promise not to talk to others about the things I knew. Not easy for me.

A "Bunker," he told me, was a place of safety in the event of an enemy attack. I did not know we had enemies. There followed a serious discussion about the eventuality of war. But my mind was on the promised visit to the Planetarium. The talk about war did not take root.

School brought those words back to my own reality. There was a little private war in Spain, something about the Communists besieging a city. And there was, of course, Goehring's success with the "LUFTWAFFE," the prized "Condor Legion." It appeared that the Third Reich assisted Generalissimo Franco in his war against the Communists. German airplanes dropped bombs on the opposition. Now I knew the purpose of "Bunkers." A bunker was there to protect against bombs.

The teacher laughed as I paled. Never fear, he said. No one would be able to penetrate General Feld Marschall Goehring's defense of German Air Space.

"Then why are we building bunkers?"

After I said it I realized that I shouldn't have said it. The teacher's face purpled. "Disobedience," he said, "Talking without permission," he said, "Four Tatzen," he said. I winced. He brought out the little bamboo rod. He held my hand steady at the wrist. His grasp was strong and tight to keep me from moving my hand out of harm's way. He brought the bamboo rod up high. It whistled as it cut through the air. It thumped as it made contact with my fingertips. Four Tatzen, two on the left hand and two on the right. First my fingers felt numb, then they burned and then the feeling returned and brought tears to my eyes. My face was red. I tried to shrink along the woodwork back to my desk. No one laughed. They'd all known the teacher's expertise with the bamboo rod, some more than others. After that I forgot what I was going to say next. I also forgot my curiosity about the activities of the Third Reich.

That year Grandmother came to visit for Christmas. So did my cousin Anneliese. I could hardly wait. Anneliese enjoyed coming to Mannheim. I enjoyed introducing her to the magic of city life. There were no soldiers in Bruchsal and Mannheim had several garrisons. Soldiers frequently marched through the main streets of the city.

There were Lutheran as well as Catholic churches and I could hardly wait to show her the inside of a "Protestant" church. It was a half-forbidden thing and therefore twice as desirable. Elfriede Goth was Protestant and she had no difficulty showing us the church.

"What about Mary? What about the Saints?" Anneliese asked.

"They don't belong in church. Statues of dead people don't belong in church," Elfriede volunteered. The church, Elfriede explained, was a house of God. To kneel before statues of Saints was idol worship.

We were stunned. I asked the priest about it the next time I saw him at mass. He was a good priest and he allowed private conversations. He just smiled.

"We don't worship the statue, we address ourselves to the spirit of the person it represents."

Now why didn't I think of that? I thought that was so clever. And of course if it applied to the saints would it then apply to anything else.

"Is it the same way with the flag?"

He looked at me. His smile froze on his lips.

"Be sure to tell your mother I said hello," he said and walked away. The Third Reich, it was like an invisible circle that imprisoned my mind and left my curiosity dissatisfied.

Mutti and Vati allowed us to go to the movies. The movie house was on the same block as the Ghetto. In fact it was part of the Ghetto. It was accessible from the street that ran between G.7 and H.7., and it had an exit to the little alley in the center of the block.

We went to see Heidi with Shirley Temple. Shirley Temple's curls were a point of envy for me. Anneliese had black, naturally curly hair. She could have all the Shirley Temple Curls she wanted. Mine was straight and hung down like a horse's tail. I was cursed with horsehair.

It was a mild December and we were allowed to visit Aunt Antonia at the big house at Werderstrasse. Since we were not given a specific time limit, we took the long way, via the Augusta Anlage. The Hotel Mannheimer Hof was there. Sometimes famous people stopped there and we were lucky and we could watch them drive up in those big cars.

We were lucky that day as well. As we approached the hotel we noticed there were a lot of

47

uniformed individuals milling around the entrance. Black uniforms, S.S. uniforms. We moved back from the sidewalk and sort of blended in with the shrubbery. Soon one singular, relatively small person in a brown uniform emerged from the building.

Having seen that face on a daily basis, staring down from public buildings there was no mistaking that identity.

"Hitler," I whispered. And behind Hitler, that gaunt, black-uniformed individual who looked more like praying mantid than a human, Himmler. Goehring and Goebbels followed closely.

I was looking to advertise the news. Anneliese held me back.

"Don't," she said.

"Why not?"

"Maybe we're not supposed to see them. Maybe they don't want anyone to knew that they're here."

"What if it had something to do with war?" I countered.

"That's even more reason," Anneliese replied.

WAR

Anneliese had a point. Besides that, we were once more where we were not supposed to be. No need to chance getting grounded. But it wasn't easy to keep quiet about that adventure.

Christmas Eve, feast of peace was overshadowed by war. The apartment was full of people. Uncle Konrad provided the music. Mutti served cold cuts and potato salad. Vati made glow-wine. I received two books for Christmas. Shinderhannes was a collection of folk tales. The other book was about the Titanic.

Anneliese and I were sent to bed early. It had something to do with Vati having to leave after

Christmas. We weren't ready to be dismissed and so we hunkered down in the hall, outside the kitchen door where everyone was gathered around the table. We heard shreds of conversation about the West Wall. Hitler was building a fortification between France and Germany. And here again was the word: "Bunker." War was mentioned several times. Soon the conversation sank down to a whisper.

Anneliese and I could not imagine WAR. We wanted to think about ballets and Christmas Trees and pretty movies about handsome princes and beautiful princesses.

They woke us up to go to Midnight Mass. We were sleepy and it was cold out there. We shivered, but we went.

The church was a sea of people. There was candle glow adrift and clouds of incense overhead. On the left side altar was the manger with the cattle and figures of Joseph, Mary, and Jesus. The organist played exceedingly well. The place was alive with sound.

As the priest elevated the host, he prayed, and with him all the congregation, that there may be peace.

We understood little of the sermon. But we could not avoid feeling what the majority of the people felt. If there is a God, I thought, how could He keep from responding to this plea. And of course there was a God. I just didn't know where He was or when He was or is. This God, how could he not answer this petition for peace?

1938 was overshadowed by war clouds. Vati had gone to work on the West Wall. Mutti and I were left alone. Early in 1939 Hitler justified the West Wall.

The Fuehrer said that France posed a potential threat for Germany. Just as France had damned every German to live in poverty with the infamous treaty of Versailles, so was France forcing the Germans to build a defense against the defense that the French were building. It was known as the MAGINOT LINE. The equivalent of the MAGINOT LINE, would be the WEST WALL, also known as the SIEGFRIED LINE.

At school we drew maps. The line of defense was the cutting edge of a knife that cut Europe in half from south to north. Able-bodied men, Vati among them, men who were not in the Air Force the Navy or the Wehrmacht, were building bunkers.

Now there was talk of war. We even discussed it at school. But I had learned to listen. I was not asking questions. There was talk of war, but there was no talk of death.

Germany, the teacher said, was well defended. The German soldiers were the best equipped on the continent. If war came, it would not be German blood that flowed.

War, they said, was no big thing. If war came it would last, at the most six to eight weeks. That's how long it would take to keep the nations around us from brutalizing Germans who had the misfortune of living beyond the border of the Third Reich.

War they said, would make it necessary to incarcerate non-Germans and to eject enemies of the Third Reich. The word "Concentration Camp" came up briefly and we were given to understand that those would be places that offered same comfort and at the same time Non-Germans would be safely kept out of harm's way. We were shown pictures of places like the garrisons at Mannheim, places with little gardens and small parks.

War, Goehring said, would be no problem. All he had to do was push a button and his air force would be up there to keep the skies over Germany safe.

War, Himmler said, would make it necessary to report all activities that could be interpreted as unsympathetic to the Third Reich. People, who did not agree with the Third Reich, would be guilty of treason. Those who failed to report such treason would be equally guilty.

At school we practiced safe procedure in the event of Air Raids.

I was puzzled. So were my friends. None of us wanted to say anything for fear that some one would think we were committing treason.

Across the street, new people moved in where the shoemaker used to live. No one wanted to ask any questions. Then Hannelore's father was taken away and her mother committed suicide. Herr and Frau Rettig took Hannelore as a foster child. She was not allowed to associate with us. And we never knew what really happened. But we were scared.

Mutti's face looked small and pinched. She did allow me freedom to be with my friends, but she was careful not to have any discussions with me. She spent a lot of time with Frau Greulich.

That summer Vati's cousin Josef and his son Seppel came up from Augsburg. I was eager to meet them. Uncle Konrad told us that they were mountain climbers. The highest mountain I knew was the Koenigstuhl at Heidelberg. You could walk up there. Where Josef and Seppel came from, Uncle Konrad said, the mountains were so tall the snow never melted.

Mutti allowed me to go to the Grandmother at G.3. From the window upstairs I could see them coming from wherever they'd been. Grandfather said they were dressed like real Bavarians. I had no idea how real Bavarians dressed. But I found out soon. They wore Lederhosen and socks that came in two stages. There was the foot part that covered the foot in the shoe. And there was the top part that went from the knee down to within five inches of the ankles. Those five inches were left bare. Again no one could tell me why. But that was O.K. as well. They both were tall, sunburned, and masculine. They both spoke as though there was always a little laughter hidden somewhere. They were wonderful and I paraded Seppel in front of my girl friends like a grand prize. There was no doubt that Annel Keller was envious. Nor was there any doubt that I enjoyed her being envious. I just don't know why it was important to me that she was envious.

I also enjoyed Seppel's company for the thing itself. Seppel was different from the boys on the street. He was different from the boys backstage at the National Theater. He was a lot different from the boys in the village. There was an open-minded gentleness about him that exuded warmth. Seppel was eager to accommodate. He always asked Mutti's permission to take me out for a walk; or as he put it, for me to show him the city. And while Mutti never granted time with me rashly, she always gave Seppel permission.

Seppel and I went for long walks through the Castle Gardens, the Rhine River, The National Theater, and the Augusta Anlage. I told him that Anneliese and I saw Hitler there. Seppel just smiled.

Seppel never talked about matters of the Third Reich. Instead he talked about his native Bavaria, the mountains, the animals that lived among the cliffs and crags, the Alpine Range that separated Northern

Europe from the southern part of the continent. From Seppel I learned a lot about eternal snows, glaciers and walls of ice that glow red in the setting sun.

It was Seppel who introduced me to Ganghofer. Now, besides reading Karl May's adventure series of Indians, cowboys, African Hunters, and Indian Rajahs, I read about heroes risking life and limb on the Eiger, the Jungfrau, the Matterhorn.

I hated to see him go. It seemed as though for the time he was with us, a sense of gentility prevailed. While he was with us, the shadow of war and the chilling eminence of the Third Reich somehow had ceased to exist.

Of course, as always in the summer, we went to the village. We left after Seppel had gone. Mutti went to L.6 Polizei Presidium to report our departure from Mannheim.

"Why does the police have to know everything?" I asked.

" It's the way we live and where we live and how we live that determines that. And don't ask any more questions please."

I did not ask any more questions. I focused on the train ride ahead. I looked forward to going to Neibsheim. Anneliese would be there. I could tell her all about Seppel.

DISASTER

Anneliese was there. But that summer turned out to be our summer of malcontent. It was a hot summer that came to a sudden end with a violent cloudburst. Uncle Johann had seen it coming. He returned unexpectedly from the field. He called for Franzl.

"Go to the priest's house. Tell him to ring the church bell."

Franzl turned slightly pale.

"What do I say when he asks me why?" he inquired. Uncle Johann's voice returned threatening.

"Do what I tell you!" he roared.

Grandmother reached for her rosary. She settled in the corner of the kitchen and prayed.

Uncle Johann called for the boys. Herr Kratzmeier, in the farmhouse behind us, called for his four sons. They all transferred the manure from the byre to the entrance of the farmyard.

Boards were placed against the entrance to the house as well.

The church bell started ringing. Wagons pulled by cows and horses flowed into the village. Across the street the Bruecke Seph and his son Edmund were putting up barriers. Daughter Agnes and her mother put up the chickens. At our place Aunt Martha herded the pigs up the front steps and into the house.

That distant rumbling of thunder had now become an explosion of sound and lightning followed lightning.

Anneliese started to cry. I still was unaware of what was going to happen. When lightning and thunder became more distant I stepped outside. There the men were manning the barricades. I sort of jumped it to look beyond to see what it was that they were barricading against. Uncle Johann reached across, hoisted me up by the scruff of my neck and pitched me headfirst into the house.

"If you want to drown, do it someplace else," he yelled.

I was severely reprimanded. Anneliese cried, Aunt Antonia and Aunt Martha joined Grandmother in praying the Rosary. Mutti corralled me and placed me at the bedroom window.

"You can see it from here when it comes! Don't worry! You won't miss it."

"But why are they ringing the church bells?"

"They do that when a disaster happens."

I stood there for a full five minutes waiting for a disaster. I looked out the window. Then I saw it coming. It was a wall of water, at least four feet high. It was a brown, ugly churning mass that swept everything in its way down toward the village, toward the church.

The barricade did not keep the water out. A lot of the water seeped seemingly unrestricted through the barricade.

The water almost reached the top of the stairs that led into the house before it slowed down and slowly ebbed away.

The clean-up was awful. Nothing smells as bad as a mixture of mud and manure. Karl, who was not supposed to curse, cursed under his breath, still manning the shovel.

"Shit!" he said. I smiled, sort of, behind the hand that hid the lips.

"I didn't know you were that smart."

Karl was going to pitch the shovel. But Uncle Johann glared at him and that got him back on task. Then Uncle Johann glared at me.

"Time you learned something too."

From that time on, Anneliese and I were introduced to the joy of womanhood, HOUSEWORK. We had to wash dishes, sweep floors, help prepare supper, and carry Vesper to the men in the field.

Neither one of us did that willingly. We rebelled in our own way. Anneliese talked and I acted. Between the two of us we managed quite a few misdeeds. Just to get even with Aunt Martha who always informed on us to Uncle Johann, we ate most of her winter's supply of walnuts. We took time out to play circus with the neighbor's chickens. I understand they weren't laying for weeks. We got into the supply of poppy seeds. We accidentally let the rabbits loose. In short, the list went on and on.

Anneliese and I, afraid of what would happen to us when Uncle Johann found out, addressed ourselves to a Higher Power. Now it was our turn to pray the Rosary. We did it in style, on our knees, all the way up to the chapel on the hill, from one station of the cross to the next. We were contrite. I was doubly contrite because I knew that Anneliese by herself would never have gotten into that much trouble.

We almost felt we were successful. Our prayers had been heard. Nothing had happened, not when we left, not after we returned to our homes, she in Bruchsal, I in Mannheim.

It stayed that way until Aunt Antonia came to see Mutti. She had just returned from a visit to the village. Aunt Martha couldn't resist the temptation. She told Aunt Antonia everything, the affair with the chickens, the nuts in the attic, Ida's little filly getting loose in the barnyard, the rabbits, I think she even added a few that we were not responsible for. It was Anneliese Kratzmeier who skinned out the dead cat. The bug collection, well I didn't mean for those beetles to wind up in Aunt Martha's bed. As I said, the list went on and on. Mutti said I was lucky that my father wasn't here. He would have paddled me. Mutti did it her way. "GROUNDED," she said, "until further notice," and yes, that included rehearsal and practice at the National Theater.

By the time I was free, it was almost time for school. Not that the house-arrest kept me out of hot water.

Mutti set boundaries. If she could prove that I had gone beyond the boundaries, I'd be grounded again.

The temptation was irresistible. This time it was an expedition on borrowed bikes, across the Rhine to Ludwigshafen. Several hours of intensive biking took its toll on my slip. That old bike seat had worn the garment so thin I could literally read through it by moonlight.

Mutti found out about that too and I was GROUNDED again. She made it plain to me what was meant by going-one-bridge-too-far.

When that stint of incarceration was completed, I was content to stay on the street. That little gang of mine was there as well. Boys and girls, shouting insults at each other. There was Ursula Mueller, Annel and Maria Keller, Inge Currant, Inge's brother Rolf, his cousin Hans and their friend Alfred.

Now we played a new game. "Der Kaiser schickt sein Heer aus!"

You could hear that call echo all the way up and down the street. The Emperor sends his army out. Two lines were formed, one for each Emperor. Each line was an army. The name was called by the Emperor and the person whose name was called, had to break through the opposite line. If that person were successful, the line broke and a prisoner of choice was taken.

Soldiers of the line took their duty serious. It was a game of skill. You had to figure out velocity, speed and the origin of the weakest link. The Hitler Youth had taught us to think of ourselves as free people. We did not easily become prisoners. And we had sprained wrists, skinned shinbones and split lips to prove it. It seemed as though our way of thinking and feeling about ourselves and others had imperceptibly changed.

So had the songs we were singing at the Hitler Youth meetings:

Wir werden weiter marschieren;

Bis alles in Scherben faellt:

Denn heute gehoert uns Deutschland;

Und morgen die ganze Welt.

The song said that we would keep on marching when everything about us fell apart. Today we owned Germany and tomorrow the world.

It was basically meaningless to me. I had no wish to own anything. But I liked the melody, the cadence, and the rhythm of the song. Mutti forbade me to sing that song at home. A lot of stuff was "VERBOTEN."

At the UFA Cinema, the big film was "JUD SUESS." It was a film about a Jewish family that was going to own Europe simply by managing all of its finances. It was a film about the evil things that the Jews visited upon the non-Jews. "JUD SUESS" was "verboten" for young people under the age of fourteen. I was under fourteen. Mutti said it was forbidden. The Third Reich said it was forbidden. Annel and Maria and I went to see it. It was all about a man who wanted another man's girlfriend, and forced her to do unspeakable things. It was a little like the plot of the opera TOSCA, except that in this film the girl committed suicide, the Jewish person was to blame, and in the end a lot of people wanted to kill him.

I was naive. I didn't understand the reason for it. My girlfriends tried to explain. In the end, the only thing I remembered about that film was a map of Europe on a table, a group of men standing around it, connecting the dots on the map and the connected dots became the Star of David. It was the same dreaded emblem that was on every coat of every Jewish person as they passed us on the street, like night shadows.

Mutti didn't catch that misdeed and I was grateful for it.

I was in school when the "BLITZKRIEG" occurred. There was no use asking Mutti about it. Vati was away, working on the West Wall. But I needed to talk to someone about that. I managed to skip school once more. I went to visit Mama Roth at Friedrich Ebert Strasse 64. It was no longer the Friedrich Ebert Strasse. It was now the Adolf Hitler Strasse. I ran up the stairs and rang the bell. I was in luck. She was home. As always, she welcomed me in, offered me sweet treats and as always, answered my questions in a way I could understand. She even told me why no one wanted to talk about it. She told me about the GESTAPO, the secret police. Mama Roth had her own way of explaining the Blitzkrieg. The world had let loose a devil on mankind, she said. The world had let loose the killing thing.

"God help us if we die and God help us if we live," she said. Either way it was going to be bad. She was somber and downcast. I had never seen her this way.

I tried being pert and cheerful. I told her that at school we had been told that the whole thing would be over with in six weeks.

Mama Roth brought out a World Atlas. She opened it to the map of Europe. She pointed towards England. She pointed out all the island nations, Denmark, Sweden, Iceland, Norway, and Scotland.

"What does that have to do with the Sudeten?" I asked.

"It's not what they teach you in school that becomes a problem; it's what they fail to teach you."

I was not going to argue with her about school. But I was interested in the things she pointed out.

"It's possible that England has an agreement with Poland. And Poland has everything to do with the Sudeten."

"Why would England have an agreement with Poland?"

"Why do we have an agreement with Russia?"

I looked at her as though she was the headmaster at school about to give a quiz. The next sentence just sort of slipped out.

"We have an agreement with Stalin."

"We have an agreement with a butcher." She said it in the same voice she used when she used to give me orders. It was something someone said about what our government was doing and she did not say that with the voice of approval. There was a momentary silence and then she continued in a softer voice.

"Some of the countries have agreements with Poland. Remember that the last war started in the Balkan. The last war was about an assassination of a royal person. Before it was over with all Europe was at war, except Switzerland. And the Swiss don't fight, they just make money and chocolate and cheese."

I countered by telling her about our superior Air Force. There was that statement about Goehring pushing a button again. I talked about all the fliers flying against England. She talked about all the fliers that would be shot down by the Flak. She talked about all the planes flying over Germany, dropping bombs.

She completed the lecture by stating, "That's why we have bunkers in Mannheim. And that's why we have Flak in Mannheim."

The last statement caught me by surprise.

"We have Flak?" I asked. She nodded her head.

"Look up sometime when you go through the city. Look up to the highest buildings. Sometimes you can see the guns."

When I left I felt disturbed. She did not soothe the disturbance within myself. She did not take away my fears. Instead, she made me aware of the "KILLING THING" she'd been talking about. On the way home I looked for those guns she'd mentioned. I saw them atop of Sparkasse, the National Health Insurance Building. Just as I had discovered the bunker in the Tennis Platz, so did I now discover the anti-aircraft guns on top of the insurance building? It was, as usual, an illegal excursion and as much as I wanted I couldn't bring it to Mutti's attention.

When I got home that afternoon I did not want to go out and play. I felt bad. I felt bad because I had once again deceived in order to satisfy my own needs. Of course I couldn't tell her about seeing Jud Suess and I couldn't tell her about going and seeing Water for Canitoba. That film was forbidden because it was all about "Untenrum," more commonly referred to as S E X.

There were so many taboos. The Catholic Church had taboos about sex and taboos about lying and taboos about disobedience. The Catholic Church did not explain why those things were considered wrong. To say God didn't like it was a little like saying God didn't like dill pickles. But did that make eating dill pickles bad? The Third Reich had taboos against sex, taboos against lying, and most certainly taboos against disobedience. The Third Reich offered no explanation other than the German female of the future must be pure of spirit, pure of race, clean of heart, and clean of body, but most of all obedient.

The Third Reich did not explain. As far as I could ascertain, the entire adult world made demands, satisfied few needs, and explained next to nothing. The child was persona-non-grata. "BASTA," as Uncle Johann always said. That meant the topic was terminated.

My attention was soon captured by something new that came into my life. Anneliese first wrote me about it. She told me that her mother had seen a Rechtsanwalt, an attorney, about a possible inheritance from India. Mutti did not want to talk about that. But Mutti and I started seeing a soothsayer. Annel Keller laughed when I asked her what a "soothsayer" was.

"A soothsayer says sooth." Annel laughed when she'd said that, then added: "What you don't know could fill a book."

"What I do know could fill a book too," I answered, my temper rising. Did you know there are guns on top of houses? Did you know that Verdi wrote Aida? Did you know that Wotan was the same as Zeus and Jupiter?"

Annel and Maria calmed me down. They said they did not want me to feel bad about what I didn't know. They said they were quite certain that what I did know could fill a book as well. They said that a soothsayer was a person who told the future by playing cards. It was a kind of superstition.

Superstition did not rate high in the Catholic Church; as a matter of fact, superstition ranked next to idol worship and was described as: "THOU SHALT NOT HAVE ANY OTHER GODS BEFORE ME."

That's what the priest said when I asked him. I could not tell him that my mother was taking weekly trips to have the cards read. Nor could I tell him that my mother disliked the clergy.

I really didn't mind those trips across the Rhine to Ludwigshafen. For once I was all legal about doing an illegal thing. The lady who read the cards for my mother was very nice. She had two big tomcats. I was allowed to pet them. I loved those cats. The lady also had a big collection of comic books. She had Max & Moritz, and Felix the Cat. One of the cartoons showed Felix flying into the twenty-first century on a bundle of balloons in one paw, and in the other an ice cream cone.

"Poor Felix," I said. "If he isn't careful, he'll get shot down by the Flak."

My mother did not appreciate my sense of humor. She told me to be quiet. I was. I listened to the conversation she had with the lady. It was something about the cards revealing that there may be some difficulty with the inheritance. It had something to do with England. England, it appeared, owned India. And England, it seemed, was not on friendly terms with Germany.

A DISPUTE AMONG NATIONS

England declared war on Germany on September 3,1939. France followed suit. Vati came home from the West Wall. The West Wall was now completed.

The radio was alive with special bulletins, telling us all about the victorious march of our troops into foreign territory. On Sundays there was a program called WUNSCH KONZERT. People could request songs to be played for their favorite soldier. There were many soldiers now. Every family had soldiers.

Uncle Konrad was the first to be called to duty in our family. It was a tearful farewell. Uncle Konrad smiled and told us not to be concerned. He would be home soon, who knows, Christmas perhaps. His new wife was pregnant. He never returned and he never knew his son.

Shortly before Christmas, my mother's family called a gathering of the clan. It was the first and only time that Grandmother saw her seven children assembled as adults. All the cousins were there, except Ellen and Hans Peter, the children of Uncle Moritz. Uncle Moritz was there. It was the only time I saw my mother's youngest brother.

I was thirteen and I was now admitted to the circle of adults and was also old enough to know and understand that the clan was divided among political lines. Aunt Antonia, Aunt Fanny, Uncle Moritz, and my grandmother were apparently pro-Third Reich. Uncle Moritz now lived in Berlin. He talked about his personal struggle and how the Third Reich helped him to obtain his degree in engineering. And then he told his mother that he was in the army now and that he was an officer. He said he had wanted to be with the elite parachute command, but that he had been turned down because he had small children. He talked about a thing called patriotism and that he was willing to fight for the good of the country if that was what was asked of him. My grandmother said very little, but agreed with him. She said it was all the fault of the Jews. It had been a Jewish Loan Concern that had taken the last cow out of the barn and had left her a destitute widow with no way to raise her seven children. She blamed the Jews for the fact that three of her daughters were forced to hire out as servants.

Uncle Johann didn't see it that way. He blamed the Third Reich for the war that could only harm the land. He said he had sacrificed and worked hard to keep the land. He'd given up the school that Moritz had handed to him on a silver platter. His mission had been to save the farm.

"For what!" he grumbled; "For another damned war? Another scorched earth?"

Anneliese and I sat quietly in the corner. I don't know if we realized that this would be the end of our childhood. For the first time in our young life we were brought face to face with the things that could divide a family. And once again we were made aware that whatever it was that had been discussed in that gathering, could not be discussed anyplace else.

Now the Third Reich was an intimate part of my life. In a way I wanted to be proud of the success the nation was having on all battlefronts. And in another way I failed to understand why it was necessary to have a war, to hurt and to hate. Someone had written into my little remembrance book: "Sei immer treu und edel, und bleib ein deutsches Maedel." Four little lines that wanted me to be true, noble, and German. What I wanted to be more than anything else was myself.

By the time I turned fourteen the war was in full swing. Uncle Moritz had received another promotion and I composed a few verses of congratulation. I was surprised when he answered my letter and told me to make a wish. If it were possible, he would grant it. No one had ever made me an offer like that. I wasn't long to state my desire. I wanted a pair of roller skates. All my friends had roller skates. Alfred skated and so did Rolf and Hans and Inge and Annel. Maria could not skate because she had a curved spine. Maria was too delicate to skate. But she was wiser than all of us, except she didn't know who composed "Siegfried" and I did.

I sort of forgot about the skates because now the war brought new dangers. Hitler said that England, goaded by Churchill, had attacked Berlin. Not just Berlin, but the civilian sector. Innocent women and children had died and now there would be an all out attack on England. Night and day, our planes would fly and attack England. The blood of innocent children was asking for revenge, he said.

Now when we went to see Aunt Antonia or the soothsayer, we had to make certain that we were near an air raid shelter in case of attack.

At school we had air raid drills. Sirens were a new addition to our life. We learned the signals for "attack" and sirens for "all clear." Alert-Alarm-All Clear!

In the beginning it was a big thrill to get up in the middle of the night, to sit in the sheltered basement and to communicate with knocks against a brick wall with the person in the other shelter. We were just one big community, going underground, having an exciting adventure. Gunfire was added to new sounds in my life. After the all clear I was allowed to join my friends in gathering fragments of missiles. Judging from the size of the fragments, the missiles must have been impressive. They had to be, Manfred explained. After all, they were designed to bring down those inferior British air planes.

Now there were lots of people to hate. There were the British, the Polish, the French, and of course, as always, the Jews. I wondered if there was anyone left to like. To be friends was natural to me; to be enemy was not.

It was at the National Theater where none of the hates crossed the threshold.

At the dress rehearsal for Aida I was almost too tall for the children's ballet and barely tall enough for the mass scene of the triumphal entrance. I was a black Ethiopian slave, so said Herr Hoelzlin, except my eyes. They were blue. He thought I was a fascinating Ethiopian. I liked Herr Hoelzlin. He was pleasant and approachable. He was the basso profundo and appeared more regal in his role as High Priest than Pharaoh himself.

The life of the theater was easy to love backstage. I loved the props and the music. I loved the smell and the sight and the sound of it all. I lost myself in a world of make-belief and thoroughly enjoyed being on stage.

Among those backstage companions was Helmut Spengler. He was the only son of a lighting engineer. Helmut spent hours patiently explaining to me the way how everything worked. He also explained why the theater could not be renovated, that its importance as national, cultural and historical landmark made it in essence untouchable. Schiller had worked there; so had Goethe, Mozart, and Wagner.

"ES MOEGEN MAENNER WELTEN BAUEN:"

"ES STEHT UND FAELLT EIN VOLK MIT SEINEN FRAUEN!"

That banner hung high above the hallway of the building where Mutti went for testing. It proclaimed, that although men were building worlds, a nation stood and fell with its women. Again and again The Third Reich proclaimed the importance of the nation's female population.

Mutti was ill. No one seemed to know the problem or the cause. But the Third Reich took good care of her. The Third Reich paid for extensive as well as expensive testing procedures. Mutti did not tell me what she was ailing from. But then, it had always been difficult for Mutti to share matters of a personal nature with me.

Vati was not available for comment either. But thank God he was available.

At school we were reveling in the victories of the Third Reich. Hitler had fulfilled his promises. We had gone to Paris for the fourth time. Once more we were signing a treaty in the Hall of Mirrors in Versailles. This time we were the victors. For a brief moment in time we were hoping that this would be the end of the war. But then came Churchill's ordered attack by air on the civilian sector of Berlin. Now the Luftwaffe retaliated. Vengeance a hundred-fold was Hitler's motto and London came under attack. Ships at high seas came under attack by the U-Boats.

Little seemed to change for us, except that groceries would be rationed.

Herman no longer dismissed his H.J. troop in front of our house. The last time I saw him was at Mass one Sunday Morning. I thought that was a godsend. There was little doubt about this early infatuation with Herman. Tall and tan, well suited to his uniform, soft spoken and always seemingly in command, he could have qualified for poster person.

He went up to the communion rail and so did I, and for a brief while it seemed as though we were kneeling side by side. It was the ultimate bliss. And then he was gone. His sister, who was our Jungmadel group leader, told me he was in the navy he spoke something about serving on a U-Boat. I did not write to him. He did not know I existed. Love seemed to be that way at times. At least I had the memory of going to the communion rail with him, kneeling side by side. I did correspond with the boys from the National Theater. Helmut Spengler was among the first to go. Manfred followed not much later.

At school I was scheduled for advancement I did not choose. My parents were called in. That was followed by a conference at home.

"The government will pay for your education, that is, if you choose to attend the gymnasium."

"You mean I actually have a choice?" I was not being facetious. It was the first time I had been offered a choice where education was concerned. I was not fond of school. That did not mean that I was not fond of learning. Learning came natural to me. It was just that I liked learning what I wanted to learn and not learning what somebody else insisted I'd learn.

No came easy and quickly. My parents did not ask me why I said no. They just accepted the fact that I had turned down the opportunity to attend the gymnasium and the eventuality of attending the University at Heidelberg.

School would not continue much longer. At the last part of the eight grade no reports were issued because of the war.

The Third Reich made out the schedule for my future. When I was fourteen I had to join the B.D.M., "Bund Deutscher Maedels," the female part of the Hitler Youth.

I was tired of standing on the street corners in my uniform and asking for donations with my little tin can. I was tired of singing those songs and marching in formation. I did what I had done so well in school. I skipped the meetings. Then there was the police officer at the door and it became clear that missing the Hitler Youth meetings was a major offense that could have some unpleasant consequences. Vati solved that dilemma. He got in touch with my mother's physician. The good doctor wrote an excuse, on the basis of my mother's illness. The Third Reich accepted that.

A WOMAN'S DUTY

The Third Reich demanded of every female person a year of duty, employed as a maidservant in a household. The choice of household belonged to the Third Reich. It was an unfortunate choice. The Department of Labor assigned me to the household of an officer, stationed at Feudenheim. As best I can remember, the man had a wife, three children and a gold tooth. I shall always remember that vague and distant smile and that gold tooth.

The woman and I did not get along. I did not like emptying chamber pots first thing in the morning. I cleaned floors, made up beds, and scrubbed kids. The eldest son, barely in his teens, explained to me that he was having erections while he bathed.

I had no way to approach that subject with his mother. Nor could I discuss that with my mother. Sex was taboo. I had no way of knowing what it meant for the boy to have an erection. In matters of sex I was woefully under-educated.

My servitude earned me ten marks a month. I liked the money, but I lacked the enthusiasm needed for a job that included chamber pot duty and the bathing of pubescent boys. Once again, I faked illness. This time I got caught. An acquaintance of the family was in the Corps de Ballet. She told the lady that I had been at rehearsal when I was too ill to be on the job. My mother cautioned me. This, she said, was more dangerous than skipping school.

"People in uniform tell us what to do."

"But — "She would have no "buts". And I sensed the fear in her voice. I could not understand the fear. And she would not discuss that with me.

71

Christmas came around and there was a gift under the tree. I was not allowed to touch it until dark when the candles were lit on the tree, the glow wine was ready and the guests had arrived for the celebration. When I finally opened the box I could scarcely contain myself. It was a pair of the finest roller skates I could wish for. And of course I had to put them on right away. I skated through the apartment. I skated out into the hall. I maneuvered myself down the stairs and out the door. And I completed my first three point landing.

"Skating is a skill. You have to learn first," Vati said.

I was an impatient learner. Rolf was an accomplished skater. So was Hans and Alfred and Inge and Elfriede. Learning to skate did not come cheap. My grandmother finally insisted that I learn how to knit along with learning how to skate, so that I could learn to knit my own patches to go on my torn stockings. My knees rarely got the chance to heel before the skin was off again.

Although the army had been to Paris for the fourth time, the war did not end. Now there were the Allied Forces and the Axis forces. Hitler explained to us how we came to be the friends of Hirohito, the emperor of Japan. We did not know much about Japan. We were told that China was an ever-present danger. China and the Chinese were referred to as the "Gelbe Gefahr." It was the Yellow Danger. At the theater we were rehearsing for "Das Land Des Laechelns," the land of smiles. The country where everyone smiled, no matter how unhappy they were. We were also rehearsing Madame Butterfly. That was a Puccini opera about a Japanese girl and a British naval officer. It was, in essence a tragedy. I was told that I could learn from it, that unions of different backgrounds never ended happily. There seemed to be a message, a hidden meaning in every performance. The Magic Flute, by Mozart, appeared to be the only exception.

Of course the radio was alive with special bulletins. Apparently there had been a big battle at Narvik and Scaggerak. The song lauded the nobility of the navy that was willing to die for the Vaterland. I asked Mutti if we knew anyone who had died in battle yet. Mutti shook her head and turned away. We were not going to discuss that either. Mutti still paid her visits to the astrologer across the Rhine. But now we only went on rainy days, when the air raids were not a possibility. It seemed that the British were going to keep us from any inheritance.

"Why can they do that?" I asked.

"Because they rule in India and because we are at war with England."

The war moved closer to us one night. There was an air raid. The bombers managed to penetrate and the first bomb fell within walking distance from the house. We sat in the basement, choking on gritty dust that seeped in from somewhere. The following morning some of my friends went up to see the building. Half of the building had been destroyed. Somewhere on the fourth floor a bathtub dangled high above our head. Part of a bed was there and an arm was extended from the pile of rubbish. Death had arrived. It was there for all of us to see.

1941 and Seppl wrote from distant Africa. He was in Rommel's Afrika Korps. His letters were cheerful. But when I asked him to describe those big tanks we heard so much about, he replied by telling me that it was hot in the desert and sand was everywhere. Then

73

one day a soldier came to the door. Mutti nearly fainted. He said he was a friend of Seppl's and he had a letter for us. That was how we found out about Tobruk. That was how we found out about the tanks.

"A tank," he wrote, "is a cross between an overgrown caterpillar and a car. A big car, more like a truck. The tank has chains and gear wheels on which it moves. It can move very quickly. It can move across sand dunes, through barbed-wire fences, through all sorts of barriers.

"A tank is essentially unstoppable unless it runs out of gasoline. One drives a tank by entering what is more like a sardine box than anything else and one enters through the top hatch. The hatch is closed. One sees the road ahead through slit-like openings. The biggest danger is not being killed by the enemy's bullet, but to be steamed alive should the hatch fail to open. For each driver in the box, there are numerous infantry persons who use the protection the tank allows to forge ahead in enemy territory. The tank has a large gun and the enemy can be blasted out from a distance. This war is deadly. And death and sun and sand is all we see."

He went on to discuss the battle for enemy positions. He talked about E1 Alamain and Tbbruk. Strange sounding places with strange sounding names. I wanted to know about the animals. But Mutti shook her head.

"There are no animals on battlefields; at least not live ones."

I thought it funny how my world was changing. For the first time I was forced to think that for every conquest announced over the radio, there were beings, human and otherwise, who died because of it. I suffered more for the non-human casualties. They had no choice. But then, neither did we.

Uncle Johann came in early autumn and brought us groceries, the fruit of the harvest. He would not see us short of foodstuffs because of rationing. He was, after all the steward of the clan's land. We were part of the clan.

Uncle Johann brought potatoes, carrots, onions and apples. He brought eggs, packed in calcium in a stone crock. Tomatoes arrived, already pureed. Green beans had been salted down, and so was the cabbage.

Uncle Johann explained how the foodstuffs were delivered to each of his sisters. Uncle Moritz had requested that his share was to be evenly divided among the sisters. Berlin, Uncle Moritz decreed, was too far away. Whatever the problem between the two brothers, the value of fairness determined the action of each.

CHEMICAL WARFARE

Uncle Johann was angry. He was as pleasant as a bear aroused too soon from hibernation. His ugly mood had something to do with an insect, called a Colorado Beetle, being dropped from airplanes in small vials on the crops below. The beetle, he said, could easily wipe out an entire potato crop. The whole village, men women and children had to walk the fields and eliminate as many of the beetles as possible. The crop had suffered, but the Third Reich, nonetheless, requested its quota of potatoes for the multitude of people depending on it.

When I brought up the question of the present state of war and that Hitler had called it a "sacred war," Uncle Johann's eyes gave off bolts of lightning.

"What sacred war," he shouted. Mutti was trying to quieten him down, but to no avail. "There is no sacred war," he roared. "War is only about money."

That was new to me. Uncle Johann was not inclined to hold back. He talked about the war industries. He saw Hitler as one person who had, at one time, a good idea. But that was before all the "Little Hitlers" got a hold of him. He said it was no longer a matter of earning a living but a matter of getting rich by spilling the blood of the common man. He said it was like a disease and that it was not limited to Germany and that before it was over, an entire continent would become a wasteland. Mutti tried to stop him, but he would have none of that. He said I was old enough to understand what was going on.

"But is she old enough to keep her mouth shut?" Mutti shouted.

Uncle Johann stopped temporarily, then added: "What kind of existence is it when a man can't speak the truth in the confines of his own four walls."

"The kind of existence that is allotted to us at this point in time!" Mutti answered.

The conversation stopped. Brother and sister, one generation separated from me, stopped the discussion. Mutti did not have to tell me how to keep quiet. I understood Uncle Johann very well.

Krupp Steel and Daimler Benz, just to mention two. Then there were the makers of uniforms. No wonder everybody was gainfully employed. But the captains of business and industry and those only accumulated wealth were the people that influenced Hitler. Hermann Goehring saw to that and so did Todt and Himmler.

I wanted to talk about that some more, but Mutti had declared an end to that discussion. I would not be able to discuss that with my friends. And the only person left to talk to was the priest. When I went to see him, I was told that he was no longer there. The priest who took his place told me that he was busy. He told me that if I needed a priest to come during time for confession. There would be a confessional and there would be a priest.

"But what I have to say is not a sin!" I said.

"Confessions are between three and five on Saturday."

Just then the first warning sirens went off and I had to rush home. Mutti worried when there was an air raid and I wasn't home. I promised The Lady, Mother of God, Mary, to make my way to the church on bended knees, all the way, like the pilgrims in the pictures of the books that came from the church, if only she would stop the war. But then I remembered the debacle from the village. I was alone with the things that I thought and the things that I felt, and war would not end.

By January 1941 Uncle Moritz was on his way to Russia. A lot of soldiers were on the way to Russia. I listened to the "Wunsch Konzert" on Sundays, hoping I would hear from friends that were no longer home. Mutti wept silently and I was afraid to ask why. I turned away and concentrated on letters to the front, wherever the front was. Vati had been drafted and was headed east. And then Rudolf Hess took a plane and flew north to Scotland.

One of my books contained a picture of Rudolf Hess, second in command, side by side with the Fuehrer. There were those who said that Hess had betrayed Hitler, had taken a plane and sought political asylum in England. There were those who thought that he had been sent on a secret mission by Hitler, and that the mission had failed. No one seemed to understand it. The Third Reich made its own declaration. The Third Reich simply stated that Rudolf Hess had gone insane.

If there was a mystery person in the tragedy that engulfed an entire continent, it was probably Rudolf Hess. After the war he was imprisoned in the Fortress Spandau. He remained in solitary confinement, the only prisoner within the walls of the fortress Spandau, until the day he died. Surrounded by guards twenty four hours a day, denied all visiting privileges, the mystery was never solved.

Annel and Maria Keller and I talked about Rudolf Hess briefly. We talked about the fact that he was a handsome man. We knew little about his political career. As a matter of fact we knew little about politics. It was a subject that was not open for discussion among our parents. Besides that, we were more interested in movie stars. Annel and Maria did get to see more movies than I did. My family did not approve of movies. My primary devotion was to the National Theater. But I did like Johannes Hesters and Marikka Roeck. Like most of my peers, I was familiar with the street songs, the hit songs from favorite movies and musical plays. I also knew most of the arias and choruses from the operas, not to mention the ballets. I knew most of the plays, classical and contemporary as well and I could quote verbatim most of the lines from Faust, Don Karlos, Othello, Der Zerbrochene Krug, and most anything that came along during a year's worth of performances.

If I thought Johannes Hesters handsome, it was the basso profundo, Heinrich Hoelzlin, who captured my devotion. During dress rehearsal of Mozart's Magic Flute, I sat at the edge of the stage apron, totally enraptured, listening breathlessly to hear him sing "In diesen heiligen Hallen," being every inch of his stature, the High Priest Sarastro. I shared the secret of my infatuation with Charlotte, Herr Wagner's only daughter. She came to me laughingly at one point and said: "Guess what? I just shook hands with the person you admire most, Herr Hoelzlin."

I shook her hand and I really didn't want to wash my hand for several days.

My year of servitude was almost complete when Grandmother came to visit. With her came Anneliese. Grandmother was seventy-eight and spry as a spring bok. Anneliese had also almost completed her "Dienst Jahr." She had been better at it than I was. But neither of us was happy with that situation. It was Katzenjammer at our house. Mutti, in order to put a stop to it, proposed a hike to Oppau. Grandmother had a friend there. It was a childhood friend and the two had not seen each other since they got married in 1889. I was looking forward to a train ride. But our Elders decided on walking.

Walking the distance of sixteen miles was nothing to Grandmother. And we were told that what was good for Grandmother, was good for us. Anneliese and I disagreed, silently; and we made ugly faces behind their backs.

Grandmother had gone through some difficult times. Her husband died in 1910. The farm was heavily indebted to a Jewish loan company. When she referred to that demise she usually did so with ill-concealed hatred for Jewish Lending Firms. "The Jew came and took that last cow out of the barn." I heard her say that more than once. It was the sweet and gentle Aunt Elise who explained that to me.

"There were seven of us," she recalled. "Your mother was just eleven years old. Your Aunt Fanny and your Aunt Anna and I had to go into service, without the cows Uncle Johann had no draft animals left. He was the eldest son and it was up to him to keep the land in the family and to raise crops. When your Uncle Moritz was old enough, he ran away to Berlin. Life was just too hard for him. Your mother and your Aunt Antonia gathered Reisig and gleaned the fields after the people had gathered the harvest. Your Grandmother used to cry at night. We heard our mother and we were scared to death of what would happen to us."

Anneliese and I were young and impressionable. We had a deep respect for Grandmother. The farm was still in our hands. There were those awful war stories of the French war of 1871. Grandmother was just a little girl child then. They hid her from the troops to keep her from being raped. Grandmother was a widow with seven children when the first World War started in 1914. My mother was fifteen when that war started and Uncle Johann and Grandmother had to hide the younger sisters that remained on the farm. They had to hide their food supplies from the French troops. They drove the cattle to the woods to keep the French from taking the two cows they had been able to acquire. It was agreed that without Grandmother and Uncle Johann there would be no farm.

APPETITES

The visit at Oppau was west of the Rhine. It was disputed territory. But since Hitler had won the battle with France, Oppau was safe.

Grandmother's friend had married an "Outlander." He was not from the village. But he had been a Catholic. Her clan had been grateful that she had found a husband. Had it not been for that marriage, she would have been given to a convent.

Grandmother cried when she saw her friend. I was deeply touched as well, but I did wish for them to hurry and get the hugging over with. The table was set with all manner of lunch meats and breads and fruits. There was cheese, all kind of cheese and deserts and fruit drinks and something called Coca Cola. I could hardly wait. These days I was always hungry. And there was never enough to eat.

"Du," said Anneliese: "Sei doch gut." When she said "du" in this way, and her green eyes blazed akin to lightning, that usually meant that I would do well to be good, in order to keep out of trouble. And I was good. My table manners were impeccable. I was good until everyone left the table. Then I devised a little game with the children of the house. As we all chased around the table, I helped myself to slices of minced ham and Swiss cheese.

Vati broke it all up. By that time I had stuffed myself close to foundering and there were miles to go before we returned to the apartment. The long walk gave me an opportunity to talk to Anneliese about my latest, emotional commitment; Herr Basso Profundo Heinrich Hoelzlin.

Anneliese failed to comprehend why an aging opera singer was worth my affection.

"Listen you" she said, "When you're thirty, he'll be sixty. He'll be as old as the shoemaker in the village."

"But he's also a basso profundo. He is handsome and gentle, and wise beyond words."

I wanted to go on listing his values, lauding his praises, but Anneliese interrupted unceremoniously. "And he is married. The church does not approve."

I knew he was married. I knew that the church did not approve. What irked me about the church was that the church always disapproved without an explanation.

"I don't want to marry him. I just want…" I stopped because I really did not know what I wanted. Was it something referred to as "Romantic Love?" Was it affection? I really didn't know. Anneliese said it had something to do with "Untenrum." But "Untenrum" was a forbidden subject and we were within earshot of adults. We fell silent. We just looked at each other.

An air raid occurred during the last night of her stay. The shrapnel had scarcely gotten cold before we were out there, gathering souvenirs.

We continued our conversation picking shrapnel out of the gutter. I knew that Anneliese had a crush on the priest, Kaplan Wildschuette. I brought that up in passing.

"And he's older than you."

"But he isn't married."

"He's married to the church."

Anneliese did not reply. She was sensitive and I knew I had caused her to feel bad. I did not pursue the topic.

In retrospect, I often wonder if our emotional attachments had something to do with the fact that neither of us had been fortunate in the choice of parents. Vati was not so difficult to live with. He was strict and definitely not the affectionate type. Neither was Mutti, or Anneliese's mother, Tante Anna. Her Father was even worse. He was ill tempered and quarrelsome, given to fits of rage. It was said that his ill temper was due to a head wound he received during World War I.

We returned with Grandmother and Anneliese to the village. Nothing much ever changed in the village. The war appeared to have no effect on the place. The cattle were still bedded down in the stalls. The Angelus still called the entire population to prayer. If there was a change it was subtle. It only became apparent in knowing its people. All of the young men were gone. Many of the older men were gone as well. There were fathers and sons, serving somewhere, side by side. The village functioned smoothly, run by the old men, the widows and the children. And there were widows.

The Arbeits Dienst now performed the work, once performed by the men now who stood guard over the Third Reich. Young Men and women of any nationality were allowed to serve, by choice, we were told, in the Arbeits Dienst. Young Germans, before turning old enough to serve in the army, also served in the Arbeits Dienst. Properly translated it simply stated labor-duty. There were camps for men and women. Separated by sex, they sometimes served their year of duty on the same farm. The camps were beyond the village and the workers were brought to the farms. Sometimes they arrived by truck, sometimes on bicycle, sometimes on foot.

The same was true of prisoners of war, who also served in this manner. There was one difference;

prisoners of war were not permitted to fraternize with the German population.

Prisoners were fed according to the farmer's will. If a farmer decided to work a prisoner without allowing food or drink, he could do so.

The village was a farming community, Catholic for centuries, with deeply ingrained catholic principles. The person, who worked for the farmer, ate, drank, and prayed with him.

Most of the prisoners who worked in the village were French. Some of them had left farms behind and knew the importance of bringing in the crop. Like Uncle Johann, they were men of the soil, bound to the soil by an innate reverence for life and respect for faith. The Third Reich could not change that. By the same token, the man of the soil picked up the gun and laid down the plow when the order came. The church could not change that.

We no longer played in the clay digs. Now we walked with the women and the children to clear the fields of damaging beetles and to search for small incendiaries designed to catch the fields on fire.

Uncle Johann had not been drafted. He worked tirelessly. Walking along the wagon trails, we could see him on the rim of the horizon, cutting the grain with that long handled scythe, rhythmically, stroke upon stroke, row upon row. He worked alone, in silence, keeping his thoughts to himself.

Once, when I carried his noonday meal, some bread, some cheese, a slice of smoked meat, and a flask of hard cider, we talked quietly.

It was not the political party that mattered. There had been the good and there had been bad politics. There had been Lords of the Manor who abused the serf. They went to war and they took the cattle and then the enemy came and burned the homestead. There had been Lords of the Manor, kind and generously disposed toward freedom for the serf. They too went to war. Sons died, fathers died, cattle were taken, and the enemy came just the same and burned the homestead. This was the third war in less than a century. Old ones, he said, remembered all three and did the best they could to silence their fear. It was the farmer's task to save the harvest, to keep the soil from being violated. Nothing else mattered.

"Without the fertile soil, there can be no crop. Without the crop, there can be no food. Without food we will die."

His words were prophetic, although I did not realize that at that moment. He did not talk about his brother Moritz. As far as we all knew, Moritz was on his way to Russia. He had been promoted again and was in charge of an armored division.

We were at war with Russia. Russia, we were told, by the Third Reich, presented a threat and a danger, because of its political philosophy. Russia stood for the essence of Communism. Stalin was an evil, blood-thirsty dictator who would no doubt overrun Europe and enslave its population. Hitler, we were told, was Europe's only hope to remain a free continent.

AIR WARFARE

I was glad to be back home in Mannheim. Nowadays the city was under constant threat from the air. I could not prevent the bombs from dropping, but I could be there, in case I was needed.

Mannheim had lost an entire block of apartment houses on the Ring during my absence. Alfred's apartment was gone. He and his family had survived. They were now part of that slowly growing segment of homeless people; without belongings, without shelter, with barely enough food to remain alive.

The next bombing was the first I experienced close at hand. We were all gathered in the basement. My mother sat there, knitting away. The Flak was shooting; the bombers could be heard overhead. The first bombs began to fall and with each new explosion there was more grit between our teeth. Then the lights went out. You could still hear my mother's knitting needles clicking away. We somehow took comfort from that. As long as she sat there knitting, whether she could see what she was knitting or not, things were O.K.. I was assumed that my mother was attuned to danger. Knitting meant no immediate danger.

When the siren gave the "all clear," we went top side. There was a strange silence, only interrupted by the crackling sound of an all-consuming fire. And there was that awful glow on the horizon. Mutti would not permit me to go and see.

"There's no need to watch some one else's calamity," she said.

If Alfred had survived the bombing, Hildegard had not. They found half of her in the rubble down below. The other half was wedged into the twisted

87

girders up above. No one would say if she had been immediately killed or if part of her was forced to die slowly. Her mother was near insanity with grief, with rage, with fear. Hilde had been her only child.

"What did I ever do to deserve that? I'm not in the party, I didn't ask for that war? Why don't they bomb some one who wanted that war?" She screamed. There were people who tried to calm her. There were some with worried faces. By now I understood the silent threat of the Gestapo and I quietly left.

Now I wanted to talk about the war, about being who I am, but Mutti would not talk. I thought I'd take the chance and try for one more clandestine trip to Mama Roth. I had it all figured out. If I ran most of the way, I could squeeze an hour with Mama Roth out of the time available.

It began well enough. There was little traffic, the air was fine, there were no clouds. I was halfway across the bridge when the siren went off. The Flak started shooting immediately. Then there was the faint hum of approaching air planes. I stood there, on that bridge. The distance was the same either way. I ducked down to the pavement but I realized that there was no protection from shrapnel and certainly not from bombs. The bridge was empty and except for the howling of the sirens, the shooting of the anti-aircraft guns and the humming of the approaching bombers, there was no other sound. There was nothing, except the bridge and the water below. I looked down from the railing. I couldn't jump and I couldn't swim.

I don't know how much time I spent there, huddled against the curb on the pavement of that bridge. Time was meaningless. I understood Hell very well at that point. If Tante Anna would find out she'd tell me that this was God's punishment. But God didn't create the war.

The "all clear" was sounded; I got up on shaky legs. I tried running, but that came ever so slowly.

Back on solid ground, I looked back at the bridge. I knew, that I would never cross that bridge again; at least not for a long, long time.

I did not tell my mother what I had experienced. I came home and quietly reached for a book. I went to bed without supper. Mutti was afraid I was coming down with something. I told her I was fine. I was just a little tired.

My perimeter of movement became very limited after that. I stayed near the air raid shelters. I no longer went on those fun-like adventurous excursions.

Vati was scheduled to leave. Not much was said about that, except that he was leaving. Mutti was left with a head-strong daughter and a frail physique. That she suffered from some sort of illness was now clearly evident, but I did not wish to see that. I was beginning to learn a technique that would allow me to eliminate the unpleasant and the fearful from my mind. I also had made up my mind that I would like to pursue a career as an actress. My home was BACKSTAGE. My mind lived there, my heart and soul lived there.

Mutti didn't see it that way. Vati didn't see it that way. And as they had done once before, they now held a conference, before he left.

"There are not that many opportunities to earn a living that will keep you safe and well-fed."

"I don't mind. I just want to become an actress."

In the end I was persuaded to go to school, to learn a trade. They'd given up on my willingness to attend the Gymnasium and possibly the University. I met them half way and agreed on a trade school. I would attend courses in typing and shorthand.

The Third Reich also agreed to that. As long as I attended trade school I would not have to go to labor camp. That part made me very happy. I, for one, did not see life in a camp, bedding down with other females, rising before dawn and working hard at physical labor all day, in my future.

Not long after Vati left, Willi came to visit us. Willi was from the village. He belonged to a Panzer division. Mutti and I entertained him and fed him coffeecake.

Willi had no news from Uncle Moritz. Nor did he know how the battle went. At Kiev, he said they drove the enemy into the swamp.

"Sometimes we win," he said: "sometimes we lose. Sometimes we just sit and wait. We don't know why."

Willi was the son of one of Mutti's cousins once removed. He was with a Panzer Division in Russia. Although Uncle Moritz was there also, Willi had no information about Uncle Moritz.

Mutti was extremely cautious. She made certain no one could listen to the conversation. But I was curious.

"When you win, what happens to the enemy soldier?"

He closed his eyes, swallowed hard, and then replied:

"The tank just rolls over everything. Sometimes over people."

He whispered softly of the horror of death, of man and beast alike. He talked of people shot and killed at close range.

"It was more merciful then watching them slowly drown in the swamps."

There were times when the enemy was successful and what happened then?

"They'd dump explosives into the top closure. The tank exploded and the people inside just fried alive."

Willi told of orders to shoot the Russian Commissars. Himmler had ordered that no Russian Commissar was to be taken prisoner.

"What's a Commissar?"

"That's a Russian officer."

"We kill them just because they're officers?"

"We kill Russians because they're Slavic. A Slav is inferior to a German!"

"And all that because Himmler orders it?"

Willi suddenly stopped talking.

"Do you kill?"

"Only when I have to."

Mutti put an end to the conversation. Willi left shortly after that. He promised to come back but he never did.

Mutti and I sat alone in the apartment that evening. The light was very dim. The shades, regulation window blinds, were drawn tightly so as not to allow any light to escape. Everything these days was regulation. I was writing a letter to Helmut Spengler on regulation paper. Mutti interrupted. She handed me a letter.

"I forgot to give this to you today," she said. It was a letter I had written to Helmut. All it said was that it could no longer be delivered. I stopped writing. Helmut had no need for letters anymore.

I wanted to find a fantasy island somewhere in the back of my mind. I wanted to erase the things that Willi had said, but I couldn't.

Mutti filled a small metal container with hot water to place it in my bed. It was cold out and the bedrooms were unheated. There was a limited amount of fuel for the kitchen stove and we dressed heavy against the cold. But it wasn't the cold that made me shiver. It was the sounds and sights of death that surrounded my being.

Mutti reminded me that I had given my word not to repeat what I had heard. It was difficult to be saddled with that kind of information; information I could not share with anyone. But I kept my word. Doom was descending on us.

I had problems sleeping. Willi's words danced through my head and I saw bodies crushed and mired in the filth of the road. Sometimes I woke myself up screaming. Sometimes the air raid siren was a blessed relief.

While we sat there in that basement and made small talk, and listened to my mother's knitting needles clicking away, light or no light; while we listened to the anti-aircraft guns, the bombs that rained down on us not far away; while we listened intently, choking back the screams that formed within us, I had one consolation. I did not have to think about battles.

In that year of 1942 I turned sixteen. There was nothing sweet about being sixteen. We had a World Premiere at the National Theater. The world did not attend. We were at war with the world. We were at war with America, and America was so far away that we couldn't even reach it. But America could reach us with bombs.

At the National Theater we rehearsed Dvorak's opera, Jakobiner. I was once more a half-sized street urchin. But that was all right. Herr Hoelzlin had a leading part. I sat at the edge of that stage during dress rehearsal, listening breathlessly, dreaming dreams of Heinrich Hoelzlin leading me to freedom, whatever that was. The Swiss were neutral. Why wasn't it possible to escape to Switzerland? In the Schweitz they had lots of food and lots of milk and they had chocolates. In the Schweitz people laughed and sang and their windows were never dark.

STALINGRAD

By Christmas my grandmother came to visit again with Anneliese. Vati was home. We all went to Midnight Mass. Aunt Antonia came as well.

In the cold moonlight, on the way home, I saw the tears glistening on my mother's face. When Vati saw the shocked expression on my face, he came and took me to the back of the group, out of hearing distance.

"You are not to say anything. You are not to ask, at least not in front of your grandmother. But your Uncle Moritz is missing in action, in Russia."

"Where?"

"Stalingrad."

I knew exactly what that meant. My grandmother had lost a son. Tante Gertrude was now a widow, and Ellen and Hans Peter had no father. All the things we were told on the radio were untrue. We had started a fight with the entire world and we had lost it. But we were not going to be permitted to bow out gracefully. We would fight and die, down to the last German alive. I looked at Anneliese. But her eyes held no hope, no joy.

"Next week we'll sneak out. We'll go and see Gasparone." Anneliese nodded her head.

How do you celebrate the feast of peace in the middle of a war?

I did ask Mutti for permission to go and see Gasparone. I was fond of Johannes Hesters and Marikka Roekk, and music and dancing.

Permission was denied. But we went to see Gasparone anyhow.

Among the popular hit songs of the day was the song of the island of dreams, Hawaii. The street urchins had changed the lyrics. They were singing:

"Eine Insel im Laufschritt verloren, ist die Krim. Sie ist hin"

We were now losing battles. Fieldmarschall Goehring's promised assistance from the air force was virtually non-existent. Werner had flown quite a few of the missions. But Werner was a prisoner of war. He went down over England. How he survived that was always a puzzle to me.

The news from Helmut Ernst was much better than the news from Helmut Spengler. It had not been that long ago that he left for the service. He had talked that over with me very well. He had the physique to join the elite, the S.S. He said he wanted to join the S.S. because that would mean that after the war he would be in line for careers with the government. That meant money. When he left he felt that we were winning. I was not free to discuss that with him. I had given a promise.

The news from Helmut Ernst was not good. He wrote he was alive and that would have to do for the moment.

Radio programs were constantly interrupted by special bulletins. There were the battles we won and there were the ships we sank.

But the war was now extended over an entire continent. German broadcasts referred to Winston Churchill as the Overlord of British Piracy. The broadcasts were saying that he ordered air raids on defenseless civilians on purpose and in order to weaken the moral of the fighting soldier. After all, why should the German soldier defend home and family when home and family no longer existed?

In the end it was not the radio of the Third Reich that told us the awful truth of the battle at Leningrad.

The radio never mentioned the air raids, American by day, British by night.

It was in the first week of February in 1943, shortly before my mother's birthday, that we gathered in the basement It was the usual thing. First were the sirens, then the guns of the Flak, followed by the approaching hum of airplanes, and shortly the percussion of bombs, dropped not far away. The basement filled with plaster dust and then the lights went out. And then my mother's knitting needles stopped to click, for the first time. I listened intently. There is something about the sound of approaching, impending death that makes the body go rigid and the mind explode with fear. But the impact of that bomb was not equal to the proximity where it landed.

The block leader finally broke free from the awful spell and went upstairs. Block leaders were too old for duty on the front and often too sick to do anything else. This one was about the same. When he finally came back down, he told us very quietly that we had received a "Blindganger," a dud, a bomb that could possibly explode any moment, and that we would have to leave the building. The problem was that no one knew for certain if and when the thing would explode.

One by one we passed that awful thing resting on our doorstep. My mother left her knitting needles behind. We were so busy trying to survive we did not see her grasping at her chest. She held my hand and we slowly walked past the bomb, up the street to another shelter, where we were comforted. I couldn't even cry.

The "Himmelfahrts Commando" as the small group of people was called, diffused the bomb and we were back by daylight. People who did that sort of work for a living, had a brief life expectancy. But they were given double food rations. Same supported families and placed a bigger value on food for the kids then survival for themselves.

My mother went to bed early that day, feeling badly. I made her Chamomile tea. But it did not help.

By noon she asked me to get Frau Grau, mother's closest companion, who lived on the fourth floor. She came immediately and called the doctor.

I was sent out of the room, but I managed to listen, as the doctor made arrangements for her to enter the hospital.

"She won't survive," he said. The ambulance came and took her away. I was trying to cope with that. I simply could not accept what the doctor had said.

By noon my father had arrived. I had no idea where he had been and where he came from so quickly and why?

We went to visit my mother at the hospital. She said she was feeling fine and there was no reason for us to remain. She requested that I go to my typing classes.

That was the last lecture I attended at school. The teacher felt it to be important that we put our typewriters up properly. He told us an anecdote of a young lady who had gone to the restroom and accidentally stuffed her skirt in the back part of her trousers. He said that was what a type writer looked like when the cover was not on properly. I thought that was funny. There wasn't much else funny in my life.

Vati picked me up at the end of the lecture. He said Mutti was fine. We went home and we fixed potato pancakes. He had always loved them. Since

Mutti didn't, it was our opportunity to have what we liked.

After supper we visited Mutti at the hospital. She looked a little pale. She appeared to have no pain. She thought we needed to go home in case there was another air raid. Doctors have been known to be wrong. My mother looked a little pale, but she certainly did not look like a dying person. The nurse on duty agreed with Mutti. We were sent home for the night.

My father and I walked home in silence. He said nothing of where he had been. From the uniform I gathered he was with the anti-aircraft unit. I could clearly see that the subject was not open for discussion. But, as he so often did, he held out the promise of a trip to Heidelberg the following day.

Vati was not very talkative. He thought, in view of the previous night's excitement, maybe I should go to bed early. And I did just that. I laid there, staring out the window at a cloudy sky. I'd forgotten to close the blinds, but that was all right. It was cloudy. No air raids tonight, I thought.

I don't know when I went to sleep, but I woke up from a pounding on the door. I heard voices, male voices, a policeman and my father. The policeman said we were to come to the hospital immediately. My mother had just passed away.

"She died, she died," my father cried. All I could think is that they were wrong. I got dressed as quickly as possible. He was out of the door and down the street. I tried to keep in step with him. He took giant steps.

When we arrived at the hospital, the door was locked. We knocked, but no one answered. Unable to get in, we returned home, trying to understand the situation.

The policeman came back and this time he told us that we had to go to the morgue.

Now the awful fact sank in. Mutti was gone, gone forever. My insides were turning to water. I whimpered. My teeth chattered uncontrollably.

"I don't want to go to the morgue. Why do we have to go there?"

"We have to identify her."

"But they know who she is. Why tell them again?"

"Because it's the law."

Nothing about me moved right. I felt as though I was dragged across the pavement.

At the morgue the attendant took us to an empty room. In the center was what looked to be a combination of gurney and marble slab. On it was my mother. A kerchief was tied below her chin. Vati said it was to keep the chin from dropping. She looked very pale. And she was very still and when I touched her finger it felt like ice. But there was a smile on her lips. I would always remember the smile. It was almost as if she was glad to be gone.

My father gave the information requested of him. He gave it quietly and softly. His face was like a marble sculpture. His chin was set. He completed what had been requested of him and turned to me.

"We're ready to leave!" he said.

He never spoke another word all the way home. At home he pointed toward the bedroom. It was time for me to retire. He closed the door to the kitchen. It was silent in there. I wished for an air raid, for something, for people to talk to, to tell my mother had died. But no one was there. No air raid, only the silence of the bedroom. I was even afraid to cry.

Aunt Antonia came the next day. We had to clean up the apartment, she said. We had to gather my things. I was leaving.

"When?" I asked.

"After the funeral," she replied.

The auspicious day for the funeral was not good, said Aunt Anna. It was because of the day of my mother's death. Whenever someone in the family died on that day, another family member would die. Aunt Anna was not happy with the arrangements. Aunt Anna was very unhappy with me. She wanted to know why I did not call a priest? Why did I not call Kaplan Wildschuette. He was in Mannheim now and I should have called him. How could I let my mother die without the benefit of the last sacrament? I had condemned her to hell. That's what I did. I shrank into a corner before the accusing finger.

Aunt Antonia came in and told Aunt Anna to stop. Aunt Antonia knew what I knew. My mother had been estranged from the clergy for years.

We went to the cemetery by way of streetcar. We were huddled together in the last car, a party of ten, dressed in black. It was February and I would wear black until the next February rolled along. Black shoes, black stocking, black dress, and black everything.

The ceremony dissolved itself into a fog of semi-existence, the details lost forever somewhere in my mind.

There was a meal prepared and the people sat and ate. Karl, Anneliese's oldest brother was there. He used to come and visit us. He was devastated and so was I. When I sought comfort from him, Aunt Anna referred to it as behavior not suitable for a funeral dinner. Nor, she said, was my appetite suitable for the occasion. The occasion, she said would not have happened if I had not been such a stubborn, selfish, self-willed female child.

I left the room wishing in a way that I had died instead of her. I was only a female child. I was dispensable. I crawled into the corner of the bed, covered myself and wished myself away.

After some time my cousin Anneliese came in.

"Du," she said. I could not cry and I could not talk; I just stayed there. When she could not rouse me, she began to cry softly. That disturbed me. My cousin was like the sister I never had and I could not see her cry. I crept into her arms and we cried together.

One by one we heard the people leave. Aunt Anna called for my cousin. I was left to myself. Arrangements were made for Vati to bring me to Aunt Antonia's place.

Somewhere during these seemingly interminable hours, Vati came in with a box. It was a strong box. In it, he said, was the information of my origin. He also had a second box. That one contained the letters I had received from Helmut Ernst. Vati had read them. At first I thought he was angry enough to strike me.

"Get your coat!" He roared.

I could not understand the problem.

"This is an S.S. man!" He shouted. Whatever possessed me to correspond with an S.S. man. We returned to the cemetery, to that fresh grave. He pushed me down.

"Swear," he shouted: "Swear on your mother's grave that you won't write to him ever again."

I swore. I can still smell the fragrance of that freshly turned soil. I could not say anything to him.

Everything he had been forced to endure in the last couple of days was unleashed like a fury. He dragged me back home. He locked me in my room. He gave me no explanation.

The next morning he escorted me to Aunt Antonia's house. Before we left. He opened up the strong box.

"Don't call me Vati," he said. He pointed toward a piece of paper. It was a document that stated the name of my real father. I could no longer feel anything. If he looked for an answer, there was none. I could not reply. But it really didn't matter whether I was half orphan or full orphan.

I put on my black clothes and took my suitcase with whatever belongings I had, but was not allowed to take my books. I followed him, like a beaten puppy, tail tucked under, without conversation to Werderstrasse 44. This was my third home in less than a decade.

At Werderstrasse 44 I was requested to enter through the servant's entrance. My hands were never clean, they told me, and dirt was hard to get off the alabaster banister.

Somewhere, sometime during that awful first week, I managed to get in touch with Annel, to give her Helmut's address and to tell her why I could no longer correspond with him.

Nor was death through with me yet. As if an unkind fate wanted to reward Aunt Anna for her prophecy, my mother's cousin died. The next funeral was at the village. Lioba and Friedel and I held hands. Once we played together as children in the clay pits. Now we were dispensable female children orphans.

School was dispensed with and I went to work at Feudenheim at a defense plant. I was not allowed to participate in the activities at the National Theater. I was now an orphan in mourning. I would be allowed to go to church on Sunday. Twice a week I was requested to go to the cemetery to water the flowers on my mother's grave.

At work the people wanted to know who died. But it did not matter that much. There were so few who did not wear black.

The house at Werderstrasse 44 was sumptuous. There was little doubt about that. There was the first floor, the mezzanine, the second floor, the third floor and the garret rooms used for servant's quarters.

Aunt Antonia and I were the only ones there, except on Friday when the cleaning staff arrived. I was introduced to the staff, and I was shown the rooms and one thing I am forever grateful for, I was allowed free access to the library.

Heart what can you wish for. Classics, Histories, work translated from any language. And there were the plays. I could no longer go to the theater, but there were the plays and I could read them and in the silence of my room, act them out. I could commit to memory any thing I wanted to. I was no longer limited to German authors. The world was at my fingertips. The books kept the demons inside me at bay. The books made the pain bearable.

Adulthood had arrived with more serious matters. At Aunt Antonia's I was introduced to the schism in the land. Not everything we heard on the national radio station was true. Aunt Antonia listened to the black station, the forbidden station. That station told us that we had lost Africa. We faced resistance from the Underground in France and the Netherlands. In Russia the sixth army had been surrounded at Leningrad. 600,000 men were marched to Siberia.

The Crimea had been lost. The Africa Corps was no more. No one knew what happened to all the soldiers.

But the national radio kept telling us that victory would be ours soon. Aunt Antonia also allowed me to listen to the Wunsch Konzert. While listening, one Sunday afternoon, they filled a request by a soldier, a song for the girl he left behind. It was stated as requested.

"This is for you Elsa, from Helmut Ernst."

They had been careful to leave the S.S. information off. Annel had written to Helmut. He knew. I listened to the sounds of the music, music from earlier, happier days. For the first time, since my mother had passed away, my heart did not feel like it wore an iron bracelet.

Spring came to the land. The air raids continued, but so far we had been fortunate. Spring and the temptation not to go to the cemetery, but to visit Charlotte and the Wagners instead, was too big to resist. They were doing "Cosi Fan Tutte" and "La Traviata" and "Cavalleria Rusticana," Herr Wagner said. I listened. I devoured every word especially what Charlotte told me about Herr Hoelzlin.

"You know the love of your life lives just around the corner from you," she whispered, then added: "Victoria Strasse 7." I swore I would be back. I did not know how, but I would be back. I told her about the factory and the trips to the cemetery. Church was the only other thing, and oh yes, Aunt Antonia did take me to a concert.

Summer came and with it the unforgettable raid on the cemetery. I knew there had been an air raid. We all knew. We just did not know where. When I went to my mother's grave to tend it, I could no longer find it. Now I knew where the bombs had fallen. There were coffins, corpses, remains of all kind and an awful sweet and acrid smell. Decaying bodies smell horrible.

By the time I got as close as a few rows from the grave, I looked up. There was a skeleton dangling from a tree.

I dropped the rake and the watering can. I screamed and I turned and ran as fast as I could, away from there. I knew that I would not return to that cemetery. I was tired of the black dresses, tired of death, tired of mourning, tired of my life. If they would beat me it would not matter. I grabbed a suitcase, stuffed it with anything but black clothes, went down the servant's staircase and ran.

I slowed down when I was out of breath. The only place I could go to, was to the Wagners.

They bade me come in. They made me comfortable. They listened to me. They quieted me down. Herr Wagner realized that I had left my Aunt's house without intention to return there. He had a potential runaway on his hands. The Third Reich did not approve of assistance to runaways. The Third Reich did not approve of running away.

After awhile Herr Wagner started to talk about the potential of police interference in the matter. I hadn't thought of that. Why everyone was so afraid of the police was something I had not been informed about. But I agreed with Herr Wagner that it might not be a bad idea to tell my aunt where I was.

Herr Wagner talked to her on the phone. It was almost like someone bartering over some merchandise. In the end Herr Wagner had gotten some concessions. I would be allowed to participate at the National Theater, at the beginning of the Fall Season. However, wearing black was not an option. It was a tradition. I would not be permitted to break with tradition.

Aunt Antonia told Herr Wagner that I was two-faced and therefore not trustworthy. In his usual, caustic way of jesting, he retorted: "Yes I know. Two cheeks above, two cheeks below."

He did not betray my confidence. He did tell me that Aunt Antonia had been quite upset when I had not returned from my visit to the cemetery. She'd gone looking for me. She'd found what I had found earlier. But the shock was twice as hard on her because she had no way of knowing what had happened to me. She was not certain if I had been caught in that raid. She readily agreed. There would be no more trips to the cemetery.

The authorities closed the cemetery the next day. They were worried about an open outbreak of typhoid. Now there were no more options about going to the cemetery.

ASSASSINATION ATTEMPT

During the summer we had a guest, a high-ranking officer of the Wehrmacht. I assumed he was from Rommel's Africa Corps. I was sent out of the room, but I could hear what was being discussed. Apparently the Corps had surrendered to the British force under Montgomery. What really shocked me was that the officer stated that 75% of the world's natural, material resources were at the disposal of the enemy. That left us with 25%. It wasn't hard to figure out what he meant.

What he discussed with her with lowered voice after that was something I did not understand. It had to do with a "Putsch," and it had to do with Hitler.

After he had gone to his room, I was once again allowed downstairs. My curiosity had unbridled reign over my mouth.

"What's a Putsch?" I asked.

"Stuck your nose in where you shouldn't have; did you now!"

She was right and I apologized. Over the last few weeks I'd almost grown fond of her. Although I had to attend church, she did not insist on my going to confession or to communion. She held the belief that my conscience was mine to judge. GUILT was not in her vocabulary. She usually talked in terms of CONSEQUENCES. She was fond of that word. Although she seemed a bit provoked that I had listened to a private conversation, she did explain to me.

"A Putsch is an 'Attentat,' an assassination."

She did not have to tell me more. I did not have to tell her that I would keep this bit of knowledge to

107

myself. That was implicitly understood. I nonetheless was curious why there should be an assassination.

She said the "Fuehrer" had lost sight of the objective he had set himself to begin with. He wanted to conduct the war personally. He had relieved his Generals of their command. He was losing the war for them. There were too many enemies, too much area to cover and not enough material to cover with.

She would not talk with me beyond that. She sent me to the library.

"Go find a good book to read," she said.

The officer was still our visitor when the next air raid occurred. It was again a night raid. We were in the basement. And though the basement provided an excellent shelter, the shooting and the bombs raining down at us not so far away, made the officer restless. He mentioned that he'd prefer to be at the front with his troops, rather than in a basement, bombarded by an enemy he could not see. At the front he could defend himself.

The damage of the bombing was evident at daybreak. The bombs had stopped short of the Stinnes' Villa, no more than a block away. Someone mentioned that we would probably be next. It was even thought that perhaps we should evacuate, rather than risk being killed. Aunt Antonia said that was out of the question. The Third Reich concurred. I was working at a defense plant and leaving would be equivocal to a soldier leaving his post. It would be considered treason. The penalty for that was summary execution.

Working in a factory was not what I had intended to do for the rest of my life. But the factory had its fascination. Huge yellow blimps surrounded it. With the threat of an impending air raid, the blimps went up. I never quite understood how they could stop an airplane, especially something as big as a "Flying Fortress." But when we were within sight of the blimps, and we saw that they were up, we knew that the planes were coming. Eventually we paid close attention to those blimps. They were more reliable than the air raid siren.

A robot could have performed the work at the factory, except that they were not in vogue at that time. We were checking for size and fit. We were counting. We did not know what it was that we were counting or fitting. We were told that that was not our concern.

Food became somewhat of a problem. Rations grew smaller. And as the ration decreased, my appetite increased. Uncle Johann saw to it that we did not starve, but I kept wishing for one meal with enough to eat, and for just a few more nights of uninterrupted sleep.

September came, and with it the beginning of the new season at the National Theater.

Dress rehearsal for "Freischuetz." At this point in time I was neither fish nor fowl, as they said, and I was assigned little parts as an extra. It meant access to the stage, and it meant strolling across the stage a couple of times, and as always, listening to Herr Hoelzlin. Herr Hoelzlin had the part of a villain in that opera. I preferred to see him as royalty, as High Priest, as a hero, rather than the "arch fiend." But it was Freischuetz and it was better than nothing.

Charlotte was there and those of my friends who were still alive. Boys were scarce. Even one of the male dancers had been drafted. Some of the girls had evacuated with their families. Most of us looked slim, and most of us were always hungry. All of us were

109

happy to be there. All of us were just a little apprehensive. It was a clear, mellow, early autumn night. But up to this point in time, there had not been a raid during the performances. Many patrons felt justified in not leaving during the performance. Perhaps, in some small way, it was the ultimate gesture of defiance. Ignore the danger and it will go away.

I had clear instructions from Aunt Antonia to come home at the first warning. First warning sounded once that night. It was followed by a "clear." Shortly before the end of the performance, first warning sounded again. But it was during the final curtain calls and the audience insisted on a standing ovation. Clear did not follow first warning this time. We did not remove our make up. We left quickly, at the urging of Herr Wagner.

The early autumn air was cool, but not unpleasant. The city streets were dark and quiet. The buildings loomed tall and massive in the shadows above the streets. Not a beam of light escaped from behind darkened windows. The only sound heard, was the water cascading down the fountains by the Water Tower. It was almost as if this city enfolded me with a pervasive sense of validation and I responded in the affirmative. I loved this city. This city was home. I never knew a moment's fear walking the city streets at night. All who lived there were Mannheim, and Mannheim was all who lived there.

I passed the house at Victoria Strasse 7. I gave a moment's hesitation, wondering if Herr Hoelzlin had made it home. It was not for me to know, but the one who lived there held my emotions captive.

At Werderstrasse 44 I let myself in quietly. I went up the rear stair case. I knew all about the importance of keeping parquet floors and pale blue oriental carpets clean, not to mention alabaster banisters.

I checked in with Aunt Antonia. She did not say anything about the make up, but disapproval was written all over her face. She hated "Schminke," or make-up, as it was known. She considered it base and trashy. She did not understand about stage lights and props. She did not want to know. She merely tolerated in exchange of peaceful coexistence with me.

I thanked her profusely for letting me go and promised to go upstairs and take off the make-up right away.

After I removed the make-up, I turned out the light and opened the window. The sky was clear, moonlit, starlit, vivacity beaming down.

I went to bed with the window open and K.M.V. Weber's music dancing through my mind. I fell asleep with the ballet, the chorus, and the solo performances of Elmendorff in my head, his baton and the magic of light and color and sound rested with me.

I woke up to the sound of gunfire. The Flak was shooting and the sound of approaching airplanes could be heard. Somebody down below shouted:

"AIR RAID! AIR RAID!"

I vaulted out of bed. I grabbed my clothes and put them on as well as I could. A dim light glowed in the stairway. Aunt Antonia was ahead of me. In the haste for safety she'd stuffed her dress into the back of her bloomers. She almost slapped me when I grabbed her by the waste band in order to pull out her dress. She was very sensitive about being touched.

Apparently we had company again, because with her was another high ranking officer and his wife.

The sound of the approaching airplanes grew louder. There was furious gunfire and then the sirens were activated to tell us that we had an air raid.

The first bomb that whistled down gave us an indication that we would not escape this time. My heart was beating in my throat. Then everything changed to slow motion. There was an awful concussion that left my mouth full of grit. The heavy metal escape doors simply opened like magic. All of us were thrown across the room, slammed up against the opposite wall. My lungs felt as though they were going to explode any moment. We looked at each other, thinking impending death.

There was another explosion not far away and another more distant. Through the open door I could see golden rain dropping down, without making a sound.

The army officer was the first to comprehend the situation.

"Incendiary," he shouted, "Fire bombs. We have to get out!"

Get out how? Get out where? What kind of hell was waiting outside? The big house shuddered. The floor rose up beneath us. The air was unbeatably thick with mortar and fire fumes. We were choking. The officer found some water. We placed the wet towels across mouth and nose, and attempted to fight our way up the stairs.

"Go for help!" my aunt shouted.

I don't recall how I got up those stairs. I do remember standing outside the building, looking up. The top floor had been completely torn away. The second floor was burning and liquid fire was still raining down on the deserted street.

I crossed the street, ran down half a block to Victoria Strasse 7 and pounded on the door like an insane person.

I don't remember who opened the door but I do remember when Herr Hoelzlin got there.

"You?" he said. Then he realized what had happened.

"Oh my God," he said.

At that point my legs just gave way from under me. He picked me up and carried me downstairs. He bedded me down on a couch in the corner. All the tears I could not cry at my mother's funeral, all the repressed feelings for the last five months burst forth like an unstoppable volcano.

"Whatever it is, it's going to be all right," he said. He held me close. He brushed my hair with his hands and kissed my forehead. I quieted down. Somewhere inside of me I felt that if I could make him stay there, holding me like that, all sorrow, all anger and all the pain I ever felt would go away. And then I just passed out.

When I came to, the basement was empty. I slowly made my way to the door. I opened it and looked out. "Goetter Dammerung" with Walhalla burning could not have been more convincingly staged. Werderstrasse 44 was totally engulfed in flames. I started toward the house, but Herr Hoelzlin had returned.

"Get back down there!" he shouted. I obeyed. I was to stay there, he said, until a doctor could be located. My aunt, he said, was all right. Every able-bodied person was over there, pulling stuff from the burning house.

He patted me softly on the head, kissed me on the cheek and made me promise to stay there until

113

someone came to get me. I settled back on the couch, trying to rationalize what sort of destiny provided for that first embrace and the Hell-fire and brimstone at the same time.

Aunt Antonia was the first to come down the stairs. A doctor could not be found, she said, then added: "Can you walk?" '

I told her I could. She helped me up. My lungs still hurt terribly. It was painful to breathe.

"We have to get our things together," she told me.

I really didn't think I had "things" left. I had a small emergency suitcase, filled with some clothing, a few pictures from better times, my mother's knitting needles, and the little remembrance book Uncle Konrad had given me so long ago.

Dawn had broken, but the sky was filled with a dusty haze. Fire and smoke was all you could smell and it hurt to breathe in.

The stuff that was salvaged from the burning house was piled all along the street. There was no water to wash, no fuel to cook with, no food available for immediate consumption. There were people smudged with coal and dirt.

I sat there, next to all those bundles. I could consider myself orphaned and homeless.

"I want you to go to Heidelberg," Aunt Antonia said. "See Aunt Elise and Aunt Fanny and tell them I'm all right."

How do you go from Mannheim to Heidelberg? You walk until you get past the devastation, till you find a point where the A Train to Heidelberg is still functional. You tell the conductor that you were just bombed out, and it wouldn't take a genius to see that.

My suitcase wasn't heavy, but if I could stash it somewhere long enough to make a trip across town. I wanted to see if the Wagners were alive. I wanted to see if the National Theater was still standing.

I hid the suitcase among a pile of stuff and walked away undetected, once again past Victoria Strasse 7. I would never forget Victoria Strasse 7.

Long before I reached the Water Tower, I knew there were other places worse than Werderstrasse 44. Clouds of dust smoke and soot drifted my way. Everything smelled of burning.

I couldn't get through by way of Water Tower. That entire area was cordoned off. But I could see that a bomb had taken the dome off the Tower. There was water and mud and debris everywhere.

I picked my way between the city blocks, scores of them still burning. The heat was immense. Hollow-eyed, empty-faced people, checking on survivors, looking for the dead, surrounded gutted, hollow shells of buildings. There was little doubt that this was the end of the city, as I knew it. Churches, apartment houses, most of the business district, the castle, all that was culturally and historically significant, had been efficiently eradicated. Napoleon could not have done a better job on the sacking of the castle at Heidelberg.

As I approached, and from the distance, it looked as though the National Theater was still standing. It was when I got close that I saw that colossal, empty hull. The Wagners were there, in a small building nearby. Huddled around them, performers, ballet dancers, opera singers, members of the Chorus, musicians electricians, and stagehands. Their faces were so easy to read. It was the end. There would be no more performances.

"It went, just like that," said Herr Wagner. "It didn't take long for all that plush and velvet to burn away."

I stepped out, onto the stage or what was once the stage. Schweska cautioned me. "Those girders are still hot."

The girders that supported the curtains lay there like so much twisted spaghetti. The props were reduced to ashes. I sat amid those ashes, sifting them through my fingers. One of the dancers sat next to me, his career finished, too young to retire, too old to start over. Even at that, would all stages wind up being reduced to rubble? Would art and culture die the way the city lay dying? Was there anything besides this war with its killing and killing and killing?

Schweska came over and talked to us softly.

"Don't look at it as an end, look at it as a beginning. We were never been able to change this building because of its historical importance. Now we can have a new building." History, he said wistfully, had finally freed us from history.

I could only sift the ashes. Last night those ashes had been castle, village, and forest. Only a few months ago they were temples along the Nile. They were the harbor of Venice.

Charlotte came and placed her arm around my shoulder.

"Think of the Phoenix".

The Phoenix rose and so would I. I got up. I had to catch the A train to Heidelberg. We embraced and said a tearful farewell.

"Who knows if we will see each other again." Those were the last words she said to me. The war claimed her two months later.

Herr Wagner could not find words. His future was as uncertain as mine. His eyes were as red-rimmed as mine. There are times when the feeling of despair is so great it simply numbs the mind. This was one of the times. Dying certainly seemed easier than living.

OLD HEIDELBERG

I backtracked, avoiding burning buildings. I was, after all, a "Mannemer," a child of the city of Mannheim, a city street urchin. My city was dying. What was there of value in this, in the city and in me?

On September 6th, 1943 back in front of the bombed out house at Werder Strasse 44, I picked up my suitcase, quietly, undetected and made my way out of town. I was not alone. There were others, mostly women and children; most of them carried suitcases like me. They carried names and numbers for identification. Somewhere east of the city the A Train was still running. I fought for a small space on the last wagon. Sometimes it felt as if I was hanging there suspended, held in place by the throng that shared that space.

I was hardly able to walk the distance from the station to the house on the Neckar River.

My aunts must have been waiting for me. They saw me coming and rushed toward me half carrying, half supporting me up the small incline through the front door and up the stairs.

"Aunt Antonia is all right," I said. They stripped my dirty clothes off, prepared the bath and gave me a night gown to wear.

Aunt Elise brought up a tray of food, but for the first time in my life I could not eat. There was a lump in my throat, big enough to choke me. The smell of fire was still in my nostrils and my head ached fiercely.

Aunt Elise brought me an aspirin to help with the headache and herbal tea to help me sleep. She told me to go to bed.

I laid there in the silence of that darkened room. I could not sleep. I walked over to the garret window, opened it and looked out across the Neckar. The river talked softly, its little waves slapping against the banks. The river was on its way toward Mannheim, unhurried, as it had been for centuries.

Across the river, two-thirds of the way up on Mount Koenigstuhl, stood the castle ruins. Napoleon had sacked that castle. Eyewitness accounts stated that you could see the glow all the way to Mannheim. You could definitely see it from the Neckar River Bridge, in the early dawn hours. Well, it was night now, and from the banks of the river Neckar, in Heidelberg, you could see Mannheim burning.

"You've got lots of company," I said, as I stood there and looked at the ghostly outlines of the Heidelberg Castle.

I finally went to bed. I fell asleep, but nightmares of crashing, burning buildings woke me up. It must have been past midnight. In the house, downstairs, there were voices. I looked around the room, illuminated by moonlight. There were no colors, only shades of blue, grey, black and white.

The bed I slept in was a four-poster. I could see the post at the foot of my bed, and the rat, sitting there, casually grooming its tail. A rat? I had never before seen a rat. This was a big rat, in the garrets of the villa, at the foot of my bed. I bolted upright, got out of bed, went downstairs screaming: "There is a rat in my room!!!"

Startled faces with startled eyes looked at me. These people would not tolerate a speck of dust or a gnat, much less a rat in the house.

The man rose immediately, grabbed a broom and led the way up the stairs. I followed.

119

"Where?" He asked.

"It was sitting on the post at the foot of my bed," I explained.

Of course, by the time we all lumbered noisily upstairs, the rat was gone. A general search was made, but the rat had disappeared.

"Maybe you just dreamed you saw a rat," Aunt Fannie suggested. Why was it that I always imagined? I was adamant. I was angry because no one believed me. I was in no mood for arguments.

"I dreamt about burning houses and screaming people. The rat was there when I woke up."

"You'll feel better tomorrow," answered Aunt Elise. She brought me another cup of Chamomile tea. She'd laced the tea with a generous helping of Schwarzwaelder Kirsch. It was the kind of cherry brandy that my grandmother considered a miracle cure. I drank it. It tasted awful, but it sort of made reality disappear. The rat was gone.

Chances were it would not return. I was glad they didn't find it. There had been enough killing for the time being. The only wonderful moment was to be held by Herr Hoelzlin to have my head stroked with something akin to fatherly affection. I tried to hold on to that moment, to keep the nightmares away.

How could anyone say everything would be all right? Nothing would ever be all right again. Everything was destroyed, bombed out. My limbs felt heavy from the effect of the alcohol. I closed my eyes. In dreams I wandered the streets. I was a little child again, with Mutti and Vati, and we were riding the streetcar, and it was night. I could see the city lights reflected in the river below, as we crossed the Neckar Bridge, on the way to Mama Rath's apartment.

I woke up in the morning. The smell of rain was in the air. The sky was heavy with clouds.

Bowl and pitcher filled with water, towel, soap and face cloth were laid out for me to wash up.

I searched in my suitcase for a dress and some underwear. I discovered the little album of remembrances Uncle Konrad had given me so long ago. It was tucked away between items of clothing. It fell open to the page where Gretel Nerreter had written:

EDELIST DER MENSCH; HILFREICH UND GUT

(NOBLE IS MAN AND HELPFUL AND GOOD)

My jaw ached and cramped. I was fighting back tears again. How could I believe in all of that in the face of all that destruction and devastation?

I cleaned up as well as I could. I went downstairs for breakfast.

Aunt Antonia had arrived during the night. She told me I had to return to Mannheim. The Third Reich requested that I report that I was bombed out and that I was leaving the city. I also had to report personal losses.

"I lost the place where I lived. I lost the city. I lost the National Theater. I lost home. I don't have any place to go. My mother is dead and my father is gone. How do I report that?"

They all sat there and looked at each other, apparently trying to figure out what to say next. But they said nothing. They even ignored my breach of etiquette. Juveniles do not shout at adults. I said I wasn't hungry and for the second time in my young life I walked away from food. I did not want to go back to that city. I wanted to stay in Heidelberg. And while we were on the subject of Heidelberg I wanted to know how come they never dropped any bombs on Heidelberg? Heidelberg had churches and theaters and concert halls and a university and lots of quaint little houses crammed in to the city area.

"How come they never bomb Heidelberg?"

Aunt Antonia tried to explain it.

"They consider Heidelberg a city of international renown."

"You mean they want it left whole so they can come back and vacation here!"

Aunt Antonia rose from the table. Her dark eyes were blazing.

"Keep talking like that, let your emotions rule your mouth and we will all disappear from the face of the earth."

"What do you mean, disappear from the face of the earth?"

I had started something. I was at the threshold of finding out exactly what type of dragon precipitated all that fear. At that point, Aunt Fannie rose.

"Consider the discussion terminated!"

Aunt Fannie rarely made concise statements. But all obeyed this concise statement. I went upstairs. I had no coat against the rain, just an old summer dress. It would have to do. I had no money. Aunt Antonia came up. She gave me money and an old sweater. It would have to do, she told me. She explained to me that when I reported at Mannheim, I would be given money and ration tickets to purchase new clothing as well. She said nothing else to me. I could see that she was angry. More than that, I could see fear reflected in the expression of her face.

122

RAVAGED CITY

The trip to Mannheim was an adventure in itself. I was lucky to get a seat on the A Train. The train was crowded with people. Many more were left at the platform, waiting for the next train. There were no schedules. Trains came and people piled on. Seckenheim was as close as we could get. The rest of the way we had to walk. At the edge of the city we encountered a police barricade. We were questioned. Only the people who had lived in Mannheim, prior to the bombing, were allowed to enter the city. I told the uniformed individual that I had been bombed out. When I gave him my address, he told me where to report. He warned me and said I had to be out by nightfall.

I made my way toward the appointed place. It was a wet and stormy day. The air was heavy with those awful smells of death and fire. I pulled that sweater around my shoulders as tightly as I could. Still I couldn't keep from shivering.

Part of a bombed-out office building served as a gathering place. I was requested to fill out a sheet of paper, give my name and address plus the previous address where I had lost everything. That I had lost everything was of little doubt.

When my name was called I went into a small cubicle. The man behind the desk had a gold tooth, wore glasses and on his lapel the insignia of the N.S.D.A.P. He was a party member. He commiserated with me, but said to be of good cheer, because the Fuehrer would eventually win the war and things would be better than they had ever been before. He asked where my mother was and I told him that she had died. My stepfather, I told him, was missing. I was about to tell him that most of my boyfriends were missing, my male cousins were missing and a couple of uncles to boot. But I remembered Aunt Antonia's bitterly hostile glare. I swallowed hard and said nothing. There was a prompter sitting in my brain saying: JUST ANSWER THE QUESTION!

When the administrator asked about my losses I told him that I had a Ghandi in oil and a Batavia in oil. When he looked at me rather puzzled I informed him: "The Ghandi was an original oil painting. It was a portrait of Mahatma, and the Batavia was a schooner that was wrecked."

He held up his hand. That meant for me to be silent. He looked at the address again. That was Werderstrasse 44., definitely not the Ghetto. He got up to check with the next person. He returned and asked if 2500.00 Mark was sufficient for loss of personal property?

Twenty five hundred Mark I thought. I had never seen that much money in one place. I thought I was definitely overpaid. After all, I had been a poor person of peasant stock most of my life. And no one ever told me anything about money. I nodded my head. He made out the necessary papers, gave me the coupons for clothing and food and a check for the stated amount. He rose, saluted and said: "Heil Hitler!" His heels clicked. I raised my hand and returned the greeting.

"Heil Hitler!" For twenty five hundred Mark and a fistful of ration tickets I could say that. I was finally learning to live in the Third Reich.

I left the office the house and the street. I wasn't nearly as cold as I had been in the beginning. It was early in the day. I was making my way toward the Neckar River. I stopped at the bridge. My insides were twisting at the thought of it. But it was a cloudy day. There would be no "Angriff" today. And I had to know if Mama Roth had survived. I virtually flew across that bridge. I ran all the way to Friedrich Ekert Strasse 64. There were no bombed out houses there. Outside the ring, on the east side of the city, no bombs fell. The Kaiser Wilhelm Kaserne, one of the biggest military installations in the city, was still standing. Culture had been killed, but Military was given a reprieve.

I went up to the third floor. The nameplate was still there. I rang the bell and she opened the door. She just shook her head. She bade me sit down. She grabbed a towel and dried my hair. She hung the sweater up to dry near the stove.

"You look like a two-bit prostitute," she said. I knew the dress was too short, the hair unkempt and I told her that I had just survived the bombing at Werder Strasse 44. I told her of Mutti's death, of Vati's disappearance, and the oath I had been made to swear. I was afraid to tell her about Herr Hoelzlin. She would not have understood. When I told her of Vati's revelation concerning my birth, she had a wry smile on her face.

"So you know about Karl Tretter?"

I told her that I knew that he was my real father, that he had promised to support my mother and that he had not done so. I even told her of my intentions of finding him.

"They'll never permit that." she said.

Mama Roth told me about the clan feud between my mother's family and Karl Tretter. Tretter was apparently Lutheran and hailed from the village Buechig. Mother was Catholic and hailed from Neibsheim. The hostility would always be there. I was the child of that unfortunate union and the clan would nurture me as long as I did not exhibit personality traits that would make me undesirable. Something inside me told me that I had already begun to exhibit those traits. It would not be a happy future with the clan. We talked for a long time. I told her that I couldn't get a straight answer from anyone when it came to matters of the Third Reich, matters of the Catholic Church, or even for that fact, matters that dealt with sex.

She smiled and said she could not help me much with matters about the church. She was Lutheran. But as far as the Third Reich was concerned, she knew why they were afraid.

"It's the Gestapo, it's Himmler, it's getting arrested and put in jail for saying anything that may lead to a doomsday philosophy, a defeatist attitude or criticism of the National Socialistische Deutsche Arbeiter Partei, in short the N.S.D.A.P. All of these things are considered treason." The Regime, she said, and she said it was a Regime that would not tolerate any opposition. That meant to keep opinions locked away in the mind. And if someone greeted you with Heil Hitler, you most certainly said Heil Hitler back. And you never said Hitler was wrong or Himmler was bad or the war was lost.

I spent three hours there, talking to her. She was a widow now, she was supporting herself. She had boarders and with the Kaserne across the street she would always have boarders. It was a lucrative business. The money was good, she said, but one had to learn to remain silent. It was a skill I hadn't mustered. I told her of my confrontation with Aunt Antonia. I brought up the possibility of staying with her. She shook her head.

"Your mother's family would never permit that."

Frau Roth would not tell me why my mother's family was so opposed to my staying with her, or for that matter, visiting with her. I asked her if it had something to do with her being Lutheran.

"No!" she said, "it's just the way they are."

We talked for a little while longer and then it was time to say good-bye. We both felt the tears but neither one of us cried. Crying was the forbidden thing; the sign of weakness and the Third Reich did not acknowledge weakness.

I made my way back to Werderstrasse 44 where I was to meet Aunt Antonia. The rain had settled the dust. The house stood there like a decapitated giant. A watchman had been employed. He lived in the basement. I went through the house, up the partly destroyed staircase. The alabaster wasn't white anymore. The malachite birdbath was a pile of green rubble. I found my room and the remnants of the bed. Couched on it was a bundle of incendiary bombs. Next to them was the metal safety box that held all of my papers. I opened it. Little bits of black flakes floated out, past me across the wall, down toward the street. All of my mother's secrets were now safely destroyed.

Aunt Antonia had returned and called out for me. "It is time," she said, "time to leave." I told her of my visit to the office of the Third Reich. She took the check. She said it would be deposited in a bank for me until I was of age.

"And when will that be?"

"When you're twenty one."

"I should live that long."

"We live one day at a time and by the grace of God."

"And the permission of the Third Reich!"

I knew I shouldn't have said that. She gathered a few things and never looked back to see if I was coming. She motioned for me to follow and she kept leading the way. All the way to Seckenheimat a running speed, like demons were pursuing her. There was no keeping up with her. She no longer conversed with me. As far as she was concerned I was Persona Non Grata.

We had to fight our way on to the platform of the train. Aunt Antonia was on the platform. I was hanging from the rail, held in place by the throng of people headed for Heidelberg. It was a silent throng. Desperate people speak no language. They just cling to what's left of life and to each other. I was beginning to understand that.

Midway between Mannheim and Heidelberg a siren announced one more air raid. The train kept on moving. The people looked up to the sky and then straight-ahead.

"Schicksal," somebody said. It would be destiny no matter how or what.

We got off at the main station at Heidelberg. Aunt Antonia looked at me firmly and in a way threateningly.

"I don't care what you do," she said: "But I simply will forbid you to talk to anybody at Aunt Fannie's house about the Third Reich. I forbid you to open your mouth, unless your're asked. And if and when you're asked it's YES MAM and NO MAM. Is that understood?"

She was smaller than I was. But she was wiry and strong. She could cross my lips with her fist and my lips would be twice the normal size. From the way she looked at me, I wasn't about to take a chance on a physical confrontation. I nodded my head and followed her quietly.

Heidelberg was another world. There were no bomb craters, no damaged houses. There were things to buy, prominently displayed in those quaint shop windows. All the streetcars worked. The A Train was in working condition and so were the trains that pulled into the Haupt Bahnhof. You could smell the forest on the Koenig Stuhl, and when you walked through the city you could smell that marvelous food aroma from the restaurants. It was hard to distinguish real from real. The idea of staying in Heidelberg was acceptable as far as I was concerned. At Heidelberg there was the sound of music and the aroma of food. I would like to have lived anywhere where there was no war, but the borders were closed. I was German. Germans could not leave any more than foreigners could come in.

They had waited dinner for us. I sat down quietly. Aunt Antonia gave the report. She told them of the ration coupons and the money. Aunt Fannie agreed to deposit the money at the Bank in Heidelberg. I was to be given spending money the following day. I was to be allowed to go shopping for new clothes, a new pair of shoes and a new winter coat.

"Is that agreeable with you?" asked Aunt Fannie. I remembered Aunt Antonia's command.

"Yes Mam!" I answered, with lowered eyes. I hoped that was correct. Then suddenly, out of the clear, Aunt Antonia turned to me and asked:

"Exactly why did you stop at Victoria Strasse 7 that night?"

My mind went into overdrive. If I blushed, if I betrayed the least bit of emotion, I'd lose that trip scheduled for the next day. There was no doubt that their curiosity was piqued. I could feel all eyes looking at me. It was SHOW TIME.

"Herr Hoelzlin lives there," I replied.

"Who is Herr Hoelzlin?" Aunt Elise wanted to know.

"Herr Hoelzlin is an opera singer at the National Theater," I volunteered cautiously.

"Of course!" said Aunt Fannie, "he performs at the Stadt Theater here."

There was a stage in Heidelberg. Suddenly Heidelberg became even more acceptable. If there was a stage in Heidelberg, there was still hope for a career. Suddenly Aunt Fannie was as dear to me as a long lost friend. She said she'd heard him perform. He was well known as a basso profundo and he was a "Nice Person," she said. I answered whatever questions they asked, nicely, politely, and I was grateful when I was dismissed from the table.

I went up to my little garret room. My heart had a dream to hold against the nightmares of the day before. There would be the exploration of Heidelberg.

The morning dawned with sunlight and blue sky and brisk autumn air. I washed up and dressed to the best of my ability, in my still smoky smelling clothes. I went downstairs for breakfast. I was told where to go shopping. I did not ask where the Stadt Theater was. I figured I'd find that, once I made it into town.

Heidelberg was small compared to Mannheim. I left with a new goal for an old life. I'd go shopping and then I'd find the Stadt Theater.

The ruins of the castle rose above the morning mist and sparkled with the essence of bright red granite. I didn't need a streetcar. The walk was wonderful. The Old Bridge was just like so much more pavement with railings on either side, stone arch railings to protect those who crossed the Neckar River. Once it was part of the defense of the castle. But it did not keep the French out. Nor did it keep Tilly from sacking the town. Tilly and his army finished what the French had left standing. Tilly did not leave until he had appropriated the ArchDuke's library in the Heilig Geist Kirche. He gave that to the Pope. I suddenly became aware of how many people must have crossed that bridge, fleeing, fighting, and as always now in the back of my mind, how many must have died.

SAILOR

Shopping in Heidelberg was a little like living a fairy tale.

I wore my new clothes. I wore my new shoes, although that turned out to be a blistering mistake.

I went in search of the Stadt Theater. I stood in front of it, perusing the bill of fare, when I became aware of a person standing behind me. I intended to smile briefly and to turn away, but the person behind me was a sailor. As a rule there are no sailors inland. Certainly I did not expect to see a sailor in Heidelberg.

He smiled in response to the puzzled expression on my face.

"Forgive me for staring," I said, "I did not expect to see a sailor in Heidelberg."

He doffed his cap, introduced himself and said, that I was correct in that assumption. He said he hailed from Esslingen. He had been on leave and was on his way to return to the coast. He said he had just purchased concert tickets for a concert at the castle. I told him I was just curious to see what was playing at the theater. I told him I had just lost everything at an air raid at Mannheim. He said his experience had been similar. He had been stationed on a U-Boat, and the ship had made it safely back to harbor. But there they had been bombarded and the U-boat had gone down as it had docked. Most of the sailors, including the captain, had gone down with it. He was among the few who escaped. So was a journalist who had gone along for the ride. He hoped the journalist would have the opportunity to write and publish his story.

We came to an agreement that war, in general, was hell.

We stopped at a little cafe, safely tucked away in the granite folds of the Heiligeist Church.

He ordered for both of us. I could hardly believe my good fortune. I was sitting here in a small cafe, being served a piece of Torte, a creation of cream and sweets and cherries.

The radio suddenly went quiet. Beethoven's fifth came on loud and clear and with it the announcement of a special bulletin. The announcer went on to talk about the glory of the Third Reich. I was more interested in the pie in front of me. I belabored it quietly. But then the fork slipped and crashed down on the porcelain plate. The piece of piecrust performed a perfect arc above my head before it landed on the plate of the gentleman at the adjacent table. The man looked at me and grinned and said: "Would you like to have it back?"

I could feel my ears turning red from embarrassment. I sat quietly, hoping I could be forgiven for having given priority to the pie. I listened intently as the announcer told of one more ship that was sunk by the U-boats. The sailor next to me said nothing. When I asked him about the bulletin, he said that they hunted in packs now. The enemy had air superiority and although we did not talk about it, the British had more sea power. He said that hunting in packs provided a margin of safety for the individual submarine. Even at that, survival was slim. The enemy had something called Sonar. Sonar was able to locate the submarine down below. Once it was located, depth charges were lowered. Once a U-Boat was hit, there was really no escape for anyone on board.

The music had continued. Most of the people were involved in their own conversation. I suggested we leave. I told him I'd like to see the Castle before I had to return home.

We spent a quiet, late, sunny autumn afternoon by the castle walls. It was a very private place. I was still full of curiosity. Had he ever been there when a ship was torpedoed?

He was reluctant to talk about it at first.

"When we shoot at a ship, we have to stay in order to know if it was a hit or a miss."

"When it's a hit, what then?"

"There is an explosion. You can't hear it but you can almost feel it. The ship blows up. Black smoke fills the air and the water around the ship becomes a sea of flames."

"What of the people?"

"Some die right away. Some try to swim clear of the ship. You can almost hear their screams for help."

"Do you help them?"

"How can we? The U-boat has only enough room and provision for the crew."

"You mean you have to leave them to die?"

"U- Boats take no prisoners." His jaw muscles twitched. He was fighting for composure. "At night I sometimes dream about it. I wake myself up screaming."

"So do I."

The afternoon sun reflected off the ruins. I said it was a pity that we had this beautiful day and all we could talk about was war. He agreed. He said he had two concert tickets for the evening's concert. If I liked, he would give me one and I could meet him at the castle before the concert. I agreed. I took the ticket and we started out back toward town. I left him standing at the bridge. He waved good-bye. I was frantically trying to figure out how I could get away to meet a sailor for a concert at the castle. I could hear Frau Roth's words echoing in my mind. "I'm afraid your mother's family won't permit that."

I arrived at the house with little time to spare. For once I had been punctual.

Aunt Antonia had not returned from Mannheim yet. Aunt Elise was busy fixing the evening meal. She was an excellent cook. The food smell permeated the whole house. It would be Wiener Schnitzel, Sauerkraut, and mashed potatoes.

The challenge at this point in time was no longer a matter of life and death, but one of getting to the castle on blistered feet, and most of all, how to persuade my aunts to let me go to the concert.

For once, I tried to be the perfect example of good behavior. I said my prayer before the meal correctly. I answered all the questions as I had been told. I volunteered no information unless asked for it. Yes I did have a wonderful time. Yes I purchased the clothing required. Yes I stopped at the little Konditorei. Yes my feet hurt a bit from the new shoes. Yes I went to the castle. Then came the big one. With baited breath: "There is a concert at the castle. I was able to get a ticket. And could I please have permission to go."

I placed the ticket on the table.

Dinner stopped. Silence reigned supreme. Aunt Antonia was the first to ask: "You mean to go to the castle to the concert alone?" I avoided a direct answer.

"I could only get one ticket!"

I looked at my three aunts and for a moment they became the three Nornes of fate, spinning an evil web. I hoped against hope but I knew that a NO would be a foregone conclusion. It was Aunt Fannie who delivered the blow.

"Without someone to accompany you, it's pretty much out the question."

"Why?" The word slipped out and beyond it in my heart and soul lurked anger.

"In the first place you are still in mourning. Respectable people in their first year of mourning for a close family member do not go to performances of any kind. Besides that, young girls your age and status do not go to a concert alone."

After Aunt Fannie had delivered the verdict, there was a moment of silence. But it was always important to me to deliver an adequate response. And I had an adequate response. I stood up, glared at my aunt across the table and said: "In that case, why don't you go in my place. You're not in mourning for an immediate family member. And you're not my age."

I picked up the ticket and tossed it at her. Her eyes met mine with equal spark. Her voice was better controlled as she replied: "Thank you, I believe I will."

For once I was speechless. I moved my chair from behind me and turned to leave the room. The same controlled voice said: "I don't recall hearing you ask for permission to leave the table." '

"I don't intend to!" I replied and left.

I watched Aunt Fannie leave the house that evening. Tears of anger, tears of sorrow, tears of grief; I cried them all and they all tasted the same way. They were salty.

No one spoke to me that evening. I was Persona Non Grata once more.

It was the following morning that I was given orders to pack my belongings and prepare to leave. I did not comprehend properly at first. I had hoped to remain in Heidelberg.

"Am I not going to stay here? "

"No," said Aunt Antonia.

"Is it because of last night?"

"No," said Aunt Fannie.

Aunt Elise broke the news to me softly.

"Heidelberg has a quota. Only so many people are allowed to have residence here. You don't qualify for residence."

"Why not?"

"You're not of age and your guardian doesn't live here."

"Then could I stay in Mannheim? I could live with Frau Roth."

"NO!" it was a definite no from all three. For a moment I thought of running away, but there was no place to run to. The Third Reich did not allow anyone to live anyplace without permission. All the feeling inside of me left. All I needed to know now was where I was going to live. I dreaded to hear that answer.

"Where will I go?"

"You're to live in Bruchsal. Your Aunt Anna will be your guardian."

As far as I was concerned that was the end to any kind of life, it was the end; period. I did not reply. I went upstairs and packed my one and only suitcase. I thought of the sailor. I wondered what he thought when the person next to him turned out to be an elderly female. I did not know his name. I would not be able to tell him what transpired.

BRUCHSAL

In the end I was glad to leave Heidelberg. The
close scrutiny of one maiden aunt was bad enough,
but three was definitely more than I could cope with.
And in Bruchsal there was Anneliese. Living with
Anneliese might not be so bad. She was my cousin,
the sister I never had, my friend, my closest confidant.
Her brother Heinz, on the other hand, was not
someone to be looked forward to. Heinz was reputed
to have an ill temper and like his father, "jaehzornig,"
given to sudden fits of rage. And there was Uncle
Karl, also quick to anger. Uncle Karl could be brutal.
And there was Bruchsal. As far as I could recall, there
was no theater. There was no concert hall. Bruchsal
did have a castle, and churches. As in most places in
central Germany, half of them were Catholic, the
other half Lutheran.

Two days later I was taken to the train depot. I
had all of my papers, according to the dictates of the
Third Reich. I had written permission to leave
Mannheim, and written consent to reside in Bruchsal.
I had ration tickets, some money and a piece of paper
that was the equivalent of an order to appear at the
Arbeits-Amt (department of labor) the following
Monday.

The train was adequately referred to as "Bummel
Zug." It was a slow train that stopped at every village.
Most villages were just like Neibsheim, my mother's
native place. There was, of course, Schwetzingen.
That little village had a castle, a summer palace. And
there was Wiesloch, that one had an insane asylum.

I sat in the corner, next to the window of the a
third class compartment. The benches were made of
wooden slats. I could feel the wheels beneath me. I

138

could pick up the rhythm of the track. For just a little while I thought of running away I thought of disappearing somewhere between Heidelberg and Brucheal. But that did not work in the Third Reich. If the Third Reich had one thing, it had organization and it had order. I was certain that if I lost a stamp from a document, if it blew off the paper and out the window, the Third Reich would locate it. There was no escape.

I got off at the Bahnhof at Bruchsal. I placed my suitcase beside me. I did not have long to wait. Anneliese saw me first. She was overjoyed to see me. And there was comfort in her presence. My Aunt Anna, on the other hand, was not so overjoyed. It was a long walk through the town, to the small three-storied apartment house on the Wuerttemberger Strasse 7. There was a filling station on the corner where the bridge became the road to town. Between the filling station and the apartment house was a little playground with a large weeping willow. I loved the willow. And I loved the little Creek, the "Saal-Bach," that ran next to it. There was something else that appealed to me. That little town had all of its houses intact. There were no bomb craters.

Anneliese talked about her girlfriends and the little Catholic Youth Group she belonged to. I said nothing. I was not a person to join any group, unless it was the Theater and Brucheal did not have one.

Those first few days sort of went by in a haze. Peaceful coexistence was possible as long as I kept my mouth closed and did exactly what I was told.

Aunt Anna's family attended St. Peters on the hill. It was a beautiful old church, with an adjoining parish house, a small convent nearby and a large cemetery behind the church. I did not like cemeteries.

Anneliese pointed out to me that the trees were pretty. The cemetery was a gated piece of land with a respectable wrought iron fence. Anneliese pointed out the grave outside the pale. Next to the fence, a small grave with a small stone identifying the occupant as female, and having died from self-inflicted wounds. Somehow, it seemed impossible to escape from the all pervasive element of death, even in a peaceful town like Bruchsal.

Anneliese was in the Choir; I was allowed to be seated with her, on the balcony, next to the organ.

The church was filled to capacity on Sundays and most of the people were women and children. Most of the people wore black. The organ was impressive. The organist was an elderly gentleman. His daughter, Franziska, was quick to introduce herself to me.

Franziska's family lived on the outskirts of town in a small one-family house. I accepted an invitation to the house. Franziska and I became good friends. That house was different than the small apartment where I lived. That house had a piano, books and a radio. People sang and played the piano, discussed news events, read books, people did the kind of thinking I loved. At Aunt Anna's house we were the only people. Other people rarely visited because of My Uncle. There was no song there was no music and there were no books. At Aunt Anna's Anneliese and I did the chores. We cleaned and swept and washed dishes and helped with the cooking. That, my uncle said, was a woman's role in life.

The amicable coexistence lasted only a few days. I found it difficult to submit meekly and quietly. It simply was not in my nature. I talked back. My brain formulated and whatever the brain formulated slipped effortlessly across my lips.

140

"Why do you bait him?" Anneliese asked, after the first battle royal.

"I'm not aware of doing that," I replied. To me it was an exercise in intellectual fencing and Uncle Karl was not the world's greatest thinker.

"You back-talk, he backhands," she said.

What was it that made my words, my deeds, a crime, a sin, an immorality? Anneliese did the same thing, but she had a different approach. When I curled up with a good book, I was lazy. Anneliese complained of a stomachache, and right away she was put in a quiet place to relax and to get well.

No matter how I tried, I could not fit into the mold that was required of me. It was a blessing when I reported to the office of labor and was told that there was a job for me. The Third Reich needed me and I was to go to work at Rodi & Wienenberger. I was not told what I was supposed to do, except that I was to report for work the following morning.

"They make watches at Rodi & Wienenberger," my cousin said.

Franziska laughed. "You're so naive, they make ammunition there."

I hadn't started to work there yet and already there was a controversy. Aunt Anna settled it with a simple derogatory remark.

"It's a factory. You're a factory worker."

Anneliese felt pretty smug about that. She was a sales clerk at the local Kaufhaus. That was a notch above factory worker. I didn't care as long as it would get me out of that house and away from the uncle for eight hours a day. Mealtime torture was still the same. I took too much spinach. I had more than my share of potatoes. Thank God the meat was apportioned by

Aunt Anna, otherwise would have come to blows over that.

I reported at Rodi & Wienenberger, as requested in the morning, on time. The office was sparsely furnished. The man seated behind the desk, motioned for me to enter. He was of medium build, blond hair, a high forehead and a firmly set jaw line. What was unique about him, was his eyes. They were definitely blue and penetrating. This man had AUTHORITY tattooed all over his demeanor. This man was also a member of the National-Sozialistische-Deutsche-Arbeiter-Partei. He wore the party pin in his lapel, made of gold and precious stones. I looked at the pin and my mind blinked a caution sign inside of my head.

He told me his name was Herr Fricker. He wanted an honest day's work for an honest day's pay. If I behaved myself, worked hard and showed up properly each day, the pay would be good. He came around the desk, stood in front of me, about a head taller than I was, extended his hand. The bargain was sealed with a handshake. The interview was over. I was dismissed. Another man came and took me to the second floor department. He placed me between two women, both working on some items, held together by screws. The women were told to teach me how to run the little machine in front of me. It was a week before anybody even asked me my name. If there was laughter in the room, it became a deadly silence the moment Herr Fricker entered. But the pay was good. I took that first week's pay and purchased a topaz ring. Anneliese had wanted it so badly. And I always had the need to see her happy.

AMICABLE COEXISTENCE

Bruchsal and The Third Reich sort of coexisted in an amicable fashion. Rarely did I see anyone saluting another person with Heil Hitler. In Bruchsal it had always been Gruess Gott, no matter who reined the country, no matter who won the war. In Bruchsal, people greeted each other with "Gruess Gott".

Within the factory compound, people did not say "God Bless." They greeted each other by their first name. Besides Herr Fricker, there were two minor authority figures. They too wore the party insignia. They were treated with respect, but behind their backs, the women made fun.

The women in the factory were not overly concerned with the government. They were concerned about husbands, sons, brothers and fathers. So many were missing, missing in action The Third Reich declared. Missing in action left little room for hope. Some of the women wore black. When the person next to you suddenly showed up in black, no questions were asked. Grief, if in need for attention, would make itself known. Most of the time, carefree chatter, jokes about sex, ribald puns, deterred from the sorrow that would not go away.

Sometimes a song would spring up from somewhere, an old folk melody, a hymn, a hit, better known from the Wunsch Konzert, and everyone would join. Not even the rhythm of the heavy machinery could detract from the melodies.

Most of the people who worked there, had lived in Bruchsal and the surrounding villages for generations. Some where newcomers. Some had followed German soldiers as they had been transferred to a position behind the war zone. Some had been enticed by advertisements that told of good pay, free medical care and free vacations. Some had found out that their men were in prisoner-of-war camps in the surrounding area and that they were working on the farms. All in all, The Third Reich had managed to accumulate many non-Germans. That, in spite of the fact, that Germans were supposed to keep the race pure. Of course it was forbidden to fraternize with a non-German male if you were a German female. There were Italians, Spaniards, Russians, French, Alsatians, Hollanders, Latvians and Lithuanians.

Chances are if he was a man, not wearing a uniform, he was not a German. And forbidden or not, romance blossomed and songs of love drifted through the evening air with strange sounding names and foreign words.

Franziska Ruebenacker introduced me to a family where the male members were German. Herr and Frau Boes had three sons. And they were all home. Willi, the eldest, had a war injury and was presently on leave. Walter, the middle child, belonged to an army band unit and was awaiting orders to be shipped out. Werner, the youngest, had just completed his training as an Air Force Pilot and was waiting for his orders. Herr Boes was a musician and the family gathered for music on a daily basis. With music came talk. Apparently no one there had ever heard about the Gestapo. Within the walls of that apartment, politics was freely discussed. So was philosophy and religion. The family was Catholic, outspoken and not always approvingly Catholic.

Within these walls, Patriarchy, as a means of social directive, was finally questioned. Most heatedly by Franziska:

144

"I don't care that all the leaders of the nations are male, maybe if they weren't our people wouldn't have to bleed to death on the battlefield."

"When has a woman ever accomplished monumental fame?"

"St. Joan of Ark comes to mind. But the grand inquisitors burned her at the stake."

"When a man puts on his belt——"

"When a man puts on his belt he loses his humanness. It's when he takes off his belt, that he becomes humane and a man." At this point the conversation was moving more swiftly than I could follow.

"Why would a man take off his belt?"

There was momentary silence, followed by a sally of laughter. Willi, the eldest, came to my side, looked at me and said:

"Looks like we have a genuine ingénue in our midst."

Franziska was quick to reply: "And whatever teaching that is necessary, I'll do it myself."

Willi laughed, backed away, curtsied and said: "I'll promise to be friend and protector, nothing more."

There was laughter and then Frau Boes arrived with refreshments. How she was able to serve food and drink with the limit of ration cards, was beyond my comprehension.

Herr Boes went to the piano and soon the songs of the country filled the air. The room was warm with the presence of happy people.

It was late when we started out for my Aunt's apartment. I told Franziska that I felt so inadequate, so totally uneducated.

"Well that's the way the Fuehrer wants his youth, totally uninformed".

"But why?"

"People who don't know anything don't ask any questions."

"I don't know anything and I ask questions:"

"Ever get any answers?"

"Not really, at least not the kind I was hoping for."

By the time we reached Aunt Anna's house, Franziska had definitely satisfied some of my curiosity. But for every question she answered, ten others popped up in my mind. If I was in the process of crossing a street and someone from the other side shouted HALT, would I stop? Of course I would; but why?

Franziska was my friend. I could not lie to her. Nor could I answer that question. What she was telling me was that I would place my life in jeopardy in order to obey orders. What she was telling me was that I never questioned the wisdom of an order or the intelligence of the order-giver. We said good night. She said she would see me at mass Sunday. She never requested my silence. She said Gruess Gott as she left. I replied with "Aufwiedersehn."

If I talked to anyone about the things we said it was to Anneliese. And Anneliese became very still. I thought for a moment, she'd stopped breathing. Then she said: "DU", and then there was a long pause. But I could read it in her eyes and I could sense it in the way she stood there with shoulders drawn in. That kind of talk had made her be afraid.

Aunt Anna told us that there was no time for whispered comments. It was way past bedtime and had it not been for Franziska Ruebenacker, she would not have allowed my staying out past ten. I apologized. I understood that life with all of us sleeping in the same bedroom certainly could not have been easy. She sent Heinz to bed first. I was next. Anneliese followed and then Uncle Karl and Aunt Anna came to bed. How we ever slept, crammed in there like sardines, three beds, five people, I often wondered how any of us could have endured that much togetherness.

The next time we met at Herr and Frau Boes, the atmosphere was more subdued. Frau Boes wore black. Walter had been killed in action. No one knew where. The official letter stated that he had sacrificed his young life for the Fatherland. Werner was in uniform and it was his farewell party. Werner was the youngest. He was in the Luft Waffe. He was scheduled to fly against England.

After coffee and cake, the usual Ersatz coffee made of roasted grain; and cake made with semolina, it was Werner's time to leave. It had been agreed that he would be sent off with a smile and a cheerful Aufwiedersehn. We walked him to the train station. The picture of all of us gathered there is one of the few possessions the war and the Third Reich permitted me to have.

147

CHRISTMAS, 1943

By the time Christmas rolled around, I had adjusted to life in Bruchsal. There was no radio at my aunt's house. Consequently there was little news from The Third Reich.

At work, Herr Fricker unveiled the Christmas present from The Third Reich. Apparently the government had arranged for communal showers to be installed. Herr Fricker pointed with pride toward the two large, circular basins, hewn out of granite, and the tiled floor in the spacious confine of the public bath. I don't recall him ever telling us if we were to bathe or shower sexually segregated or integrated. He did say that the showers could accommodate as many as twenty persons at a time. However, the showers were not ready for use because the water had not been hooked up. That was to come later. As history would have it, allied air raids made that unnecessary.

Before we could plan for a Christmas celebration at the Boes's house, Werner turned up missing. It was assumed that his plane went down over England. Nothing else was known for weeks. Now there was only one son left for Frau Boes.

Prior to Christmas, I asked and was granted permission to go to the village. I was grateful to be allowed to go there. I was certainly not allowed to go to Mannheim. I wasn't certain if that had anything to do with my summoning Herr Hoelzlin to the rescue. I did not talk about Herr Hoelzlin again, even to Anneliese. And yet that one night, when he calmed my fears and made that terrible ordeal of the bombing less terrifying, was enough memory to see me through those first few weeks at Aunt Anna's house. The stage and all its attractions was still a greater part of me.

148

Within my mind and my imagination I staged dramatic performances of Schiller's Ballads.

"Zu Dyonis dem Tyrannen schlich, Damos den Dolch im Gewande," my lips whispered the words and my mind staged the scene. It was better than nothing.

Mother Nature called off my visit to Neibsheim. Before I could arrange for the trip, the heavy snows set in. Mother Nature taketh and giveth. I could not go to Neibsheim, but we would have a white Christmas.

The Third Reich did not celebrate Christmas in Bruchsal. Maybe it did not celebrate Christmas at all. Little news came to us from the outside of the confines of the small town.

It was said that the Afrika Korps had been dissolved. It was said that the war was slowly turning upon itself and inward. For anyone to say that Germany should sue for peace was considered treason. Franziska told me that. And she told me that anyone suspected of treason would be taken into Schutzhaft, protective custody.

"Just for saying something?" I asked. I found that to be incredulous. We were a free people. That was what the Third Reich told us. We were a free people, born to rule.

"Think of it," Franziska said: "If you're a free person, German, born to rule and the Fuehrer is not a German, how does that fit."

"But the Fuehrer is German! Isn't he?"

"What were you taught about Hitler? The first facts?"

"He was born, April the twentieth at Braunau on the Inn."

"Remember your geography lessons; Is the Inn a German or an Austrian river?"

149

"But he made the Austrians German with the Anschluss."

"Can you make a cat a dog by calling it a dog?"

Franziska was right. Franziska was always right. But it was a dangerous way of being right.

Most of Anneliese's social activities centered around the church. Anneliese belonged to a Catholic Youth Organization. She also belonged to the St. Peter's Choir. Anneliese had a wonderful voice. She was also a beautiful person. Black curly hair, slender and lithe of limb like a willow, she represented everything that I was not. She was submissive, feminen, schmiegsam and biegsam, they said. She was attractive and she had a beautiful voice. There was little doubt why the choir director selected her for the solo at midnight mass. Franziska's father, Herr Ruebenacker, was the organist. He agreed with that choice. The Ruebenacker family was aware of the strained condition in my aunt's household. There was always Uncle Karl with his terrifying temper. Franziska, shortly before Christmas, proposed the possibility of my staying with her family. It would be her mother, her father and herself.

"Don't say anything to your aunt, let me do the talking." Franziska was well aware of my shortcomings in the field of diplomacy.

The idea of possibly staying with the Ruebenackers, of having a bed of my own and a room of my own, kept me from becoming terribly depressed that Christmas of 1943. There was a small tree, decorated with home made decoration and decked out with little white candles. Tante Anna lit the candles on Christmas Eve, shortly before we went to midnight mass. We sang silent night and then the candles were extinguished. Uncle Karl complained about the smell of the candle wax and all that singing. I held back the tears and remembered better days. But I was grateful that there were no sirens wailing away and no air raids.

Midnight mass and the bells were ringing. We slushed through snow, knee-deep and up hill toward the church on the hilltop. St. Peter's was to Bruchsal what St. Peter's was to Rome. Considering that the town only had about 12000 residents, the church was a magnificent edifice. Beyond it and surrounding it on three sides was the "Friedhof," the cemetery, a place of peace, the domain of the dead. It always seemed to me that St. Peter's sat on that domain like a brooding hen.

Anneliese had a new dress for the occasion. Aunt Anna had connections. She was good at getting things that no one else could.

Anneliese looked beautiful, as she stood there, next to the organ, ready to perform her solo. She was scheduled to sing the Ave Maria. There were no microphones. Her voice would have to carry that distance from organ to altar. And the church was packed. Side altars and High Altar all of them were heavily decorated with Christmas Green and Candle White. The fragrance of pine needles, candle wax and incense was intoxicating.

I was seated next to Franziska Ruebenacker, in the choir section, a little back from the organ. The organ itself was monumental. It took up most of the room on the balcony. The pipes were polished and the woodwork lustrous.

Herr Ruebenacker looked at the choir director. The choir director looked at Anneliese and for a brief moment in time the church was silent, waiting with respectful anticipation for Anneliese to nod her head.

151

Anneliese nodded. The choir director gave the signal. Herr Ruebenacker started the organ. Sound was wedded to sight and fragrance. Anneliese's voice rose to the ceiling, floated through the entire church, hesitantly gentle at first and then with full force.

"Sends shivers down your spine, don't it?" somebody whispered near us.

Had there been an opportunity for applause, there would have been a thunderous roar of applause. But this was a church and there would be no applause in a Catholic church.

It was difficult for me to express the mixture of feelings; that reverence for talent, a certain envy because at that moment she had center stage. I had lost all hopes for center stage.

After it was over, Franziska grabbed my arm and led me to Aunt Anna.

"That was certainly a beautiful performance," she told my aunt. She kept on talking on how proud Aunt Anna should be. And when the glow of success duly reflected from Aunt Anna's face. Franziska popped the question. Would Aunt Anna mind if the city cousin would take breakfast with the Ruebenackers? She, Aunt Anna, would have her hands full with all the people wanting to compliment her on her daughter's success, and all that. And then it was said and done and I slushed my way to the Ruebenacker's at Franziska's side.

FRANZISKA'S PLACE

Franziska's mother was a small woman, trained from early life to please the man and raise the children. There had been twelve children. The Ruebenackers were devout Catholics. Franziska was the youngest and the only one left at home.

At table I was seated next to Franziska and to the right of Herr Ruebenacker. It was considered a place of honor.

It was a small, but immaculate dining room. The furniture, of heirloom quality, was polished and the decorations for Christmas were laid out. But the first thing to catch my attention, was the piano in the corner, next to the window. A house with a piano would have music. And music was soul food.

Breakfast consisted of cornmeal mush and Hefe Kranz, a breakfast cake made of yeast dough.

At breakfast it was once again discussed to ask me to come and live with them. Franziska missed her older sisters and brothers.

Franziska said that the family practiced a thing called DEMOCRACY, although the final decision of the head of the household was binding. The word DEMOCRACY was new in my vocabulary. I had grown up in a world where demands were made, orders were issued, and individual voices were not recognized as such.

It was agreed, on that Christmas Day, that I would became a member of the Ruebenacker Family. It was also agreed that the task of getting Aunt Anna to agree, would be left to Franziska. Herr Ruebenacker did lend his support.

"I think it would be an excellent experience for your niece; don't you think?" The old man said it in such a way that Aunt Anna felt it to be irreverent not to comply. And somewhere between Christmas and New Year I moved to a new place, with a room of my own, a bed of my own and far away from Uncle Karl's scornful disposition.

1944 was ushered in quietly. There were no fireworks because of the possibility that it may confuse the people, what with air raids and the war. Nor were there bells. That could be confusing as well.

My new address was Augarten Strasse 14. And I could write and receive all the letters I wanted to write and to receive. I wrote in the family living room at the table. The little garret room was too cold. Herr Ruebenacker believed in living with nature. All sleeping quarters were unheated.

Herr Ruebenacker also believed in teaching. He taught me many things. He enjoyed going for walks in the country side and I became his companion. He taught me how to measure the height of a tree from its shadow. He taught me about the Roman custom of decimating a population. He pointed toward the edge of a cliff in the distance.

"That's how the Romans practiced population control. They lined up their prisoners, then they counted to ten and every tenth person was asked to take three steps back. At the tip of the sword of course."

"But that's terrible."

"Is it any more terrible than to reign fire and brimstone on an entire population?"

He was always quick to make me understand that all participants practiced cruel customs. To him there was not a clear-cut boundary between guilty and innocent, between right and wrong, there was simply an evil that was let loose on the world by the world.

154

"Integrity," he'd say; "That is what a person must never lose; integrity."

Herr Ruebenacker felt strongly about personal integrity, about giving one's word, about keeping it, about keeping a secret.

"I'll tell you a secret," he said.

I looked at him. He towered so far above me. He was tall and straight and white-haired and a man of principle.

"I'll tell you a secret and I expect you to keep it!"

"Of course I'll keep it."

And I kept it. No matter how I was tempted to talk about it. I kept his secret. Long after he had died, long after all concerned with the secret had died, I still kept the secret.

In those early days of 1944, I sat at night and looked out across black outlines of small-town houses, covered by heavy winter snows. I looked across the night skies and listened to the silence. There were whispers now about an offensive in the Ardennes. Why there was need for an offensive when we had already conquered France, I failed to comprehend.

Franziska's fiancé came home on leave, and for just a little while there was joy and laughter.

Franziska's fiancé served in the army in Russia. He told of the sorrow of the Russians. And just as Herr Ruebenacker taught me all about integrity and mathematics computations, so did Franziska's future husband teach me about policies of scorched earth. And now, for the first time, there were lessons about dictatorship. And yet, Hitler's name was never mentioned and the concepts of The Third Reich remained unassailably discreet.

GRANDMOTHER

I finally saw a break in the weather, and holding Aunt Anna to her word, I paid my respects to the village, Uncle Johann and my beloved Grossmutter, the Grand Dame of the clan.

I attended Mass at the village church with Uncle Johann and Aunt Martha. And I listened quietly, while the Village Priest railed away about the evils of big-city-dwellers.

The priest was still talking about that as we left the church. I wanted to pass by, but Uncle Johann insisted on small courtesies due to the clergy.

"This is my niece from Mannheim," Uncle Johann said, by way of introduction. The Priest looked at my uncle and then at me.

"Oh!" he exclaimed: "A big-city-dweller!"

I nodded my head. I was going to be quiet. I was not going to embarrass the good Uncle Johann. But the priest insisted.

"People in big cities forget the way of the Lord," he said, then added, "They live in sin."

Funny how quickly the mind steps down from the brain, into the mouth and across the lips.

"I suppose that's why God allowed fire bombs and block busters to be unloaded from airplanes on innocent women and children and on the newborn who haven't had the opportunity to sin."

I wanted to add a few more choice remarks while the priest looked at me as though I had just sprouted horns on my forehead. My uncle's arms came around my shoulders. That big paw of his swept me away, while he said his good-bye.

"Sorry we have to leave. One of my cows is going to calve!"

156

We rushed away from church. I could read my uncle's eyes quite well. I had committed a no-no, a breach of etiquette, and I meant to apologize. But he grumbled under his breath:

"We'll talk about that later."

Aunt Martha turned and glared at me.

"You know your grandmother just wants to die, so she won't have to look another one of her children into the grave. Well it seems to me like she doesn't have to worry about her children but she better start worrying about you. The way your mouth opens and the stuff comes out, you won't live long."

She had scarcely finished her speech when Uncle Johann stopped. He raised himself up to his full height, towering over her.

"Weib! Abba!" He thundered.

Aunt Martha lapsed into silence. I was afraid to speak. But there was a big lump in my throat and I could feel the tears coming into my eyes.

We reached the house. Aunt Martha went in. Uncle Johann directed me to the small copse behind the cow stalls. I sat down on a bundle of twigs and waited for doomsday to descend. He settled down beside me lifted up my face below my chin so that I had to look into his eyes. That's when the tears began to flow.

"I just want to go home," I sobbed.

He shook his head. "You can't go home. For you there is no more home. So forget about that."

I curled up as small as I could and continued to cry. He continued to preach.

"You see all this around you? Well maybe next year this time it won't be here."

I stopped crying. "Next year maybe the war will be over and we'll have won and we'll have all the things we don't have now," I countered.

He shook his head. "Next year this time the war will be lost."

I couldn't believe he said that.

"What makes you think we'll lose the war?" I asked.

"Be realistic! We lost that war the moment America entered on the side of the allies."

I closed my eyes. I held my hand before my eyes. I wasn't certain what it was that I was shutting out. But I could not believe that we would lose the war. This was the Third Reich, the Reich that would last a thousand years. I had been told that since I was a child. I had been taught to revere the flag, to honor the Vaterland, that Deutschland, that Germany; to respect its leaders and to accept unconditionally all that I was told and to follow orders without question. And now Uncle Johann, undisputed head of the clan, tells me that the Third Reich would lose the war.

He placed his arm protectively around my shoulders.

"This is what will happen," he said. "By next summer you'll hear thunder, except it won't be thunder. It will be the distant guns. By fall and winter you'll hear them all the time. When that spring after that winter comes around we won't be plowing or planting. During the day we'll be forced to help the army dig trenches. At night the farmers will go out and dig even deeper burrows. What would feed the cattle will line those holes and what crops that can be hidden away will be hidden away to keep us from starving to death. One army or the other will take the cattle. We'll be lucky to have the house, a few chickens maybe, some rabbits, the cats, and dogs. And if it gets bad enough, we'll lose them too. I think we can count ourselves lucky if we'll come away with our lives, because this will be battleground."

We sat there in silence. What he told me was the thing you read in an adventure book, or a history book, but it doesn't happen, here, now to yourself, to your family and your friends.

"Just how do you know?" I whispered, when I finally found the words.

"It has always been that way."

"And the Third Reich can't change that? "

"How? With airplanes we don't have any more?"

"The navy?"

"Gone!"

I remembered the sailor in Heidelberg. And there was Werner's uncle. He had gone away. He was a sailor. And Werner had gone away.

Uncle Johann rose, "Time to put an end to this. Your Aunt Martha is right. If you don't keep your thoughts to yourself, you won't survive the war either."

"It doesn't make sense." I replied. "I am German and I can't know the truth about anything. I can't talk about this land, this war to anyone because if I did, I could be arrested and executed as an enemy of the Third Reich."

There was a grim smile on his face, "You are absolutely right. And that is so because the only part of the Third Reich that still functions is the GESTAPO."

We left the copse.

"But why must all these people sacrifice their lives for a cause that can't win?"

159

"There was never a cause. Wars are fought over money!"

"In a capitalistic nation maybe but not in the Third Reich," I said.

Uncle Johann shook his head sadly. "There was a picture once, in a newspaper, of Hitler and the person next to him was a bank president. There is Porsche. Porsche promised to build the Volkswagen. Porsche is making money-building vehicles for Hitler's Army. Krupp is profiting with weapons. They're capitalists. The difference between a capitalistic government and ours is that in other lands everyone has a chance to be a capitalist. In ours in the Third Reich, Hitler makes up our minds about that by himself. Enough!"

My conference was at an end. Uncle propelled me into the living quarters. I was told that after the meal, I was to be taken to Bruchsal. Uncle Johann had arranged my transportation. I don't know where the car came from. I don't know where the gas came from that fueled the motor. But I was warm and seated and I did not have to walk through snow and slush.

The Ruebenackers were glad to see me return. They were concerned. Franziska saw at a glance that I was disturbed about something.

"Is everybody all right?" she asked. I told her that everybody was fine. I also told her that Uncle Johann and I had had a conversation. She just nodded her head. She did not ask for the contents of that conversation. I went up to my room. It was cold up there. It was also closed away from the world, a world I no longer understood. I looked out across the rooftops, rooftops that sort of became one grayish mass at dusk. I heard the door opening softly. I knew it was Franziska. I turned as she approached me. The tears could no longer be denied.

"I'm so homesick," I cried. She put her arms around me. She allowed me the luxury to cry without shame.

The snows gave way to early spring rains. Life continued in its drab, day-by-day, mundane pattern. Frau Ruebenacker saw to it that I had a good breakfast and that my lunch was packed. Franziska gave me her coat. Mine did not keep the cold out, she said. Mine was department-store-off-the-rack-wartime issue. It was falling apart faster than I could stitch it together. At the factory, Herr Fricker increased the weekly pep talks in sound and fury. Sabotage, he said. There was too much sabotage. The guns, the ammunition, nothing reached our troops. By the time they received a shipment, the boxes were filled with sand. That was the first time I heard him mention the fact we were not making watches. He came blazing down the assembly line. He screamed at me, something about my not working hard enough and fast enough. I unwound the bandage on my left hand and showed him the palm of my hand. There were blisters that had never healed. Blood and liquid oozed from it slowly. He looked around with eyes like steel.

"Who reported that?" He shouted. No one answered. The woman next to me bowed her head. She did not have to say anything. Uncle Johann was right. It really didn't take much to become an enemy of the Fatherland.

ALSATIANS AND AUDITIONS

Once a week I lunched with girls from work at the local restaurant. There were six Alsatians who came to eat as well. They were kind and friendly. It was after I ordered soup, and raised the spoon that one of the Alsatians looked at me attentively.

"Do you always shake like that?"

The spoon clattered out of my hand on to the table. I was trying to hide my hand. The girl next to me patted me on the shoulder.

"Go on, eat," she said and than proceeded to explain. "She's just a little nervous. The war you know, lost her home and her folks."

The table became silent. The Alsatian looked at me, then shook his head.

"How old are you?" He wanted to know. I had to think for a moment.

"Seventeen," I replied.

"No one that young should be trembling with fear, just eating soup," he said. The table was silent again. The Alsatians conversed in French. I liked the sound of it. I could not understand it but there was music in the way it came together.

It was in early spring that Gabrielle, one of the girls at the factory, told me of the talent show. She said the government was offering scholarships for five hundred people. Singers, dancers, actors, all kind of stage performers could be offered the scholarships.

"In Bruchsal?" I wanted to know.

"No," she said. It was held in Karlsrnhe. She said she was going. She had prepared a song. It was from an operetta. She said I could come along if I wanted to try out. She had been aware of how much I missed the theater. Did I want to go? I said yes without thinking. But on the way home the euphoria about a possible audition gave way to the stark reality of having to get Aunt Anna's permission. By the time I reached the Ruebenacker's house I was in a frenzy. I told Franziska of the unexpected offer.

"Aunt Anna won't let me go." As far as I was concerned, that was the way it was.

"Nothing much will probably ever come from it," Franziska replied, "Why don't I cover for you?"

Not until I was on that train to Karlsruhe did I think about the danger. Aunt Anna had not permitted a trip to Mannheim. Because of possible air raids, she'd said. I couldn't go to Heidelberg, because you can hear the big guns from the Ardennes, she'd said. Nor could I go to Schwetzingen. The people from the National Theater at Mannheim were performing at the Schloss Theater at Schwetzingen. There was nothing there to bomb. All that Schwetzingen had was a castle and commercial asparagus fields. I'd been unable to contain myself and asked her if she was afraid I'd trip on an asparagus there. And she'd said just for that I couldn't go. But I knew better. That entire clan would rise like a solid wall to stand between me and the theater.

And now I was on my way to an audition, a national audition in Karlsruhe. It took longer than usual. The rails had been detoured because of a small village that had been bombed out of existence. No one really knew why. When we had discussed that at the weekly lunch one of the Alsatian said that it was probably a mistake. But the village was gone with all of its houses, its people, its animals, its church and the minister. No one had survived that air raid. As we passed in silence, I could see Uncle Johann in my mind's eye. I could hear his voice. But I could not afford that little what-if game. I was going to an audition. I was going to get my chance. I could not tremble and I could not be afraid. Besides there was that consolation that Aunt Anna did not know. And if she did not know, she would not have to fear about my safety.

Gabrielle was excited. She said she was certain to win a scholarship and then she could join the Front Theater and perform for the troops. No more Herr Fricker. No more Rodi & Wienenberger.

The place for audition was not far from the train station. It was easy to find. There were so many people there.

Gabrielle went one way and I headed in the opposite direction to a room designated for actors. I was given a number, and I was told to be seated.

It was at that point that I realized that I had not prepared any material. But then, there were same lines from Goethe's Faust, the prison scene. I had no problem with memorization. I could do that. I could do Schiller. "Zu Dyonis dem Tyrannen schlich…"

One by one the people went in and came out. There were only two or three left when my number came up. I was ushered into the room. At the far end was a small platform that served as a makeshift stage. Not much room for action, I noted. There was a chair on that stage. Not many props I noted. Between that stage and myself were five people, seated around a table. I was given a choice. I could do a scene from any noteworthy play, or I could improvise. I looked across the people at the stage and its one and only prop.

"Improvise," I said. The speaker a middle-aged individual who apparently led the group, turned to me.

"You are expecting a telephone call." That was my only cue.

I walked up to the stage. I sat down on the chair. My mind projected Aunt Antonia on the phone. I picked up an imaginary phone.

"42982" I said. Funny I would have remembered that number. And then I knew that it was up to me to entertain. And so I entertained with every nuance of personality that Aunt Antonia ever displayed. When I heard the first laughter, I knew that I had made it. I simply responded to the audience. That had always been Herr Elmendorff's advice. Respond.

On the way home Gabrielle told me that she had not been able to get a scholarship. She said she was certain that the people simply did not appreciate beauty and talent. She said they had told her that her voice was not strong enough. But then, she said, it was after all a national competition. She had competed and that was enough.

I had been sitting there quietly, watching the landscape pass by. When she asked me how I had scored, I showed her the slip of paper they had given me. She didn't say much, except: "Well, it doesn't take talent to improvise. You just have to ham it up."

I agreed with her. I did not tell her that they had given me a choice. FRONT THEATER, or private lesson, paid for by The Third Reich. Of course the real problem I faced, was telling Aunt Anna that I had that scholarship, and getting permission for that weekly trip to Karlsruhe. The Third Reich took care of Herr Fricker. All I had to secure was Aunt Anna's YES.

Back once again, at the train depot in Bruchsal, I bid a hasty farewell to Gabrielle and hurried to the Ruebenacker's house.

"Really hadn't planned on that had you?" Franziska said with a grin.

The war and The Third Reich came to my assistance. Aunt Anna listened to my confession absentmindly, said nothing about that scholarship.

"Some other time," she replied. "We have to go to Neibsheim."

That was all she would say. When I told Franziska, she thought it best to leave things alone until the return from the village.

"E'm geschenkte Gaul, schaut ma net in's Maul," she said. She was right of course. You don't look a gift horse in the mouth.

"Exactly why don't you look a gift horse in the mouth?" Franziska grinned.

"Because you can tell his age by his teeth, stupid." Live and learn, I thought.

RUSSIA

I did not think that Russia could be the reason for the Gathering. How large a Gathering, I did not know. What was abundantly clear, was that this was more than a social visit. Uncle Karl was coming along. So was Heinz, Anneliese and of course, Aunt Anna. Since Uncle Karl came along, it wasn't quite clear where our presence was requested. Uncle Karl hailed from the lower village. He was a Frank. Aunt Anna came from the upper village. Not that Neibeheim was a big place. Neibsheim had at most seventeen clans. Very few clans counted more than five families.

We entered the village via Gundelsheim. From all the people afoot, it looked as though all of the clans were well represented. Most of the clans had called family members from the surrounding area to the meeting. And some of the people we met were definitely not local people.

"This place is full of outlanders," Aunt Martha grumbled. My curiosity was piqued, and I was about to ask a question when Uncle Johann gave me one of those warning glances. I would have to remember to keep my mouth shut. I was under age and what was worse, I was female.

"They are not outlanders," Uncle Johann replied, "They are refugees. They hail from the West, the Saar, Alsace Lorraine, the Pfalz."

That answer did not satisfy me at all. Refugees came from war zones. I thought the war in the West was over with a long time ago. I was afraid to bring up the subject.

Uncle Johann, apparently the head of our clan, said that the meeting was to be held in the lower mill. That was Frank territory. That was Uncle Karl's clan.

167

I looked at Anneliese, but she didn't know any more than I did.

"I don't know why we're gathering. I think it's about somebody coming back from Russia."

"Uncle Moritz?" I asked hopefully.

Anneliese shook her head. For Uncle Moritz, the gathering would have been called in the upper village. I suppose I knew it was folly to think that Uncle Moritz would ever return.

There were many people at the Lower Mill, most of them old, most of them female, some growing children. And almost all of them wore black. The man, addressing the people, had his hands in his pocket. He had indeed returned from Russia. He took his hands out of his pockets and held them up. This was how he had returned. There were no fingers left. He also lacked one leg.

No one besides him had made it, he told us. And he knew for a fact that Edmund, the son of the Bruecke Sepp was not returning. Nor would the Klammer Karle return. And young Hedwig, over there, in the corner; he pointed at her, she was going to be a widow. Hedwig stood there, her face a marble mask.

And how did he get back? Some of the Russians helped him. He said he crossed a partly frozen river on the corpses that had accumulated on the surface of the icy water. At night, when it was very cold he crawled inside the cadavers of the horses that had died there. By the time he'd made it as far as somewhere up there near Pommern, he stopped at a farmhouse. No one answered as he knocked on the door. When he walked in he saw the man, the woman, the children, slumped over the table. When he looked closer he noticed that their tongues had been nailed to the tabletop. He knew that the Russians were ahead of him. He could not take time to do anything for that family. He was behind the Russian line and near disputed territory. There were the Russians ahead, in front of the Russians, the Germans. Closer than that, the battlefield, disputed territory. He had known a kind and sympathetic side of war and enemy, and now he had seen the brutality. Now, all he wanted to do, was to survive and to tell his people that the Russians were coming.

I looked at Anneliese. She was close to passing out. But we were there for a meeting and we would have to listen to all of it.

It was apparent that this man was not from the village. But the village would protect him, would hide him, and would keep him untill he could be safely on his way.

If this man was not from the village, neither was the next. He was not missing fingers and a leg, but he had another, a direr message.

The Russians, he said, were almost to the border, whatever was the border these days. It was certain that the war would only end when the Russians reached Berlin.

He said he wasn't too worried about that, yet, what worried him was the war from the air, and a new kind of plane that this war was fought with.

"They call them Jabos to the west of us. Their makers call them Thunderbolt. They have guns in the nose of the plane and the tail of the plane. They shoot at everything that moves and they drop bombs as well."

"We are farmers, why would they shoot at us?" someone asked.

"Your work feeds a nation. What better way to stop a war then starve your enemy?" he replied.

The men and women in that room had trouble believing that.

"Ask the widow of the guard at the railroad crossing at Waghaeusel. He tried to hide in the guardhouse. The Jabos blew that away. There was almost nothing left of the guard."

Now there was a new and immediate danger. There were airplanes that shot at civilians, unarmed civilians, and the crops had to be planted, otherwise there would be famine next year. It would be useless to run, the man said. If they were overhead, the edge of a forest provided the only means to protect those valuable animals as well as the farmer. Plowing was best done on cloudy days, at night, at dusk, most importantly; tending crops was to be done when the pilots can't distinguish one thing from another. Plow if you must and plant what you must. Don't travel on a train, because the Jabos follow the rails and shoot at any moving train. Don't frequent the road near the train. A farmer a couple of miles up the road did that and they're still picking up the pieces from his team and from the farmer.

I looked at Uncle Johann and he looked at me. Now I understood perfectly well what he had told me only a few days ago. I just didn't think it would arrive this quickly. It seemed to me that the actions of the Third Reich dealt awful blows to the common man for whom the Third Reich promised to exist. My mind was still with that family at the table. And those, who perpetrated that misdeed, were coming our way.

I asked my uncle for permission to take Anneliese out. She was at the point of collapse. My uncle helped us to the door.

He stood there for a moment. The other thing, he said, that needed discussing, was how to get rid of the Burgermeister The Third Reich had appointed for the village. The only salvation for us would be in not having anything, least of all members of the N.S.D.A.P.

We walked back in the evening hours with our ears fine tuned to the hum of planes, thunderbolts, and red-tailed fighter hunter planes.

I was troubled because I knew I had the opportunity to start my lessons in Karlsruhe. But the only way I could get there was by train. The agreement had been made. A teacher had been engaged for me and the Third Reich had paid the lady and myself. I was bound to obey. I thought about that all the way home. I even thought about it as I told Franziska about that town meeting. Franziska was well aware of the danger, but had not thought it to be that extreme. She shrugged her shoulders.

"You just can't let a situation scare you out of living," she said. All the fear in the world wouldn't keep a person alive when it was time to die. She said that, knowing that the letters she had written to her fiancée were returning, and that no letters from him arrived. Her jaw was set. She simply assailed life with a grim determination to survive. Silently I vowed to do the same. Franziska, after all, was my model for life.

I went to work in the mornings. If the Jabos were here, I was unaware of them.

Summer came. There was little news, and what news there was, was not uplifting. Ration cards were less. It was 125 gram of butter per person per month. Meat was possible once a month. Bread was hard and heavy and rationed down to one loaf a week. Milk was available only for babies and nursing mothers. There were times when I felt tempted to become a mother just to know the taste of milk once more. My shoes were held together by cord. One of the girls at work had figured out how to unravel sugar sacks to make yarn for sweaters. I paid a fortune for two sugar sacks. But it was not enough for one sweater.

People looked tired and drawn and haggard. They quarreled easily. And then one day at work I stood near a tank of chemicals and the next thing I knew I was out like a light. I came to in Herr Fricker's offices, bedded down on a couch. He sat there and watched – his face void of any feelings. When I tried to get up, he told me to stay until the nurse came.

I was given a day's leave and I was told to stay away from the chemicals. It was a solution meant to clean parts that needed to be perfectly clean.

Two weeks later an officer from the Wehrmacht visited the factory. Herr Fricker brought him over and showed him what we were doing. When I looked up from work, I looked into the face of the man who had shared those air raid adventures with us. He smiled and shook my hand and told Herr Fricker that he knew me from a visit to Werderstrasse 44 at Mannheim. He said he hoped I was well and then continued on his way.

LAKE CONSTANCE

After the officer had gone, Herr Fricker sent for me. In his office, he explained to me, that he thought perhaps the work was too strenuous for me and maybe I would like to be transferred to the jewelry department downstairs. I could have kissed his hand, but I just concurred. He also told me that in view of my health, perhaps a visit to lake Constance would be good for me. Two weeks at Lake Constance in the shadow of the Alps. I could scarcely believe it. I forgot about the trains and the Jabos. I forgot about danger. I only thought of the lake I had never seen.

I told Herr Fricker that I would have to get my aunt's permission. He just smiled and said not to worry about that.

My clothes were a bit on the shabby side. The Third Reich had given me ration tickets for a new pair of shoes. Aunt Anna had found a seamstress who made me a dress and a tan summer coat to match. The money came from an allowance from the Fatherland. Aunt Anna conjured up the dress material, the coat material, and the new hat to match. I loved it. Awed by it all, I whispered my thanks. I loved my ticket to ride. Aunt Anna said nothing. She had been very accommodating. Franziska was happy for me.

"It's about time you see something of this world," she said. She embraced, bade me farewell and told me to have fun.

Unter Uhldingen was a small village on the lake with a little Inn, a room with a view and sunrise over the lake. It was like touching infinity. I did not know that I was still capable of feeling joy.

The small village of Unteruhldingen was on the far side of the lake. But we were given tours of the

173

Meersburg, where Droste Huelshoff once wrote her now famous poetry. A lady read the poems from the original manuscripts. I requested permission to touch that page and the lady, with a smile, granted it. I tried to explain to her that there was something wonderful about touching the page that contained the thoughts of the author. Time simply slipped away.

We went to the isle of Mainau, actually a peninsula, rather than an island. The place was famous for its orange and lemon trees. I looked in vain for just one fruit. It had been years since I'd seen an orange.

A movie company was on the island filming. We understood that Willy Birgel was starring.

The most impressive site of one particular tour was that of the famous Pfahl-bauten, thatch-roofed huts, erected on wooden posts, with wooden walkways to the shore. Those were the earliest human habitats. Within the huts were wooden benches, holding the display items of Stone age implements. Touch any of those and you go even farther back in time, I told myself. Almost subconsciously, gingerly, I reached out a hand.

"Touch one of those and the guards will take you away." The voice next to me belonged to a man who hailed from Bretten, also on the same vacation packet than mine. Nevertheless, I could not refrain from just one little touch. The guards did not see me. To me that was a long-remembered thrill, just to reach out and touch what another hand had touched and held eons ago.

The Bodensee, also known as Lake Constance, was famous for capturing those ultraviolet rays from the sun, bouncing them off the snowfields and returning them to the lake. My skin turned red and

174

then a nice deep, dark tan. On my throat, the sunshine had created painful blood blisters. Live and learn.

Sunburn pain across my upper chest was a physical discomfort. Looking across the lake at night and seeing the lights of Swiss cities, was a psychological discomfort. Switzerland was neutral. People were free. Food was not rationed there. They had oranges, bananas, and chocolate, all they could eat. We received the equivalent of six slices of bread, one slice of lunchmeat, one ounce of butter and two ounces of pasta per day. Water was not rationed.

There were about twelve of us on the same vacation, compliments of The Third Reich. And we discussed those distant lights. It was the same masculine voice, handing out the same negative reply.

"Forget about crossing the glacier, forget about scaling the Alps. Even if you made it, you wouldn't get across the border. That border is closed so tight, not even a cricket could get across."

He was, of course, right. I told him so as we sat at the lakeshore, watching the sun set. It was the perfect ending to what had been a perfect day. Then, with nightfall came the distant hum of engines. There was the sound of sirens, also distant. The quiet night air by the lake carried all sounds. In front of us the little wavelets caressed the shore. Not so far away, the Flak started.

"Bombers," he said. He just sat there quietly. I felt like someone had suddenly poured ice in my veins. There was only lakeshore. There was no shelter. But he calmed me down and pointed toward the east.

"Don't worry, they found their target," he said. The night sky was soon illumined.

"That's Friedrichshafen," he explained. He didn't have to say much more. Friedrichshafen had the hangars of the dirigibles, The Hindenburg, and the Graf Zeppelin. The Hindenburg burned up so long ago in New York. The Graf Zeppelin was primarily there. Judging from the light in the sky, it would not be there much longer.

Two days later we were on our way home. The train crept tediously across the land. Sometimes it seemed like it was hopping from tunnel to tunnel. Those of us, who came from the same region and made the return trip together, cowed silently into the seats. Jabos, fighter-hunter airplanes were our constant companion overhead.

When we pulled into the train station at Bruchsal everyone literally bolted from the turnstile. I covered the distance from the station to the Ruebenacker's house in the shadow of buildings. I'd made it that far alive, I wanted to stay alive. I left a message for Anneliese. I wanted her to know that I had returned safely.

Monday morning and Herr Fricker, giving me a glance of approval, smiled and said: "Brown like a Spaniard." A smile softened his usually hard and cold facial features. He wanted to know how my vacation was. I told him. I was still excited about those lake dwellings. I told him about touching those ancient implements. Then I remembered.

"Once we played in the clay digs at the village and there were things, human bones and stuff made of metal," I told him.

He listened attentively. He seemed to know about that. "If I remember correctly there was a Celt, a Gaul, and a Roman."

I looked at him. How could he know? But he just smiled, placed his forefinger to his forehead in a slight salute and left. In that small increment of time, there was a kinship that transcended social proprieties. It was something that had to do with the land, its history and its people. It had to do with being deeply and innately German.

On my next trip to Karlsruhe, I found myself practicing my lessons on the train. It kept me from thinking about the Jabos. It was a cloudy day and the train had no delays, at least not till we arrived at Karlsrnhe. There had been an air raid. The track had not yet been cleared and we had to disembark long before we reached the depot.

On the way into town there were open craters where houses once stood, and hallowed empty walls that once were churches.

Within a block of the teacher's house I began to experience a sense of panic. Two weeks ago I had been here, I was taught how to breathe from the diaphragm, correctly, to the count of seven. I had been taught how to enunciate. Now, there was no teacher. There was no house. There was a crater and one wall standing and a heap of rubble. The tears came to my eyes unbidden. I fought them back. I bowed my head. I folded my hands and whispered a prayer. The smell of those ruins told me that no one had escaped alive.

I made my way back to the train station. I sat there and waited for the train back. Exactly what kind of crime had this Third Reich committed that such retribution was visited upon its people?

I boarded that train. I didn't even care about the Jabos. What difference did it make? If it wasn't now, then it would be later. There would be no escape.

When I arrived at the Ruebenackers, it was obvious that there was distress as well. Franziska's fiancé was now reported missing.

"He is dead," she said. "I know he is dead." Then she walked away. Her mother was distressed. Her father called after her, but she would not heed his call.

Long after I had gone to bed, I heard the door. Below in the living room there were earnest conversation and then the small, pitiful cry. I buried my head between the pillows.

DEATH AD INFINITUM

We went to mass the next morning and the morning after and after that each day for two or three weeks. It would not change the outcome, and Franziska had been right.

Her father remained her main stay. He sustained her with his strength. Her mother nursed the grief away with love.

Weeks later, when Frau Ruebenacker noticed that I no longer took that trip to Karlsruhe, she asked, softly and timidly. I told her what I had found on that last trip. We looked at each other. What we felt was bereavement without end, death 'ad infinitum.'

It was in July that the small town of Bruchsal was jolted out of its submissive doldrums. It was not in the papers. And there was no town crier in Bruchsal. But the new was there. Someone had listened to the black sender on the radio. There had been an assassination attempt on Hitler's life. It had failed and there were arrests. Among those we had personally known, was Rommel. He had been a junker, lower nobility, a knight of yesteryears. He had disagreed with Hitler. Some of us quietly went to church and prayed. Rommel had always been known as fair and just and honest. When it was discussed at the restaurant with the Alsatians, one of them said: "They'll give him an opportunity to kill himself. If he doesn't do that they'll assist him."

I learned to understand what the Alsatians told us. A week later it was announced that Feldmarschall Rommel had died as a result of an accident. Hitler and the Third Reich gave him a magnificent Funeral. The band played: "Ich hat einen Kameraden…"

That bit of choice news also came by way of forbidden radio broadcasts. I told Anneliese about it. But she didn't want to know. She was afraid. Aunt Anna would not talk to me about that at all. Franziska had a choice comment. Although she did not mention his name, there was no doubt that it was Hitler she had in mind. "Verfluchter Schweinehund."

I hoped and prayed that no one was listening from behind a picket fence.

The "ATTENTAT," as it was referred to, was not mentioned at the factory. No one spoke about it. Nor was it mentioned again at lunch. One of the Alsatian was no longer with us. No one asked what had happened to him, including myself. We were afraid.

It was in August that Herr Fricker requested my presence at the office. He wanted to know if I wanted to take a short trip to Stuttgart. It seemed that he wanted a small package delivered there. I gave it little thought. As far as I was concerned, it would be a minor variation on a theme. Instead of going to work, I'd be boarding a train. I would be home at the usual time. He offered me triple rations for that day and double pay. The double pay did not tempt me near as much as the additional ration tickets.

When I came home that evening, I told Franziska. I was so happy to give her those ration tickets. That would help with the food. But Franziska shook her head.

"That is not going to be an easy trip," she said. When I asked her why, she told me that part of the track across a steep trestle had been taken out. Any train passing that gorge, would have to perform a ballet on a kite string.

"Whom do you want your stuff to go to in case you won't come back?" she asked. I thought she was kidding at first. But she wasn't. And since she insisted, I told her that it was to go to Anneliese.

"Does your Aunt know?"

"No, and I don't want her to know."

"Why not?"

I thought about it. And I was honest this time. "I don't want her to worry about it."

I put that one tomorrow out of my mind. Franziska and I were going to visit Frau Boes. There had been good news. Werner was a prisoner of war. And unless we killed him with something we shot over there, he would be safe.

"What could we possibly shoot over there?"

"Hitler has a new weapon. He calls it the "Vergeltungswaffe"

"V.1."

I had difficulty understanding. But when we arrived at the Boes House, Franziska had enlightened me about rockets. I still found it hard to believe that anyone could send a rocket all the way from the North sea coast to England.

Frau Boes was happy. Her youngest son was at last safe until the end of the war. But the end of the war would not allow itself to be discussed that easily. Between war and peace, there was an uneasy time of inhumane brutality. The accounts from places where Russian and Poles were victorious were frightening. Murder, rape, torture of any kind. On the eastern border people were killing themselves rather than falling into the hands of the victorious conqueror. Nothing much was known about the West. But it was said that the Jabos took off from an airport near Nancy. And those sounds we mistook for distant thunder were the big guns of the heavy artillery.

"The Ardennes?" I asked. No one answered. They all nodded their heads.

Now the Third Reich had committed us to battle on all borders. The British swept down from the north. The French would come in from the west. American bombers would keep us in constant fear of our lives. Our own lack of natural resources would keep our troops from defending the Third Reich.

"And Hitler, that sovereign idiot, fired his Field Marshals and took over command of all armed forces," Franziska said.

There was a momentary silence in the room. Then, Willy replied: "You must have a death wish to make a comment like that out loud."

"What's the difference how we die? We die!"

Herr and Frau Boes sat, petrified by Franziska's comment. Willy spoke again: "Before anyone else wants to say something, may I remind you that there are people waiting for execution in the Zuchthaus, for displaying a 'DEFEATIST ATTITUDE.' And it's not going to be death by the firing squad; it's death by the guillotine." Willy had said it quietly, but with the edge of certainty in his voice. Herr Boes suggested we all change the subject. I felt that I had little to say. I was unable to converse. The idea of the guillotine in the prison at Bruchsal was just too frightening. Nor was there anyone I could talk to about that. It was apparent that people could die from talking.

STUTTGART

Franziska and I returned home from the Boes House in silence. If I wanted to say anything, Franziska pressed my hand. She cautioned me not to speak while we were walking down the road. For once, I didn't have to ask why.

Nor did she have much to say after we entered the house. She said she really didn't care whether she lived or died. With most of the men gone out of her life, brother, cousin, friend, fiancé, with most of the country in ruins, and with the enemy winning, there really wasn't much to look forward to in life. She didn't even say good night. She just went into her room and closed the door. I went upstairs. I faced a trip to Stuttgart. That trip may prove to be dangerous, but that was better than the long days at the factory, fraught with ominous premonitions.

Herr Fricker was waiting for me in his office. He had an envelope in his hand. He also had a small brown package. Both were well sealed.

"You'll meet a man there at the station. As soon as you get off the train you are to look for him. He wears a small cockade on the left lapel of his jacket."

He handed over the envelope and the package. He said nothing else. He smiled and pointed toward the door. I was dismissed.

I left the building and headed for the train station. Oddly enough, the only thing I felt, was a sense of freedom. I was leaving town, taking a trip on the train, heading for Stuttgart. The scenery would be stunning.

My ticket allowed me to ride second-class. It was not as good as first, but certainly more posh than third. The sun was well up on the horizon. The train traveled at a good speed. Now and then we were

183

stopped in a tunnel. Then the all-clear sounded from some small town and we were on our way.

Two-thirds on the way, the conductor arrived. He asked for my ticket and I showed it to him.

"Are you the only person in this compartment?" he asked.

I thought it was a rather stupid question. He could plainly see that there was no one else, but me. I nodded my head. He waited around for a while, as though he expected someone beside myself in the little cubicle. But when no one else showed, he made ready to leave. Before he left, he told me that the train would shortly be passing over a stretch of rail that had been replaced.

"Not much solid ground under it. It's best not to move around while we're passing."

After he'd said that, I got up and looked out of the window. What the conductor had said became so much more meaningful when I noticed that we were on an overpass. Below, way below us were the tops of the pine trees from the Black Forest. Somewhere down there were thatched roofs and steep red-clay-tiled roofs from little churches. It looked so beautiful, like someone had placed a painting in three dimensions below us. Then I saw what the conductor had cautioned me about. Less than a mile ahead, for the distance of a mile or two, there was track, supported by wooden piers, track and no ground. I stood as still as I could. I could feel the train inching on to that stretch of rails. I could see the sunlight reflecting from the newly placed rails and I could feel the train moving forward, slowly, and cautiously. I was afraid the beating of my heart might upset the delicate balance of train, track and motion. And now, I felt, I had a definition for Hell. Hell would be forever caught in time on that piece of track, trying to get to solid ground. I closed my eyes. I don't know how long I stood there with my eyes closed.

"It's O.K., you can open your eyes," the voice said. It was the conductor. "We have to go kind of slow here, although it's quite safe," he added. I couldn't say anything. My teeth would not unclench and my hands appeared to be permanently riveted to the window frame. The train picked up speed. The conductor smiled, tipped his hat and was on his way. The only thing I could think of was that we'd be passing over that on the way back. I suddenly felt the urge to go to the restroom. I may have been constipated for three days prior to that trip. But I wasn't anymore.

The train station at Stuttgart was large, and up to that point in time, relatively undamaged. I got off the train. My knees were still shaking. I stood there, my hand clasping the envelope and the package. I felt that standing there forever might still be preferable to mounting that return trip.

Less than five minutes had gone by. Then the man stood there before me.

"May I delight you with this little trinket?" he said as he reached up to the lapel of his coat and unfastened the cockade Herr Fricker had assured me he'd be wearing. I reached for it as he took the envelope and the package. He was gone even faster than he had appeared. I turned, put the cockade in my pocket, and then made for the train, homeward bound. This time there were several people in the same compartment. I asked them about the stretch of train that I dreaded so much. Yes, a lady told me. The Jabos had bombed the rails, and the train would have to proceed in this fashion, till the overpass could be

fixed. She said the people were quite used to it. How could you possibly get used to it. As we approached and the train slowed down, I placed my arms around my knees and clasped my hands tightly, to keep my knees from shaking. No one in the coupe' spoke. We all felt the
same thing. It was like the nightmare I dreamt so often in early childhood. I was balanced on the sharp blade of a knife, performing a high wire act while I crossed the valley below. This time I did not look out the window. I tried hard not to breathe.

It was late when the train pulled in at Bruchsal. Herr Fricker met me at the station. I fished the cockade out of my pocket and gave it to him. I am not certain if I was angry or enraged. But I was not afraid, at least not of Herr Fricker.

"You didn't tell me about the train ride," I said. He shrugged his shoulders, smiled a little and said:

"I didn't know. I just found out." He paused for a moment, then added: "If I had told you, would you have gone?"

I thought about that for a while. I was beginning to accumulate some unpleasant feelings about high places. There was that bridge at Mannheim. And now there was that mile of train track.

"Probably not," I replied.

He tapped me on the shoulder, gave me a little salute and walked off.

"See you in the morning," he called over his shoulder.

Franziska had been waiting up for me and opened the door to her room as I stepped into the house. Her mother had gone to bed early and her father wasn't feeling well, she told me. She asked about the train ride, and after I told her how it had been, she

186

cautioned me not to talk to people about the trip. Something about the whole affair didn't seem right.

"He has a car! Why didn't he go by car and deliver that himself?"

She had a point. I had to agree. The times were dangerous and the less said about something, the better it would be.

Herr Ruebenacker became seriously ill and took to his bed. The doctor diagnosed pneumonia. Some of Franziska's brothers and sisters came to visit. I felt in the way. I took that weekend to go out to the village. I derived strength from that place and wisdom from Uncle Johann.

The village too had undergone change. Uncle Johann was very angry. His blue green eyes blazed lightning again, and his voice crackled with static.

"Sikhs," Uncle Johann spit it out. He couldn't shout it out, but he sort contemptuously spit it out under his breath. "Whatever possessed that man to bring in the Sikhs? "

The Third Reich had gifted the village with Indian Sikhs, straight from India, as fighting troops. I thought they were quite impressive. They were tall, wore turbans and had black beards. They looked exactly like those illustrations in the Karl May Adventure Novels. Except these Sikhs were real.

Lioba and Friedel and I talked about it. The girls in the village found them attractive. As a matter of fact they found them so attractive that not a single case of rape had been reported. The girls loved the dark eyes, the black beards, the turbans and above all, they loved the gentle manner, the way the Sikhs seemed to worship them; "Almost like we were goddesses or something," Friedel said. Uncle Johann saw it differently: "They eat our food, they drink our cider, they bed our women and all of that, compliments of The Third Reich. Thank God they don't eat meat."

I was going to say something about the possibility of the village getting a much-needed transfusion of new blood. But Aunt Antonia cautioned with her eyes. Uncle Johann was clearly upset and it would never do to take on a bull in the confines of his own paddock.

There was no longer a need for the goose herd. The geese were gone, so were most of the chickens and the ducks. By order of the Third Reich, farmers were not permitted to kill the laying hens. The village was required to hand over a quota of eggs, butter, and milk. Much of that went to the army's command post. The Sikhs, thank God, he said, did not eat meat. They did however; take a liking to the goats that were kept two houses to the east.

I had to take the message to Aunt Anna that it would be difficult to get any kind of foodstuff from the village to Bruchsal. Times were tough, Uncle Johann said, and they would be getting worse. Uncle Johann had also heard some things on the black sender. It's amazing how that illegal radio wave supplied the land with knowledge it could not get from any other source.

Uncle Johann said the Offensive in the Ardennes was not going very well. And out in the forest somewhere between Bretten and Brucheal, there were German fighter planes unable to get in the air. They were out of gasoline.

But Hitler had once more addressed the nation. "Der Rhein muss Deutschland's Strom und niemals Deutschlands Grenze sein." Never, never can the Rhein be Germany's border. Uncle Johann said that the order had been given. The Hitler Youth and the Volksturm, those would be the soldiers to defend us. Young boys age fourteen to eighteen, and old men fifty and older. Those would be the fighting troops. Hitler's highly prized youth, the future of The Third Reich, now became cannon fodder, blood sacrifice. Uncle Johann's jaw was set grimly. Behind the Volksturm and the Hitler Youth, was the S.S.; and the S.S. had orders to shoot anyone who made an attempt to escape. They'll die before they'll let the enemy cross the Rhein, Hitler said. And they did.

This time I had to walk home. And this time there was nothing to bring to Aunt Anna, except Uncle Johann's remark that the worst would be coming soon. There had been no Thanksgiving in the village, because some of the harvest had been destroyed by incendiary leaflets, dropped on the fields as the wheat ripened. The sun set them on fire and the grain, ready for harvest, scorched the land. I could hear the sounds of distant gunfire. It rumbled away in the afternoon air. All that was missing from the cacophony of war was the Jabos flying overhead.

This war, this awful war was like a flood that could not be stopped. And now there was something else Lioba had told me. It was a whispered kind of thing that had to be kept secret. She would not even tell me where it came from. But it was said that Hitler was working on a secret weapon. It was something that would allow Hitler to kill every German rather than hand the country over to the enemy. He'd have to hurry. From the way things were going the Jabos were decimating the population at breakneck speed.

On the way back I stopped at Aunt Anna's. I gave her the message from Uncle Johann. I told Anneliese about the Sikhs. I kept Lioba's whispered commentary to myself.

Things were going badly at the Ruebenacker's. The old man was dying. The doctor said there was little he could do. There were no drugs, no medication. What little was available, was being saved for emergency cases. This man was old. We understood. And there was nothing we could do. Franziska remained at her father's bedside. Sisters and brothers arrived. I knew that I would have to leave. Before they could ask me, I offered. The offer was accepted. I packed my one and only suitcase and resolutely made my way toward Aunt Anna's. Hell would have been preferable.

Christmas was approaching. But it was hard to have the spirit. This time I did not have to share the common bedroom. A little attic room across the hall from Aunt Anna's apartment was available. I roomed there with Liesel Wittmeier. I loved my cousin Anneliese, but I hated her father's frequent appearances outside my door, letting go with a stream of verbal abuse if I failed to rise at sunrise. I was lazy, shiftless, immoral, no matter what I did, I was the proverbial bad seed and he'd stand outside the door and curse and rail. At supper he counted the potato chunks in my plate. I would have given anything to find another place where I could eat. But there was none.

REQUIEM

"They're having a High Mass Sunday," Anneliese told me on that weekend. I could have cared less.

"You really want to go to that High Mass!" Anneliese insisted. I shook my head. To be up there with the choir, to hear the organ play and to know that the organist was not the same; I couldn't bear to sit up there in the balcony for over an hour.

"Mother said we have to go!" That was Anneliese's final comment. She would not tell me anything else. I was not talking to Aunt Anna. I had no way of knowing why I had to go to High Mass. But I took Anneliese's word for it and I went.

From the moment I took my place next to Anneliese, I realized that there was something else she did not tell me.

T

here was the organist. He hailed from the Cathedral in Cologne. It did not take a genius to figure out why he was playing in Bruchsal. What city had not fallen prey to air raids and what Cathedral had not been destroyed?

From the moment that man placed his hands on the keyboard, it was evident that we would be hearing more than just a High Mass. Then Anneliese pointed to the other side of the balcony.

"They'll be singing today." One by one as those faces swam into view, I recognized them. We would be listening to the organist from Cologne and the soloists and ensemble from the National Theater Mannheim. Eyes blurred with tears, voice choked with feelings, I just sat there.

191

"They sing in churches now, because most of the opera houses are bombed out," Anneliese whispered. I could not reply. I was in shock.

From the moment I heard Herr Hoelzlin's voice I knew that this would be my special Christmas present. No one could change that. No one could spoil it. No one could take it away. I felt like running over to the other side where he was. But that was unthinkable.

"I told you, you had to go to High Mass today," said Anneliese very quietly. I looked at her. How did she know? What was there about her that always brought me something special without my knowing, my asking. I just looked at her. But the tears made it difficult to see clearly. I held on to her hand. She held on to mine. We could have been twins, but she arrived a week to soon and I arrived in a different body. We were complementary, a set, always together, always apart. It was not an easy thing to fathom.

I saw Herr Hoelzlin briefly. And he did see me. He acknowledged with a smile. But I could not go there and touch him, feel his hand against my cheek, his arm around me to comfort and protect. AGNUS DEI QUI TOLLIS PECCATA MUNDI ——

After the mass, the choir and singers from Mannheim were made to exit separate from us. I saw him glance my way briefly. I saw him leave. By the time we were dismissed they were gone. It was as if I had dreamt the whole thing up. Never mind, I told myself. So Christmas came a little early this year.

Death came, if not unexpected, it arrived unwanted. Herr Ruebenacker had died. But to me it was as if I could still feel his hand on my shoulder. I could still hear the voice that lectured.

"I'll tell you a secret——"

I kept his secret well.

Franziska was like a statue made of stone at the funeral. She did not cry. She did not speak. She just looked with empty eyes at that hole in the ground. Shortly after that, I was told to come to the Ruebenacker house. Franziska's mind had snapped. There was nothing I could say or do to bring her back. There was nothing anyone could do. She had lost too much. I walked away from that. There is nothing more difficult to cope with than that utter sense of helplessness in the presence of another's demise.

I walked back to Wuerttemberger Strasse 7. The wind was cold. Snow and rain pelted my face. I would not spent Christmas here. I had no idea where I was going to spent Christmas. At the rate things were progressing, there was no assurance that I would still be alive by Christmas. The Jabos attacked, night and day, but mostly days, and mostly they shot at anything that moved in the street. I had to learn to walk near the buildings.

Food was scarce. I had a slice of bread and Ersatz Coffee for breakfast. If we took our break at the Rappen, I had some sort of soup for lunch. Soup was double the amount for the food ration ticket. That meant for half the amount of tickets, I received twice the amount of bulk–potatoes, lentils, mostly vegetables with very little meat or fat. But it filled the stomach. I could eat enough to walk away satiated.

Now there were only two Alsatians left. No one said a word. We were all afraid to talk. Incarcerations and impending executions at the penitentiary were common knowledge and no one talked about that. No one talked about the guillotine. Talking about that was an open invitation for arrest. The sound of laughter had gone away. Nobody laughed anymore.

193

One of the girls from the village had come to town and I met her on the street, coincidence. When I inquired about the Sikhs, she told me that one of the Sikhs, for whatever reason, had killed five of his comrades and then shot himself. Since their religion decrees funeral by fire, they had been given permission to burn their dead. According to her, there was a huge funeral pyre, flames shooting everywhere, and the smell, that awful smell of human flesh being consumed by fire. I concurred. I knew that smell. If I lived to be one hundred, I would never be able to get over that awful stench of death.

According to her, things were not going well in the village. Trenches were being prepared for battle. Food was carefully hidden away. The town crier had been called to active duty, although he was over fifty years old. Two families in the village had radios. They listened to the black station, the forbidden station, and news, legal or not, was passed on by word of mouth. The Kratzmeiers had lost all of their sons. There were now many families where all the male members had been killed. Clans would die out. If I had been depressed before I met her, I certainly wasn't much better after she said good-bye.

NO-MAN'S-LAND

Melita, the girl who worked next to me, cheered me up considerably. She had a plan for getting away for Christmas. It would involve some travel, but we had an invitation to visit her relatives near Freiburg. We would have to travel by train, but the train was still going and the track not yet damaged. I couldn't say YES fast enough. Melita promised wonderful people and wonderful food. There was just one problem. We could not tell Aunt Anna the truth. What we needed was a third party to lie for us.

We came up with an ingenious idea. We would tell Aunt Anna that we were having a bunking party at Liane's. Liane agreed to that. Aunt Anna would not bother to go there and check on me. Nor would she let me leave if I told her the truth. To burden Anneliese with the truth and make her my co-conspirator was unthinkable.

However, there was always the possibility of something going wrong. So the night before we left by train I decided to tell Liesel Wittmeier. We had become roommates and friends in that little garret room. Before I could get around to it, our attention was directed to a noise on the street below It sounded like a heavy truck but it did not sound like tires marking the pavement.

"It sounds more like chains being dragged," Liesel said. We almost collided in our hurry to get to the window. The benefit of having a room in the attic with a window that faced the main thoroughfare was the unlimited view of the traffic down below.

What we saw was a little unsettling there were tanks, German Tanks, one towing the other, in tandem, two by two, clanking their way along the Wuerttemberger Strasse, going from west to east.

"That's the wrong direction," Liesel whispered. I don't know why she whispered, no one could have heard us if we shouted. But we only spoke in whispers these days.

"Or else Rueckzug," I replied. Our troops were retreating. The tanks were retreating no doubt. And apparently there was not enough gasoline, so they were towing to cut back on the gas. But where did they come from? Where were they going to make a stand. Hitler would be unsuccessful with his offensive in the Ardennes.

We were going to be battleground.

"Schlachtfeld," Liesel said. Strange how the word Schlacht translates into Slaughter. We were scheduled to become a field of slaughter. That was if Hitler didn't kill us first. At the rate we were going the Third Reich would not last a thousand years. And for us it couldn't end soon enough. But we couldn't even say that to each other for fear of causing each other's demise. I crawled back in bed. Liesel did the same.

"At least the guns aren't shooting," I said.

"They've agreed on a Cease Fire for Christmas," Liesel answered. Christmas Peace, I thought. I suppose while no one was shooting, it was an excellent time to secure what little army there was left. I put the pillow over my head. But even that did not that did not keep out those sounds of metal dragging against cement

I had trouble falling asleep. I thought about that trip by train. We would be south of the Ardennes.

If I had a prayer left, I prayed that the enemy would not become aware of what was passing down below. I needed one night without air raid.

When I finally fell into an uneasy sleep, I dreamt I was crossing the Neckar at Mannheim, at midnight, in a streetcar and I could see the bright lights from the city dancing in the waves. Mutti was smiling down at me and Vati cradled me in his arms.

I woke up to a grey dawn. I rose quietly and earlier than usual. I wanted to get away before Uncle Karl's usual outburst of abusive language outside the door to our room.

I put in a full eight-hour shift at work. By late afternoon Melita and I boarded the train to Freiburg.

The train was overcrowded. The only seating available was on our suitcases in the hall of the third class car. There were hazards I had not thought of. The train progressed slowly. In places debris from previous Jabo attacks had to be cleared off the track.

Darkness descended and a pale moon illuminated freshly fallen snow. The cold night air permeated the hallways and compartments of the trains. We shivered, clinging to each other for support and warmth. We tried sleeping, sitting on our wretched little suitcases. We were not alone. Inside that railroad car miserable little piles of humanity huddled protectively against each other in those dark, uncertain hours.

The train came to an unexpected stop. We were somewhere between Offenburg and Freiburg. The conductor came around and told us this was as far as the train could go. Beyond that point was NO MAN'S LAND. Although there was a temporary Cease Fire, to go beyond this point would mean to enter disputed territory.

Why this came as a shock to me I have never understood. Except maybe somewhere in the back of my mind was the idea that cities with German

197

sounding names like Offenburg and Freiburg could not possibly be anything but German. War was now a thing five years old. The Third Reich was a little older. I was older than the two. Offenburg and Freiburg were in their second millennium of existence. And now they were disputed territory.

We picked up our suitcases, buttoned our coats tightly against the cold and set out for a place I did not know. It wasn't far, Melita said. But the snow was knee deep. The cold air bit into our lungs and for the first time I began to realize that it was possible for us to freeze to death.

Melita set the pace. My mind said one foot before the other no matter what. I turned away from the hostile environment and thought the good thoughts, like hot food, warm rooms, gentle people.

Hell had so many faces during those days. And walking forever in snow up to the knee caps, with ears and finger tips turning numb, was one more way of thinking of Hell.

By the time we reached the farmhouse our hands were numb. We rang the doorbell with out elbows. When the man came to the door we nearly fell into the room.

Although we had been expected, according to Melita, we had also been expected to know the dangers and we were not expected in this way.

We knew how to endure pain. And pain was the first thing we were given. In order to save the exposed flesh of fingers, we had our hands submerged in cold water. It was hard not to scream.

Two hours of anti frostbite therapy, hot tea and small sandwiches, and a general feeling of love and warmth and finally a warm bed and sleep.

We awoke the following morning. It was Christmas Eve. There was joy and laughter. There was a large Christmas tree, decorated with ornaments created by past generations as well as those created by the present children of the house. Melita introduced me to her cousins, her uncles and her aunts. It was almost as if war had not touched this small place. The sun shone brightly on the snow. Looking out the window was like looking at a life-sized picture postcard. No one talked about the war. The women prepared food for the evening's festivities. We were handed hot chocolate. When I made an attempt to ask where all the bounty came from, Melita placed an index finger on her lips. I thought about Franziska's wisdom. Never look a gift horse in the mouth.

The men and the boys spent a greater part of the day outdoors. Christmas, they said, was for all creatures. There would be hay for the grass eaters, the rabbits, and the deer, grain for the seedeaters, the birds, the squirrels, plenty of fodder for the livestock, and extra portion of oats for the horses.

"They have horses?" I asked. They took me out to the stalls. There was a mare and a colt, both handfed, both aware of the loving care extended to them. There was a bond here between man and beast, between man and nature, between man and man that seemed to surpass and protect, like a shield of love. I felt it but I could not understand it.

It was Christmas Eve and a party was in progress. Some of the neighbors had arrived. We drank hot mulled cider; we ate ham and cheese and potato salad. No one checked my plate to tell me that I had too much. We sang Christmas songs. The wax candles on the tree were lit. All other lights were turned off, and there, in the glow of the candles, arms around each other, we sang Silent Night.

Going to Midnight Mass was too dangerous to consider. But we said our prayers and we made our wishes known to God, each person, silently unto himself.

Christmas day arrived and we were given a generous breakfast. Then we were told that we would have an opportunity to hitch a ride with a German army contingent that was leaving. No one mentioned the word "Rueckzug." But it was an open secret that the army was in retreat. We would spend one more day at the farmstead. Then we would be taken, under cover of night, to the place where the convoy was assembled.

When we said good-bye, I expressed the hope of seeing this place again. The Patriarch, male-uppermost-head-of-the-small-family, shook his head.

"You'll never find this place again!" He said. When I asked him why, he explained that this disputed territory was sometimes French and sometimes German. When it changed hands, it also changed names. The name we knew would disappear from the map. All traces of having been German would disappear from the land and its people. That, he said, was the secret of survival for the land, the animals and the people. I had difficulty understanding that. But he said more than anything, the land was important, not the nation that owned the land, but the land. This was a way the land could survive. And that was so similar to the things that Uncle Johann always said. "Die Scholle" the land and the soil, without it people died from lack of food and shelter. The land would be there for another millennium or two. The Third Reich would not survive that long.

It was December 26th, 1944 just two hours before sunrise when we were loaded into the truck. There were twelve soldiers on the truck and ten trucks in that convoy.

The person in charge agreed to let us ride all the way to Bruchsal. He told us they were going that way and said nothing else. The soldiers about us in the truck looked thin, worn out, and cold and old beyond their years. The man next to me provided a blanket for Melita and me and told us that the long ride would be cold and weary.

Slowly the soldiers began to talk about themselves and about their families. One sitting beside Melita said he had a daughter about her age. He did not know where his family was now. He only knew that his wife and daughter had been bombed out twice. He said there had been no mail for weeks.

For a little while we discussed what was possibly worse, facing enemy fire as a soldier, or awaiting bombs from somewhere up above as a civilian.

A soldier described a thing called the Geneva Convention, something that was supposed to determine the rules of battle.

According to the dictates of the Geneva Convention, civilians should not die.

The Jabos, I thought, those little planes with their guns and bombs, certainly did not adhere to the Geneva Conventions. The Field Hospital at Bruchsal had been marked well with the red cross on a white field. But that had not kept the planes from dropping their bombs on it. I had seen that myself.

We rode through the landscape, mostly secure in the knowledge that the sky was overcast and there was a temporary Cease Fire till January second. By the time we were close to Bruchsal, the sky had cleared. We were somewhere near the "Michelsberg," a hill scarcely tall enough to qualify for the term "Michael's Mount," when the convoy came to a stop. The truck pulled out of sight. The commander ordered his troops to the side of the road, away from the vehicles. There was a tunnel within reach and we tried to take shelter there. But the planes were down on us before we could get to it.

The soldier, who had given us his blanket, now made us lie down among the shrubby growth in the ditch and quickly covered us with his body.

When the attack was over, we crawled out from under him. He no longer responded to anything we said. He did not die in the Ardennes, but died there, beside the road, protecting us, during a period of Cease Fire.

We felt guilty about it for a long time - if we had only not attempted that trip. We left the stranded convoy and walked back, the rest of the way into town.

Back at Wuerttemberger Strasse 7, Aunt Anna stood there like the wrath of God. She never asked me why it was so important for me to go away. She only knew that I had lied. Uncle Karl threatened to beat me within an inch of my young life. But for once it did not matter.

"Go ahead; beat me to death; see if I care!" I said. That awful feeling in the pit of my stomach was worse than death. I died, a long time ago, when Mannheim died. I died when that soldier died. I died so many times. One more time would not matter.

Anneliese and Aunt Anna placed themselves between the man and myself. I reached my room and closed the door. Liesel hurried to lock it behind me.

"Why do you do these things?" she asked. I had no answer for that.

1945

1945 and I was back at work. I was eighteen. My life was simple. Church on Sunday, interrupted by six days of work. Brought up by the family, the Catholic Church, and the Third Reich, I had learned to submit, minimally, to regimentation – regimentation totally void of the joy of life. Fear reigned supreme. The trick was to survive, day by day, without being shot at, starved into submission, or otherwise eliminated. And there were people who were being eliminated. They just disappeared.

Without a trace of German defense, one flight of Allied bombers followed the next. They were unstoppable. We could hear them. All around us, the death toll from air raids mounted. Only a few miles from Bruchsal, the village of Wiesental disappeared from the map. One of the Alsatians, still remaining with our dinner group, told us the unknown details, as we hurriedly wolfed down a plate of soup. The squadron leader of the approaching flight of bombers had apparently encountered difficulty with his plane. Rather than risking bombs and plane in an explosion, he dumped his load of bombs over Wiesental. The rest of the squadron, thinking he was on target, unloaded as well. That was how Wiesental, a small farming community of less than 1000 population, became the recipient of a massive dose of T.N.T.. After it was over with, there were no survivors.

At Pforzheim twenty-five thousand died within the space of half an hour. At Bruchsal, the Jabos, hunter fighter planes armed with bombs, shot at anything that moved on a daily basis.

I walked along one day, looked up and saw the dreaded red tails. One of the airplanes dove, almost without a sound. What happened next was like the time out of joint. Ahead of me a woman just sort of floated of her bicycle. Then little red flames, like little red flowers, suddenly sprang up from the pavement. The plane had passed and the roar of the engine now came from behind. There was a sharp pain on my left side. Then there was blood, red sticky blood oozing through my dress. My knees sort of buckled and I sat down on the sidewalk. Then everything went red and black and there was the smell of hot metal and sulfur and lots of noises, screaming, yelling, and the sound of explosions. The last thing I remembered was that I had to hold my side because I was bleeding.

When I came too, I was propped up against a building near the sidewalk. Someone was checking the wound on my side.

"You're lucky," the voice said. "The woman ahead of you is dead."

I saw the bicycle. I saw the body on the street, covered with a cloth. I began to shake uncontrollably. The man whose seemingly disembodied voice had addressed me, standing next to me, examined the bleeding, told me to pull myself together. He asked if I could walk. I stood up. My knees were still shaking. He asked where I lived and I told him. He wanted to know if I could make it to the house by myself. I held on to the building and said yes. There was no more hospital left to go to. There was no doctor. There was no means of transportation. There were ten others besides me that had been on the street, and some of them were no longer alive, and some of them were screaming in pain.

"You were lucky," the man said, as he helped me on my way.

I don't remember how I made it home. I do remember taking off the bloody dress. Liesel came and helped me. Aunt Anna came and fixed a makeshift bandage around my waist.

Aunt Anna was a strong believer in herbal medicine. The herbalist who supplied her with teas, potions, and healing poultices, came and examined the wound. He explained to me that a metal fragment had torn some of the flesh and the skin on my right side. I used to refer to the man as Aunt Anna's witch doctor. I owe that man a debt of gratitude, and Aunt Anna an apology. The teas helped me to sleep. The poultice healed the wound without infection.

Uncle Karl kept his distance. Anneliese made certain that I was supplied with food and drink. She even located a book somewhere. It had to do with the Pyramids of Egypt. That book took away the memory of that airplane and that pilot shooting down at us.

A few days after the incident, there was a knock on the door. I thought that to be curious. Aunt Anna never knocked. It was Aunt Anna just the same. She said there was a priest to see me. By now I had learned to control my responses. But the words tumbled out just the same.

"The last priest I talked to said that all this hell, fire, and brimstone rained down on us because we were evil. And I told him that little children who get killed in air raids don't know how to be evil. And he nearly hit me."

Aunt Anna backed away a little. She looked at a loss for words.

"This one isn't like that," she said.

I shook my head. I really didn't want to see a priest. I was angry and I felt I had a right to be angry.

"This priest is a Jesuit," Aunt Anna said.

I found that rather interesting. I put the book aside, propped myself up on the pillow and silently consented to the visit.

He walked in, straight, tall and ascetic in appearance, definitely not a local person.

"I plan to hear confession," he said authoritatively to Aunt Anna. Being a good Catholic, she agreed and left the room.

"I'm not in the mood for confession!" I countered immediately. He placed his index finger on his lips and motioned for me to be silent. He looked toward the door. He waited until he was satisfied that Aunt Anna was not listening in, then he said:

"Your friend the Alsatian told me to come and see you." That made all the difference in the world.

"You mean this hasn't anything to do with BLESS ME FATHER FOR I HAVE SINNED?" I asked.

He smiled and shook his head. He said the Alsatian had told him that I thought differently and talked differently from the others. The Priest referred to me as the Alsatian's THINKING PERSON.

I told him I was about to give up thinking as a bad venture. Thinking could get a person into trouble.

"Only when you say what you think, without thinking where and who you say things too."

I had to agree. It was a skill I hadn't mastered yet. But I was working on it.

The Priest told me about the black sender. It was the B.B.C. At least two or three people in Bruchal were able to get information that way. It was a well-kept secret.

The priest also filled in the missing parts of that "little" air raid on the people in the street.

"Those Jabos came from the 358th fighter group. They're based at Toul-Ochey."

"How do you know?"

"Your friend, the Alsatian."

My friend, the Alsatian, had a warning for me. He said I needed to leave Bruchsal, the sooner the better. When I asked why, the priest said he did not know. He only knew that it was advisable to leave Bruchsal now. I shook my head.

I don't know if the good Father understood, but it was not feasible to leave. The Third Reich had appointed unto me that I remain in Bruchsal. I could not leave. I had to show up for work, or be arrested. I had to receive my food ration ticket from Bruchsal, or starve. And last but not least, my aunts and uncles determined where I lived. I had a legal guardian because I was not yet 21. And if I had my choice, I would want to go back home to Mannheim.

The priest shook his head sadly. "Mannheim is under siege."

"You mean what's left of Mannheim is under siege!" I responded. I could feel the tears and I did not wish to cry. Why was everything so totally helpless? The priest said I should be grateful. After all, I lived, where 23 others died only two days ago.

"What for?" I said. Maybe the lucky ones were those who died. He would not hear of that. He could not remain very long, he said. And he did not tell me why he could leave and others couldn't. Nor did he tell me how he could express an opinion and give me news that was forbidden when it was well known that the church, Catholic and Lutheran, had agreed to remain neutral in matters of politics.

208

In the end I agreed to the confession and he agreed to allow me my definition of SIN. The priest smiled and said:

"Why don't you join the Jesuits? They could use your outspoken intellectuality."

It was at that point that I could no longer fight the urge to share my opinion. Catholicism, I said, was patriarchal in nature, and yes, so was National Socialism and sometimes it was difficult to differentiate.

"Impossible," he said.

"Not so," I countered. "The church orders me to be subservient, so does the Third Reich. If I disagree with the church, I can anticipate hell, fire, and damnation. If I disagree with the Third Reich, I get exactly the same. The Church has a list of don'ts and list of books I can't read. The Third Reich has a list of don'ts and books I am not supposed to read. The Church is ruled by one man and so is the Third Reich. Now, show me the difference."

"We do not kill our enemies."

"Was it the Church, the Roman Catholic Church that burned old women and called them witches? Was it the Church that killed opinionated people at the stake and called it justifiable by calling them heretics? Did we not burn St. Joan of Arc at the stake? And all because she wore chain mail and refused to ride side saddle?" A small grin played across his lips. The little room we were in was no longer cold.

The priest again placed his finger to his lips: "Remember your Aunt; if she hears us we're both in trouble. Besides that, we no longer burn people. But the Third Reich still uses the guillotine."

He was right. In the end I had to agree that a couple hundred years had elapsed since the Church had burned the nonbeliever. And he was right. Apparently the Third Reich continued to kill. The VERGELTUNGSWAFFE V.I. and the V.II. landed on British soil and killed people by the thousands. A devil had been let loose on the world and the killing would not stop until -------.

Neither one of us put that thought into words but we both knew. As far as I was concerned, the devil was Himmler. No matter what station you listened to, what debate you participated in, what trusted group or friend gave fear its name, it would always be Himmler. Himmler controlled the Third Reich. He called the Gestapo into existence. Himmler was head of the dreaded S.S.

The priest finally called an end to the session. He did hear my confession. That was the only way we could keep the secret that we shared. Confession bound us to silence. Aunt Anna knew that.

When the priest bestowed his blessing and touched my forehead ever so gently, it was like a weight falling from my shoulders. I was hoping he would say that he would return. He was such a good priest. He allowed me to think and to express my thoughts and he did not condemn me for thinking. In some small way he made me want to live again. He left quietly. When Aunt Anna came back he was gone.

"Did he hear your confession?" She asked. I replied in the affirmative. She did not ask me where I knew the priest from or why he had come. She brought me tea and soup. Anneliese put another poultice on the wound. She asked nothing. She looked at me and she knew I did not wish to talk. My mind was in a thinking mode. Where had it all gone wrong? Was the Church not there to serve the people? And when did the thing turn itself around and the people were there to serve the Church? Was the government not there to serve the people? And when did it happen that the people became the servants of the Third Reich? And were all these leaders, these heads of government not male? When did this Patriarchy begin to extract the blood sacrifice from the people? Why were the women made to suffer? Why were the children killed? Was it for money? Was it for glory? Was it for honor? What honor is there in killing women and children? Ours or their, it makes no difference. And did the Commandment not say: THOU SHALT NOT KILL? No one could answer these questions to my satisfaction.

JUDAS

I fell asleep that night and in my dreams I saw the priest, begging me to leave. But I was glued to the ground. I could not move. I don't know what's worse, the nightmares about Jabos gunning down people, or being glued to the place you are.

My next visitor, the following day, was not so friendly and he did not bless me. It was a policeman. Herr Himmler's personal representative, I thought. This time Aunt Anna did not leave and I did not care. He wanted to know why I had not been at work. Aunt Anna looked at me warningly. I never said a word. I just raised my nightgown, undid the bandage and let him look at the soggy mess. The wound was not large, but it was draining well. So it really looked worse than it was. He motioned for me to put my shirt down. He asked my aunt how long it would be before it healed up. And now the climate in the room changed. Uncle Karl entered. He was a big man, with an ugly scar on his head and a reputation for meanness. The policeman was only half his size, but he did wear a uniform. It wasn't long before the policeman was outnumbered. Liesel had entered, so had Heinz and Anneliese. Heinz was also wearing a uniform.

"We don't know," my aunt said: "But when she's well, she'll go back to work." The policeman turned, clicked his heels and saluted: "Heil Hitler." To which my aunt replied: "Gruess Gott!"

We could hear him clicking down the stairs rather hurriedly. Uncle Karl growled. "Don't be causing any trouble now, you hear?"

The fact that he addressed me and made a civil statement left me speechless.

"What'll happen next?" inquired my aunt of her husband. They walked out talking to each other, leaving me totally confused. The Third Reich had strange ways of dealing with its people. I wasn't too sure that the policeman came because the priest had been there the day before. But I could not get up. I felt dizzy and the wound felt like somebody was tearing my skin apart. Hell, I imagined, was being in pain and being unable to run away. I wanted to see the Alsatian. I still had more questions than answers. But to see the Alsatian I had to be able to walk, to get back to work, to go for lunch at the Rappen.

The guns, from the not-so-distant Western Front, grew more demanding. The shooting went on night and day. The Jabos, also known as Thunderbolts, continued to fly across town. They'd drop a couple of bombs here and there and shot at anything that moved. Then came the day when there was only one plane flying overhead. He was definitely not one of ours. Nor was he a Jabo. It was said that he took pictures.

"Pictures of what?" I asked. Now I learned a new word, "reconnaissance," that was what Heinz had said. As far as I was concerned, Heinz didn't know that much, but he wore a uniform and he was leaving at the end of the week. He had been taught to handle a gun, to march in step and to keep his uniform neat. He was so young. I felt sorry for him. I felt sorry for my aunt. She cried a lot but she kept it hidden. The sadness and the anger in that apartment was oppressive. I went back to work. The wound still pained me, but it would be easier to be at work than at home.

Herr Fricker honored me with a visit at the assembly line. He looked at me with those steel like blue-grey eyes.

"Are you well enough to work?" he asked.

"Not really," I answered; then added: "but I was afraid the policeman would return if I didn't come to work."

He definitely had the ability to rivet me to the spot with his eyes. His answer came slow and precise. "I did not send a policeman to your house. If one showed up there, it would have been someone else reporting your absence from work." His gaze wandered slowly, purposely, up and down the assembly line. No one said a word. Herr Fricker made it obvious that I had an enemy among the people. As he walked away, I tried to follow the path his eyes had taken.

"Who are you looking for?" Melita asked.

"I'm looking for Judas!" I replied. Not another word was said for a long time. Then someone started a song and everyone joined in, as if to expel those negative vibrations. Someone from Herr Fricker's office came to me and whispered in my ear that I was wanted in his office. I rose quietly. I knew that all eyes were following me as I left the room.

Herr Fricker's office was small and unassuming. There was a desk, a bookshelf, a couple of chairs besides his swivel chair. Apparently he liked freedom of movement when confined to a small space.

He looked at me, as I entered the office, and pointed to one of the chairs. I was requested to be seated. It would obviously be more than the usual three-minute visit. Again, his eyes held me captive. The atmosphere and the silence was literally breathtaking. I composed myself, telling myself that my

214

survival could very well depend on what I said in his presence.

After awhile he began to talk.

"Make no mistake, Fraulein Elsa, I am a member of the N.S.D.A.P. because I believe in all the things it stands for. When I say HEIL HITLER, I mean exactly that, I mean to wish good health to the Fuehrer. If the Fuehrer is no longer in good Health, the country will also be in poor health. I am firmly committed to the victorious conclusion of this war. And I believe that without the Fuehrer, without the Third Reich, without the final victory, there will be no more Germany and no more Germans."

He paused. I looked at him. I wanted to ask him about Himmler. I wanted to know about the Vengeance Weapon. I wanted to know about that whispered thing that Hitler would kill all the Germans, rather than hand them over to the enemy. But he spoke again before I could ask anything.

"Before you speak Fraulein Elsa, remember that my devotion to this government and this cause is stronger than my personal respect and admiration for you."

"Does that devotion include devotion to Herr Himmler?"

It was out before it could be stopped from crossing my lips. Herr Fricker placed an index finger to his lips and shook his head in silent disapproval. His eyes took in every nuance of my demeanor. He broke the silence at last and said: "Now you may speak."

I sat there, in that office, trying desperately to think of something to say. I was, after all, theater oriented, with a scholarship for acting. I remembered the few lessons I had been taught. I was, visibly controlled, breathing in deeply. 'Hold the breath to the count of seven and slowly exhale', the voice in my brain said.

I felt the calming effect of the exercise. I thought very carefully. The content of my words could not have anything to do with the present state of affairs in the land. I allowed my face to relax into an inquisitive smile.

"Did you know that Zarah Leander wears long skirts in all of her movies because she is bow-legged?"

First he flushed red with a touch of anger, then he blanched and grimaced and laughed out loud. It was a natural laughter just slightly beyond control. He rocked back in his chair. He looked at me like a cat that had just discovered a promising mouse between his paws.

I prayed silently. He rose. He stood behind my chair and looked down at me. My body said DANGER. But my lips smiled. There was nothing I could do about that situation. He had the power and I was at this point in time, his pawn, his toy. And so I tried one more foil.

"Do you know what was in the envelope that I handed over to that person in Stuttgart?"

He stepped back. "Do you play chess?" he asked. I nodded my head.

"That was MATE," he said.

He returned to his chair and was engulfed in thought for a moment. When he broke the silence once more, he looked up at me and casually remarked:

"Before I dismiss you, allow me to give you one word of caution. There are people who belong to the part for monetary gain. They will turn you in for what you say, for what you do and for what you fail to do, for money and for no other reason. Be careful before you go out among them." He nodded his head and turned away from me. I was dismissed.

I made my way back to my workstation. I walked into the room with a smile on my face. I walked in tall and straight.

"Was that him laughing?" Melita whispered as I settled into the place next to her. I nodded my head. A king's ransom could not persuade me to relate to her what had transpired in the office. From now on I would know that I had could trust no one.

SOLDIER/WORKER

Rodi & Wienenberger, compliments of the Third Reich, had a new worker. He was a German soldier, in uniform, wounded and recuperating at Bruchsal. He was tall. He was blond. He was attractive. He was the persona of Siegfried. If Siegfried ever existed, he would have looked like that. The Third Reich had no intention of losing him as a viable soldier. They found a private clinic to nurse him back to health. For physical therapy he worked at Rodi & Wienenberger.

He was every girl's fantasy. It came as no surprise that every girl made a effort to share her meager lunch with him. He was young and otherwise healthy and endowed with an excellent appetite. A lot of girls were able to share their lunch with him, including myself. To make things more exciting, it was decided to make the lunch-thing into a competition. Top winner would be his date on his-last-day celebration. Before he was to leave for whatever slaughter he was scheduled for, we were going to take him out to the RAPPEN for dining, a bit of drinking, and dancing. Aunt Anna did not know about that.

The competition was stiff, but in the end, I won. I lost a few pounds because I gave up all of my lunch. The soldier did not know that.

I was eighteen, he was twenty-two. He hailed from the Black Forest. He loved to carve things out of wood. The art came natural to him. As part of the competition, he presented me with an absolutely beautifully carved fawn. It became one of my few treasures. It did not survive the war. A displaced person from Poland took it from me.

There was now a brief interlude, something akin to ROMANCE. I was number one. He was my Knight

218

in shining armor. For one night I could pretend that I was the princess rescued from the dragon. Aunt Anna did not know I had a date with a soldier. Soldiers were forbidden, SS or not.

The Band was a local five-man affair. But they could play waltzes, tangos, two-steps, and polka. We drank the wine. It went straight to my head.

"I've never seen blue eyes beaming like that," said the soldier.

I told him it was the wine. I was not accustomed to drinking.

The food almost made me ill because I was not accustomed to eating that much. My cheeks were flushed and I knew that my ears would be burning bright red. They always did that when I was excited.

We danced and we talked. We both agreed that this would happen only once. There would be no kiss goodnight, good-bye, or otherwise. He said he was engaged to a girl from his village in the Black Forest. It had been ordained in this way from the day he was born and she was born. I understood the arrangement. I certainly would not give him cause for a sense of guilt.

The band signed off with Lily Marlene. We sang every verse. We knew every verse and we certainly knew every feeling the song conveyed.

I did not cry when he left the party. I would see him again. I knew that. But I would never touch his hand again or be held by him to that intoxicating rhythm of the dance.

I went home and filled the rest of the night with dreams of what-if. What if there was no war? What if the soldier could stay here forever? What if there was no girl in the village in the Black Forest? What if I loved him? Was that possible? Did I not love Heinrich

Hoelzlin? But there was a war. There would be a farewell and he would be sent to battle again. There was a girl waiting for him. And Heinrich Hoelzlin had a wife. And there was the song from the operetta Zarewitsch, Warum Had Jeder Fruehling Auch Nur Einen Mai!!!

Unfortunately, spring had only one May, one Beltane. Maybe God meant for me to become a nun. But I could not possibly be meant for the cloistered life. I could not tolerate obedience and total discipline without question as it was.

Cannon fire woke me up in the middle of the night. The big guns were roaring. As I rose from the bed and looked out the window I saw that awful red glow in the distance. It was not sunrise. It was BURNING in the west. I wanted to cry, but there were no tears. There was no sleep. There was only the torture of lying silently, thinking of tomorrow and tomorrow and tomorrow.

Sunrise came early enough. It came with a cloudless horizon. Breakfast was meager, and this time I would eat at least part of my lunch, if not at lunch then on the way to work. I did have an excellent appetite.

Sunrise also brought that single, solitary plane in the sky. He did not shoot. Nor did he drop bombs. He was just hanging up there in the sky, like a raptor, riding the wind.

There was no Flak fire from the ground. Melita told me there was a shortage of ammunition. I only wished that the shortage was world-wide.

No German planes took the air in defense of the air space. Melita told me there was a shortage of gasoline. When I asked her what any one plane could be doing up there most of the day, all alone? It was apparent that he wasn't there for his health. He was in harm's way.

Melita told me that he was taking pictures. We could not understand for what reason he could be taking pictures of the town. It was a small town of less than twelve thousand people. It had a train depot. But they had bombed that out of existence already. It had a field hospital. And they had bombed that one out of existence as well. Aside from that it had a castle, a couple of inns, a public bath, and churches. There was a monastery, a brewery, and a Seminary. There were three schools. One of them had been converted into an emergency hospital and that had already been bombed out as well. So why take pictures?

The only remaining Alsatian, still having dinner with us once in awhile, gave his dire prophecy one more time.

"Leave the town if you can!"

But as he had done before, he would not tell us why.

Herr Fricker stepped out the door of the building with a worried glance at the sky.

"I'm going to have to be gone for awhile. Do you suppose it's safe for me to leave?" I heard him ask one of the supervisors. The man shrugged his shoulders.

"Could be reconnaissance, he's not dropping bombs. As a matter of fact, he's not carrying any."

I wanted to look, but I knew better. Herr Fricker did not allow us to waste time looking out of windows and doors. He was very unhappy with us when he caught us doing that. Looking out the window, Lore noticed the man on the street down below massaging his testicles. Soon every woman on the floor was at the windows, leaving the machines unattended. We laughed. I had never seen a man attending to a private itch before. I laughed and turned around. The laughter froze on my lips. There, behind us, like the wrath of God, stood Herr Fricker. I had not forgotten that. So I made believe I didn't hear anything and attended the machine.

That day there were no Jabos. No Thunderbolt came out of the sky. No bomb was dropped. There was no gunfire from the front. It was an ominous silence. I concentrated on breathing deeply and saying without a flaw the word: Schwalbenschnabel. I said it as fast as I could. I said it to keep from looking in the direction of the German soldier, and in the direction of the girl whose nemesis I had been. After all, I'd won the competition.

"SCHWALBENSCHNABEL
SCHWALBENSCHNABEL
SCHWALBENSCHNABEL."

I said it to keep that ominous feeling in the back of my mind from spreading over my entire body.

It was foolish to think that the dreaded Jabos, alias thunderbolts, would not return. But my curiosity was slightly peaked when Liesel told me that one of the dreaded Red Tails had been shot down over Buchenau. Buchenau was within walking distance. I wanted to go and see what the pilot looked like. I wanted to see the enemy face to face. I wanted to see if he had horns, because surely he must have been a devil to shoot at unarmed women and children, walking on the road. I had been told that one of the babies that had been hit was barely six months old. The child had been decapitated by a shell fragment.

Aunt Anna said NO. The enemy was the enemy, she explained. War was war. To be face to face with the enemy did not take away anger. The deadly anger within would have to be overcome by prayer. I disagreed with her. As far as I was concerned, this was a justifiable hate. Aunt Anna said no hate was justifiable.

In the end, Liesel went alone to see the pilot of the infamous Red Tail. I stayed home because Anneliese did not want me to go. Anneliese was afraid. I understood her fear very well although I did not share it. My mind worked on impulse and my impulses were not fueled by reason. Of the two of us, there was no doubt in my mind that Anneliese was more intelligent.

Instead we went to church that weekend. Sunday morning and St. Peters Church was crowded. The priest gave a sermon on the importance of Easter, the importance of sacrifice and the importance of fasting. We would have no problems with fasting, I thought. Our rations had been cut drastically. For one week the individual adult person received 250 grams of meat, 1000 grams of bread, 125 grams of butter, fat, or oil, 350 grams of lentils or beans or dried peas, and 1.25 liter of skim milk. It was a good diet. There was usually less than 1600 calories per day. No, we would have no difficulty in fasting.

My mind would not stay on Mass. I kept thinking of Liesel and of Buechenau and of the dreaded Red Tail pilot. The priest had just consecrated the host when the first flight of planes became audible. No respite from air raids, even on Sunday, even during the forty days of Easter.

The priest handed out communion. The populace approached the communion rail and knelt down. Now the shooting was audible. The priest hesitated for a moment. The woman kneeling opened her mouth to receive the host. No one rose. No one acknowledged the inferno that was happening not very far away. That was OUTSIDE the sacred enclosure. We were INSIDE.

Up in the balcony, the choir was poised to sing. The organist struck the first bars.

"EIN HAUS VOLL GLORIE SCHAUET WOHL UEBER ALLE LAND—"

The song dated back to the times when one hundred years of war had been let loose on the land. The choir sang without wavering. The congregation joined. The sound of sacred music rendered the cacophony of the profane tonnage of explosives ineffective. Had the church suffered a direct hit at that point of time, those hundreds of people would not have felt the terror of death.

We left the church. The air was heavy with the smell of sulfur and dust. The sun would not reach through the curtain of black that rose on the horizon. Somebody whispered that it was Buchenau. Why, no one could understand. Buchenau was a farming community without industry, without railroad terminals. Buchenau had only 800 people.

When I met Liesel after church, she told me she had been able to get out before the bombs were dropped.

"Big bombs," she said. That had not been a minor attack by Thunderbolts. Yes, she had seen the infamous pilot of the infamous Red Tail. The Landsturm, by the police and the infantry, had heavily guarded him as well. Farmers had gathered there, armed with pitchforks and spades; armed with any weapon they could find. Liesel said she had never seen such anger before. The emotional violence was terrifying, she said.

Now it no longer mattered. Buchenau had been leveled to the ground. The farmer, his cattle, his wife and child, his church, his village of a thousand years, was gone.

"See what you have done?" I said to the Third Reich. I could talk to the Third Reich because no one could see it. It existed in my mind just as I existed as a number on its index. Buchenau would cease to exist, and so would the Third Reich. Contrary to Herr Fricker's belief, the Third Reich was not destined to exist for a thousand years.

THE ENEMY

If Aunt Anna would not permit me to see the
downed pilot of the Red Tail, she certainly would not
agree to allow me to see the pilots from the bomber
that went down. But I would see them.

The anti-air guns had made a lucky catch. There
were twenty-three prisoners in all. They were well
dressed, well fed, and up to this point, unaffected by
the environment they had created. There were
Canadians, Australians, and Americans. Dressed with
fur-trimmed leather jackets, their appearance had the
aura of wealth.

One of the Americans lit a cigarette.

"You're right Liesel," I said. They definitely did
not have horns. Some of them wore jackets that had
writing on them. Liesel pushed for us to go forward
for a closer look.

"Can you read that?" she asked.

" I N C E N D I A R Y," I spelled it out. I did not
know much English, but I knew that the word meant
to kill with fire.

"KILLFIRE" I said. We could not understand
why anyone would write that on a jacket.

We discussed it again at the Rappen. And again
the Alsatian warned us to get out of town. Alfred,
cousin to Melita, too young to be taken by the
military, had found a leaflet. The leaflet stated:

BRUCHSAL IM LOCH
WIR FINDEN DICH DOCH

Bruchsal lay cradled in a valley, surrounded by
low hills. The Alsatian said the leaflet had something
to do with the location of the town. It was difficult to
approach by air.

The Alsatian also told me of the V.I. and the V.II.

"Those things have killed some twenty thousand people," he said. Melita looked at him.

"Yeah, and then the Americans bombed Berlin and killed twenty-two thousand," she responded.

I shuddered at the thought of so many people dead and dying. I remembered Mannheim.

"It smells awful when people are killed. I remember the smell from the last bombing I was in at Mannheim."

Melita suddenly turned to me.

"That reminds me," she said. "You had a letter from Mannheim!" She dug around in her purse and came up with a large, unopened letter.

"How did you get it?" I asked. She smiled.

"I guess I have kinfolk all over the place. Some blond girl with a crooked back handed it to my cousin Annerose. My cousin was talking about me working at Rodi and having a friend that once lived in Mannheim. That's how your friend found out about you.

It would have been Maria Keller.

"That's Maria," I said. Not only did we discuss Maria. We also discussed Annel, whose only claim to fame had been Herr Bertold's untimely death.

I could hardly wait to open the letter. The news was not good. The news was never good.

Der Feind Steht Vor Dem Tor!

She had written that in big, bold letters. The enemy was at the gate. The Rhein had been crossed, first at Remagen and then closer to home. Cologne had lost its magnificent Cathedral. And now the Rhineland was under constant shelling. Endless flights of bombers flew overhead.

Sometimes the sky is dark with planes, descending like a plague of oversized locusts.

There were now air raids as well as shelling. Eighty percent of the city had been laid to waste. Of the three hundred thousand people once living there, less than eighty thousand remained. Some lived in the suburbs, some in makeshift basements and some in bunkers. Water was no longer available and the water that could be carried from the river had to be boiled. Fuel for the stoves was no longer available. People crawled out of the rubble at night or during cloudy days or when the shooting stops to gather food and fuel from the ruins of bombed out houses.

Sometimes there are body parts attached to the wood.

Maria was descriptive. But I could tell from the letter how terrible existence was for her. Most of the houses of the inner city were destroyed. Not a church was left standing. Nothing to testify to the splendor of the city, nothing historical was left.

They did not bomb the Kaserne.

I understood what she said. The enemy preserved the barracks, the Kaserne in Sandhofen, in Feudenheim and near Kaefertal. That meant that Frau Roth was still alive and well. She lived across from the Kaiser Wilhelm Kaserne and it had been left intact. That was the good news. The bad news was about Ursula, who was killed in an air raid, about Rosi, who was killed in an air raid, about Cecilia, who was killed in an air raid. The list went on. And there had been no news from Helmut, as well as no news from Alfred, Hans, and Rolf. No one knew what had happened to Inge. A blockbuster had killed the two elderly gentlemen with their little greenhouse on F.6 instantly.

I went home and thought about all that she had written. I wanted to go back to the city I loved. That was no longer possible.

Liesel was frightened as well. She said there was an air raid on Dresden. Thirty-five thousand people had been killed and the city had been destroyed. Dresden was a place of culture, of education, of art, of history and of religion. The tens of thousands of people who had been crammed into the city were refugees, women and children retreating from the approaching Russian troops. I was trying to concentrate on the mathematics equation of that staggering number. Eventually a dull numbness settled in over my mind, my spirit, my soul and my body.

In my dreams at night I wandered through the blocks at Mannheim. Houses that bore a striking similarity to skulls, with their remnants of walls, black squares and triangles where windows used to be. In my dreams I was being chased down the maze of burned out streets through piles of rubbish, chased as always by huge dragons with red tails. In my dreams I called for all those friends and kin that once peopled my landscape. In my dreams I kept asking the government, "WHY? WHY? WHY?"

But the Third Reich did not answer. I was afraid to think about Hitler, Goehring, Goebbels, and, God-forbid, that devil Himmler. If I thought about them, then I would talk about them. If I talked about them I could be arrested. If I would be arrested I could as easily as not be guillotined.

But I could think to myself about those men, those leaders, and those famous male individuals who participated in the bloody sacrifice. Stalin had changed horses in midstream, so to speak, and without fear. Now the Communist was the ally of the capitalist - strange bedfellows indeed. Stalin, after all, was responsible for the death of millions of his own people. The world surely knew about Siberia. And here it was whispered that Churchill purposely provoked Hitler in order to bring America into that war on the side of the allies. The Emperor of Japan killed his own. He killed the Chinese and the Pacific Island people without a second thought. The Emperor, it was said, was a god. All the leaders of all the nations involved in this war, were male. True, there was a queen on the throne of England. But she was only a figurehead, and the people who ruled that country were old pot-bellied men. I bet they weren't on 1600-calorie-a-day rations. Uncle Johann had said it was called a Patriarchy, a worldwide political manifestation that allowed the males of our kind to determine life and death of every individual alive, without having to answer for it. The only ones to answer were the vanquished and the losers. The only ones to suffer were the victims, the women, the children, the mothers, and the sisters. But the Catholic Church said it was God-ordained. God gave man to woman as a companion, as a mate, as a protector, as a never-ending source of joy. Well, in this case I would like to request of God to take back his gift. Man, that precious gift of God, was about to protect woman right out of existence.

"Would there be this kind of killing in a Matriarchy? Probably not." I thought.

APOCALYPSE

In a war zone, things only get worse. And worse
was yet to come in late February 1945. There had
been whispers that the enemy had a list of Targets.
The British and Americans, referred to the list as THE
BOMBERS' BAEDECKER. Germans referred to it as
the DEATH LIST. Later documents were to prove
this as a fact. Now Bruchsal had a DEATH LIST
NUMBER. It was "GH-552." The Alsatian told us
that and once more to:

"Get out of town."

How could we tell him that we could not get out
of town? Herr Himmler's police, secret or otherwise,
would not permit us to leave.

What was really upsetting was the stream of
refugees that entered the town. The Third Reich and I
had a serious conversation about that. The Third
Reich looked pale and "abgemagert," just like us. The
Third Reich was a mere shadow of its former self.
Although the German newspapers did not tell us so,
we had lost everything in Africa. We had lost
everything between our country and the Russian
Border. We had lost so many brothers and fathers and
grandfathers even. We were bleeding from the inside.
Cities were going down in flames all around us –
Cologne, Mannheim, Stuttgart, Karlsruhe, and
Pforzheim. In Pforzheim, it was whispered, twenty-
five thousand people died in one night. Survivors
wandered aimlessly into Bruchsal.

The woman, a widow with three children, who
came to our door, had a different tale to tell. The
Czechoslovakians were victorious where she came
from. Whatever vengeance inspired them, they had
entered the village where the woman had lived, and

her people before her. They rounded up women and children. They rounded up the young, the very young, and the old men. They herded them to the village square. There they bludgeoned all the men and boys to death with clubs, in front of the women and children. The women and children were given two hours to pack up and leave. The woman who told us that could scarcely speak. Her hands trembled. Her back was bent as though she carried the weight of the world on her shoulders. And so, once more we made room to accommodate a woman and three small children. Some one had found a pot-bellied stove to put in that cold little garret room.

Uncle Karl could no longer curse and fume about pig-headed lazy teenagers like myself. He could no longer curse and fume. His eyes were turned toward the direction of the guns that relentlessly pounded away in the near distance. In the evening hours, we went to church to pray. We prayed for those who had to endure. For once we all were in agreement that the dead were more fortunate than the living. The organ played, and we sang: "Wir Treten Zum Beten For Gott Dem Gerechten…"

The little hymnbook said it was a battle hymn, a prayer before the battle. Die Schlach as it was called in German. No difference between that and the word "SLAUGHTER".

It was on the first day of March in 1945 that I became intimately acquainted with the meaning of the word "APOCALYPSE." It was a cloudy morning with a rare taste of spring in the air. I wanted to take in the taste and smell of it in great gulps. Somewhere, along the way to work there was a slight misting not quite rain and a little more than dew and just enough to carry the fragrance of granite from the cobble-stoned street. It smelled like the lions in front of the Zeughaus Museum in Mannheim. I was homesick for Mannheim. It saddened me to know that the city I loved, and the small remnant of its population, was fighting for survival. I pushed that thought away and concentrated on the road ahead. At least, the day was overcast. There would be no Jabos. I still smiled when I thought about the old man who had pointed at the Jabo, flying low across the Wuerttemberger Strasse and said, "There goes one of Goehring's razor blades." I was momentarily puzzled by that remark, but then I recalled Goehring's speech stating that not even a razor blade could get across Germany's territorial air space without being detected and downed by the Flak. There had been no anti-air craft guns for quite some time. There would be none this day.

Melita and I went to lunch at the Rappen. The table, where we gathered with the Alsatian and other people, was empty. Melita looked at the table. A man in a black uniform was seated. She backed out of the restaurant and decided it was best that we return to Rodi.

"The Alsatian is gone," she said. She would not elaborate on that.

We ate lunch rather hastily in the small break room provided for that purpose.

It was just after one in the afternoon when all the machines at the factory suddenly came to a halt. We sat there with our heads up, trying to listen to what we could not hear. The assistant supervisor came to our lines and requested that we would go to the basement immediately. We did not understand that. The sky was overcast. The guns were silent. Then, from the distance we heard the sound of the approaching

233

planes. Those planes were not the usual Jabos. They were bombers. But bombers had crossed the sky before. I stood for a moment but the supervisor insisted that we hurry and get out of there.

As we passed the front door, I saw the little man with his crutches. This time he was not stopping to cure an itch. He looked like he needed help and so I rushed out of the door to assist him. The supervisor screamed an obscenity at me and told me to get in the basement. But two more workers came to help. We were able to get the man on his crutches down in the basement.

The last people to enter were the wife of Herr Fricker, a baby in her arms and her mother at her side.

Where did they come from?" I whispered to Melita.

"They live upstairs, next to his office."

The basement was filled with people, some three hundred who worked at the factory, plus Herr Fricker's family. Now the sound of the planes threatened to drown out the silence of the people.

The first bomb detonated in close proximity and once again the percussion of the explosion and the dust pervading the air returned. The lights went out, detonation followed detonation. The basement of the building had been carved out of solid rock, like catacombs, beneath the building. From the violence of the explosions we knew that we were under attack. We did what we had always done, sitting in a basement, undergoing this agony, year after year. We prayed silently. We were Catholics and Lutherans and we all folded our hands in the same way and whispered the same prayer.

We began to cough from the dust and the smoke around us.

The explosions ceased momentarily. The supervisors came down, provided us with water and rags and said we had to get out immediately. We looked at each other, "Get-Out-And-Go-Where?"

An order was an order. The woman with her child looked devastated and resisted. The supervisors were almost brutal in routing her. I offered my hand. I took the child. I had the woman on one side and her mother on the other. I made certain our mouths were covered with wet rags.

When we got to the top of the stairs and looked out of the factory entrance we could only see clouds of black dust and smoke rolling aimlessly through the deserted street. Two men handled hoses at the doorway, one to the left of us and one to the right. One of them shouted:

"Don't go toward town, go up the hill away from town."

I had been well trained. I took orders when I recognized them to be needed. With the child in my arms, a woman on either side, I turned right, up the hill along the gray wall that seemed like a protective barrier between the town and us.

Only once did I look back. That backward glance was like a moment suspended in time. The building we had just left behind rose from its foundation, permitting a sword-edged splinter of daylight to separate the building from the ground below. My mind signaled danger. We needed to get away. I found an entrance into a house and hopefully, I thought, to a basement. We literally broke down the door and stood at the tap of the basement stairs when the concussion from the exploding building caught up with us. Frau Fricker was visibly thrown down the stairs. Her mother held on to me and the baby. We were cast down to the ground, like helpless rag dolls. I still held on to the baby. I heard the woman cry out and then I heard her sob. Someone took the baby from me, handed it to her and said, "You see, the baby is fine." I picked myself up, I helped the old woman up and together we went down the stairs. That was when the second flight of bombers arrived.

Again we had the smell of dust and grit between our teeth. Again we witnessed the detonations, the building trembling, the smoke accumulating, and again the silent prayers of women and children.

When it was over, one of the air raid wardens went outside. He came quickly down stairs. The house was all right, he said. But the smoke was so thick; it was not feasible to breathe.

For those of us who had gone into that basement there was a temporary safety. We could leave. We would not be able to go toward Bruchsal, we were told. There was now a firestorm. It was the thing that was deliberately let loose on the cities. Detonations, explosions from blockbusters would cause the high winds. Incendiary bombs dropped after that, would set everything on fire. The heat and wind would be so intense that it would suck everything into its burning maw. It was fiery Gehenna.

The baby cried and it became evident that milk would have to be found. For me it was an excuse to get out of there. I thought of Anneliese. She worked at the department store in the heart of town. I could not cope with the thought of her dying in that fire, but I simply had to know.

"Go up the hill, around the town," the Warden suggested. And that was what I did. It was a mechanical thing, one foot before the other. I stood above the Seminary and I looked down and saw that

236

the house on Wuerttemberger Strasse 7, was still standing. I was almost afraid to go down there. But I had to know.

Anneliese met me in front of the house. We held on to each other tightly.

"I went home to eat lunch," she explained. Lunch at the house had saved her. We both looked across the bridge not very far from us. We could feel the heat. A solid wall of fire stood there, upright, orange red, flame locked into flame. Beyond it was a multitude of people, dead or dying. I turned away from it and remembered my errand of mercy. I hated to tell that to Aunt Anna.

"Frau Fricker's baby needs milk," I said. She looked at me as if I had lost my mind.

"You can't mean to go back into that?"

I nodded. I don't know how she found the milk. The rations were so strict. But she found a small bottle and she filled it with milk and she handed it to me. Anneliese let out a little shriek. But I went on. It was something, for some reason, I felt compelled to do.

I found my way back. I found the door. I entered the basement and went down the stairs. She was still sitting there, cradling the baby. I handed her the milk. I don't even recall whether she thanked me for it or not. I left as quickly as possible. I could feel the immense heat from that burning inferno at my back. I wanted to get away.

Eye witness accounts and records would document that more than one thousand flying fortresses left England that day. Bruchsal was one of the first targets. Others were Ulm, Reutlingen, Neckarsulm, Heilbronn, Goepping, Ingoldstadt, and

237

Neuburg. None of these cities were of military or industrial importance.

In that brief 40-minute space of time, Bruchsal received 894 five-hundred pound blockbusters and 50,000 incendiaries. All of that was unleashed on a town with less than 12000 people. One thousand people died immediately, cremated alive by the firestorm.

I stood up there, on the stairs, between the Seminary and the Brewery. The wind brought the sickening smell of burning flesh to my nostrils. I walked down slowly and carefully. I knew I would not stay there in that town that night.

Halfway down the stone steps, across from the small park surrounding the pavilion, I stopped and looked out across the landscape before me. Down below, the town was wrapped in a funeral shroud of black and gray. Now and then the flames put an unearthly glow of red and orange at the lower edge of that ominous cloud.

I roused myself from that reverie only to come face to face with Herr Fricker. I did not expect to see him there. But he stood there, in front of me, with his bicycle. And he looked at me. He never said a word. He just looked at me with those riveting, blue eyes. But this time the eyes did not intimidate me at all. I was aware that the color of his face was that of the pavement below his feet. I spoke up before he could say anything.

"Your wife and child and your mother-in-law are all right." I told him where he could find them. "The factory is gone," I added.

He just trembled a little. But his jaw was set tightly. He would not permit himself the luxury of human emotion. My anger got the best of me. And reason did not keep a tight reign on my lips.

"Heil to the Fuehrer," I said: "And Heil to the Fatherland. The Fuehrer and the Fatherland are sorely in need of it."

And then I walked away. Fatherland, I thought, whatever happened to mother country? Heimat? People who had lost home and family were known as Heimatlos. Well, from the way it looked from my point of view, before it was all over with, we would all be heimatlos. And many of us would not be alive.

I wandered slowly down those big stone steps toward the Wuerttemberger Strasse. Anneliese was glad to see me. Uncle Karl wanted to ask questions but seemed to be afraid to ask. Well, I had just one more surprise. I wasn't staying. I was going home, not to Mannheim where I belonged, but to the village where we all belonged.

THE CLAY DIGS, PART II

I summoned up courage to tell them that I wasn't staying.

"I'm going to Neibsheim!" I said.

"You can't make it, you're too exhausted," said Aunt Anna.

"I'm leaving," I replied.

"It's late in the day and you've had an awful time," said Anneliese. I tried smiling through tears.

"I'll be back," I told her.

It was roughly an eleven-mile walk. But I walked, just as I had walked away from Mannheim not to long ago. I walked, one foot before the other. I suppressed the pain from blistered feet. I denied the weariness in my bones, and I walked along the Landstrasse, one foot in front of the other.

I entered the village at the main thoroughfare by the church. They saw me coming. They stood back. There were people in front of the barnyard, in front of the house, wanting to know something. And there was Uncle Johann in the middle of the street, ram-rod-straight. I read his lips although he did not say it out loud. But the word as always was ABBA. I did not know the meaning of the word. But I knew why he said it. And I walked toward him as straight as I could. I walked at his side on to the premise, into the house. He closed the door behind me.

"Get those stinking clothes off her, clean her up, feed her, and give her something to sleep."

I never thanked him, I only said what he wanted to hear: "They're all O.K." .

Part of my clothing was scorched. I had black marks from soot and ashes on me. But I was not injured.

Aunt Martha mumbled away about leaving where I was safe and coming here where I was not. It was obvious that I had to go back. Grandmother said nothing at all. She just fingered the rosary beads and whispered her prayers. I could hear Uncle Johann talk to the people outside. He seemed to be telling them that I was incoherent. And that was all right as well. Warm milk and bread and cottage cheese were placed before me. I ate without tasting the food. Aunt Martha brewed the tea. They raised poppies for the oil in the seed and Aunt Martha knew what the seedpod was good for. I never asked a question. I drank what she placed before me.

I woke up the following morning. I was slightly disoriented. Once again I woke up in a strange bed. The reassuring village sounds. The cattle lowing, the wagons clattering noisily down the street, made me feel more at ease. At the foot of the bed were my clothes. Aunt Martha had washed them and had even repaired the socks. Unfortunately she couldn't do the same for my blistered feet.

I dressed and went to the kitchen and found Uncle Johann seated there. Hot milk and bread for breakfast was fine with me.

"The bombs didn't reach the Wurttembergerstrasse," I said. I knew that would be foremost in his mind. I told him all that I knew. "As far as I can tell Bruchsal is gone. Everything in the middle of town up the edge of the inner city, looked to be in flames."

He sat there holding his mug. Uncle Johann drank Ersatzkaffee. It was some sort of brew made with roasted malt and similar to coffee.

"That's not the first time they've sacked the town," he replied.

241

"With all the people in it?"

"With all the people in it."

He put his mug down, rose and, stretched. Then he turned to me with a command.

"Eat your breakfast, we're going for a walk," he said. I glanced wearily at my blistered feet. Aunt Martha wanted to say something, but he cut her off: "Abba Weib!"

Aunt Martha fell silent. She handed me a healing cream to put on my feet. I finished my breakfast and prepared for the walk. Uncle Johann was the Patriarch of the Clan, and what he demanded was done without question.

But he was also compassionate. He hooked up the team of cows to the wagon and we drove off. We sat there silent, side by side, he thinking his thoughts, I thinking mine.

He stopped not far from the clay digs and put the team below the protection of some trees. Jabos had been known to shoot and kill teams along with the farmers who drove them. Uncle Johann took no chances.

After helped me down from the wagon, we walked the short distance to that familiar spot where such a very long time ago, we children, had played with rocks that looked a lot like bones.

"Remember this place?" Uncle Johann asked.

Of course I did. I remembered the bones and Lioba and Friedel and Wolfgang and Anneliese and the Kratzebackerle, the little Kratzmeier girl.

"It's all gone Uncle," I said and I held back the tears. All the innocence of youth was gone, all the joys and all the feeling of good things. "It's all gone Uncle, all the people, Bruchsal, Mannheim, all my

242

friends, and all there is, is smoke and fire, and death, and hunger, and fear."

He did not reply. He sat there silently, apparently lost in thought. When he spoke again, he did not speak of yesterday.

"You played with some bones and we found an ancient burial place."

That made me sadder. I didn't want to hear about a burial place. I had come from a "crematorium."

"There was an ancient Roman, you know. There was a Druid, and there were Franks. Most of them were important, most of them warriors. Most of them men."

That part interested me.

"Why is it always men," I said: "Why must men always fight and kill and watch their women and children be killed. Why do men lead nations into war? I don't see them suffer. I don't see them die. Do you think Churchill is going to get killed? Or Stalin? Or Roosevelt? Or Hitler?"

Uncle Johann raised his hand, bidding me silence.

"Rest assured, Hitler will not survive the war. But many who made money on it, no matter who they are, will."

"What do you mean money?"

"Wake up girl, war is not fought for ideas. Wars are fought for land and money – possessions wealth, status. The loser pays and the winner keeps it all. That's how it will be with this war."

"What about the Third Reich? The Reich of the worker and the farmer?"

"The Third Reich is dying. Those who believed in it are going to die with it."

I shook my head. He was saying things I did not want to hear. I was so tired of death and dying.

243

"Herr Fricker believed in it "

"Who is Herr Fricker?"

"Herr Fricker runs Rodi & Wienenherger, correction, did run Rodi & Wienenberser. The factory blew up. Herr Fricker believed in the Nationalsozialistische Deutsche Arbeiter Partei."

"Did he die?"

"No "

"If he is smart and if he is fortunate he'll make a fortune and live to enjoy it. If not, he'll wish he had died."

It was my turn to be silent. What Uncle Johann was telling me was not music to my ears. I had trouble believing that people could kill to make money. But he was usually right.

"So what about that Patriarchy thing? Why do men rule just to ruin? I don't remember anything from history where women ruled and killed for gain?"

Uncle Johann smiled. He had accomplished his goal. He had reached a part of me that would help me to overcome the terror of yesterday and all the terrors that lay ahead tomorrow. He would extend his hand, give me support, give me strength. But he would also explain that Patriarchy thing.

"There was no Patriarchy prior to Christianity. The Nordic Cultures held all clans people, male or female, equal. When the pagans were converted and when the Druids were outlawed, this land took on the face of the South. The Jewish people had a Patriarch. The Christian Church adopted that model and with it went all the nobles and the Blood Royal.

We talked at length about the pagans and their way. We talked about religion. We talked about God. We even talked about democracy and a land where people had a choice.

"All the people? "

"Well, at least the majority." Then he said something he had never said before.

"You should never have been born a woman. YOU should have been a man."

He did not allow me to ask why, nor did he give me any further information. Instead he said it was time to return to the village. We had lunch in the village at the house of my mother's birth and my uncle's birth. We ate boiled potatoes, sausage, and cheese, and drank hard cider.

Aunt Martha made a package for my aunt. Uncle Johann told me that I must now remain where I was destined to be at this point in time, at my Aunt Anna's house. He said fighting would now be imminent. The Germans were digging in for a battle. The trenches were completed. The guns were stationed. And not far from us the Allies were doing the same thing. He paid for my transport with eggs and flour. I was hoisted on to a truck, covered with a tarpaulin. As we drove away, I could see Uncle Johann standing there, in the road, head slightly bowed, hands folded. He was praying.

They were glad to see me at Wuerttembergerstrasse 7. To Anneliese it meant that I was still alive. To my Aunt Martha that there was just a little bit more food for all the hungry mouths. To me it meant that I was back in the garret in a bed that I knew. If I could ignore that awful smell from the devastated city, I could get some rest.

"They're preparing for battle at Neibsheim," I told my Uncle Karl.

"I could have told you that," he grumbled in return.

"What about Grandmother?"

245

"She sits in her room and prays. She doesn't want to live anymore."

Aunt Anna turned away. If she felt grief because of that, she did not wish for anyone to know. Emotional displays were taboo.

The topic did not stay with Grandmother. The topic returned to the hazards of travel at that point in time.

"Women don't have any need to go out in public when it's war time like that," said Uncle Karl, then added, "Respectable women don't go."

I felt the heat of temper sort of tippy-toeing toward my lips. I saw no difference between men and women.

"I certainly didn't see any man getting up and breaking his neck in the effort to go to the village to bring back food."

Uncle Karl launched himself forward. Aunt Anna placed herself squarely between Uncle Karl and myself. Anneliese grabbed his hands and I made a quick exit. I hurried to the safety of the little garret room and closed the door behind me. Nothing much had changed. Except now, when I returned to my room, there would always be the frail women and hollow-eyed children, with questions unanswered and fear ever present and utmost in their minds.

The town smoldered, the stench growing worse, depending on the direction of the wind. There was no getting used to. But after the second or third day it was possible for people to get into Brucheal, to begin the dreadful work of removing the dead and to pursue the almost hopeless task of digging for survivors. The few teams of horses remaining were now compelled to a sorrowful duty. Horse-drawn flat wagons, that once transported produce, now carried the dead and what human remains could be found up to the cemetery. It was told that Frau Klein, in an effort to secure a coffin and a private gravesite, took the remains of her husband up to the cemetery in a wheelbarrow. Most of the dead would be buried in a mass grave.

If the city had been destroyed, Herr Himmler's police department was still active. Again the police man stood at the door and informed me that all the people who worked at Rodi, must now return to work.

"But it's bombed out," I said. He shrugged his shoulders.

"Come to work or go to jail," he said.

"Oh, is the jail still standing?" I asked naively.

I felt the danger. I replied that I would be there right away and he left.

I did not look forward to returning to the bombed out building. This time I took the direct route through town. Those flat wagons, passing by with their load of corpses, piled in rows, stacked three high, the awful stench that emanated, I would never forget as long as I lived.

DEATH THROES

In front of Kaufhaus Knopf, where Anneliese had worked only a week ago, bodies were lying in the display windows, some of them with the valuables they had with them. It was hoped that some one would pass by and identify them. By now the process of decay had set in. Some of the bodies were distended with gas that had accumulated within. I tried closing my eyes and holding my nostrils shut. Getting past that corner and up the incline was like crawling out of a nightmare.

There were not many people at what was left of the factory. Walls were still standing. We were asked to clean the reusable bricks and to gather reusable parts of whatever remained usable. Melita was there. I was grateful to see her, grateful to know that she was alive. Barbara was there. Helga was there. But many were missing and no one made the effort to know if they were alive or dead. We all felt so overwhelmed, we no longer wanted to know anything. No one spoke of Herr Fricker. The supervisor at work assigned us our own personal little rubbish pile where we could clean bricks and salvage usable parts. We did what we were told, gingerly. We were afraid of what might surface beneath the still smoldering ruin.

At the end of the day, Barbara turned to me and said, "This may be the last time we'll see each other again. I'm going home."

I looked at her. She hailed from a small village. That village had barely escaped attacks by the Jabos. I understood her feeling. I knew her fear. No one wanted to be separated from the family that was left. No one wanted to return to this town, this stench, the sounds that went with it.

248

"What if they summon you?"

"They'll have to find me first," she replied.

We said good-bye. I never saw her again. I remembered what some one had written in my little poesie book.

Menschen Begegnen Sich,
Lernen Sich Kennen, Werden Freunde
Und Muessen Sich Trennen.

I would recall that, again and again. People meet, get to know each other, become friends, and must part. I cried but without tears.

The date for the funeral ceremony had been announced from the pulpit. Since very few corpses had been identified and since there was a real danger of an outbreak of cholera, most people who had survived attended the service of all whom could be found and who did not survive. A trench had been dug. It was dusted with lime. The remains were placed into it, lime was placed on the already decaying corpses and dirt was shoveled over that. Those of us who belonged to the choir at St. Peters' were given the dreadful duty of singing the Requiem.

It was cold. It was wet. It was heart wrenching. And somewhere in the back of my mind a thought formed. This awful thing was repeated countless times all over the land. And nowhere in this gathering would be found one single, solitary man, responsible for this war. It was like uncle Johann had said. War was the hell that was let loose on the little people so that other people could benefit from it, financially. And in the end, when these wealthy people died, all their wealth would be left behind and they would take with themselves no more wealth than those poor, mutilated bodies in that trench. I slipped away from the funeral. I stopped by the fountain next to the

249

church, where tall young fir trees grew. I picked a small branch, bruised the needles, and greedily drank in the fragrance. The fresh scent of pine was the only comfort I could turn to.

If there were other funerals after this one, it was not made public. The search for human remains continued. The guns from the western front continued to hammer away, night and day as well. Now everyone alive and able, or barely able, was pressed into service. The Volkssturm, one of Hitler's last creation, a unit of old men, was put to digging trenches. Boys ranging from 14 through seventeen became the first line of defense against the Allies. An infantry detail of same three hundred men had been quartered with the farmers. It became evident that the already devastated town was going to be disputed territory. A member of the Nazi Party had requested the defense of the city.

"How can you possibly want to defend what isn't there anymore?" I asked Liesel.

"Don't even ask such a question. If a member of the party hears you, you'll be executed."

Liesel had a point. Aunt Anna had only one response, "Shut up and pray."

The aforementioned party member requested armored vehicles. Remaining officers of the army realized that anyone left would not be able to cope with battles. But the party member of the Third Reich insisted. Armored vehicles rolled in. The Third Reich person was pleased until it became evident that the bomb craters were too large an obstacle for the armored carriers to overcome. Whether he liked it or not, the tank details had to be moved to Ubstadt. The few survivors alive in Bruchsal offered silent thanks to a silent God.

Melita brought me a letter a few days before we were dismissed from the former site of Rodi. No one told us why we were dismissed. We were told to go home and wait for further orders.

"It's from Mannheim;" I said.

"It'll be the last one," Melita replied.

"Why?" I wanted to know.

"Mannheim fell."

This meant that all the land between Mannheim and Bruchsal was now a battlefield and No-man's-land. The letter was lengthy. Maria Keller had a way of giving details. The city had fallen, she said, but not without a fight. Only old men and boys were left to defend it. They died quickly. From what Maria wrote an American Captain took the city. He had apparently made it to Kaefertal first. There he found out that the phone line to Mannheim was still functioning.

The American Captain Steinitz called to City Hall and demanded that the city be handed over by an official in charge, who was to hand over the city bearing a white flag. But the only person left at City Hall was an electrician.

Maria wrote in her letter. Apparently the American Captain was not satisfied with that answer and ordered heavy artillery fire. Maria was now an expert on how to sit in the basement of a bombed out building, enduring artillery fire.

Around 5 P.M., there was a short pause and the electrician was asked to find the mayor of the city so that he could hand over the city. The poor man went to a basement in K.5, where he was told the Commander of the German troops had been. Well, no one was there and the only person left was the electrician. The American Captain finally consented to the surrender of the city by phone.

Her letter continued with the dreadful details of the battle zone.

I told Melita and let her read the letter. But she knew already. She had heard from her relatives that Mannheim had no water, no electricity, only 20% of its housing, and a hundred thousand people homeless. There was little food.

I said Good-bye to Melita. Neither one of us wanted to say that this could possibly be the last time we saw each other.

It was Good Friday. Aunt Anna gathered her flock and we all made the pilgrimage to St. Peters on the hill. The Jabos were flying. We sought shelter on the side of the road. Aunt Anna nearly slipped on a cow turd. It was funny in a way, but we were much too scared to laugh. And for once I did not open my mouth. She recovered her balance and we continued on our way. Neither turd nor Jabo would keep Aunt Anna from her duty as a Catholic. There was no Mass on Good Friday, but we gathered for prayer service. Aunt Anna said we could use all the help we could get, because what we went through was nothing compared to what we were facing. That was all she would say. Aunt Anna never spoke of the unspeakable, the murder, the rape.

Was it like that? I addressed the Christ we prayed to. Was it like that with foreign soldiers and robbery and torture? Was that the reason for dying on the cross, so that we would not do the inhuman thing to man? Good Friday; That day was all about sacrifice and victims and death. But it was spring. There were willow kittens, soft and delicate, the first flowers issuing from the ground. Now they would die with a dying world.

SURRENDER

It was unfortunate that the Third Reich would
choose to give up its ghost on Easter. Easter, after all,
was a celebration of life. But the Third Reich did not
have celebration-of-life in mind for us. We were
being prepared for the final sacrifice. First came the
HIMMELFAHRTS KOMMANDO. These were the
troops in charge of explosives. When they were not
locating duds to disarm, they were blowing up things.
Aunt Anna was up in arms. The Himmelfahrts
Kommando was going to blow up the tunnel. The
Tunnel was adjacent to St. Peter's and the cemetery.
In a way it was a blessing that the explosives
contingent was rarely ever sober. But the idea of
exploding anything in this town seemed absolutely
ludicrous to me. If there were others who felt the
same way, they were afraid to voice their opinion.
Someone had a good idea though. They provided the
fellows with lots of alcoholic beverage. Some charges
were set. One of them accidentally demolished a
family burial ground.

While the detonating squad sobered up, the
enemy moved into position. So did the S.S., Hitler's
Black Knights. Between Bruchsal and Bretten, it was
said, entire convoys of tanks could be heard. The
battle lines were drawn. To the east of us, fourteen-
year old boys and old men formed a defense
perimeter. Behind them the dreaded S.S., just in case
the little boys and old men turn away from disaster.

Easter Sunday! The church bells did not ring.
There was no Easter Sunrise Service. There were no
Easter candies or cakes, no Easter eggs or rabbits
made of chocolate. There was no new Easter dress, no

new shoes, no Easter Bonnet, no walk in the sunlight. There were no flowers.

At the St. Michael's Chapel on Michael's Mount not far away, the people gathered for an impromptu service. They were singing: "St. Michael Der An Gottes Thron Held Mit Den Englein Wache." It was a hymn to St. Michael, Patron Saint of German Catholics. Halfway through the service, shelling began. The people dispersed. Easter Sunday or not, the war would continue.

One more person shared our basement refuge. We did not know where he came from, and he did not offer that information. He did tell us that Bruchsal would not be surrendered without a fight. He had the news straight from the 'Himmelsfahrt Kommando,' the detonation squad. The man said there had been a four-mile long convoy of American tanks and armored cars and troop transport trucks on the Autobahn. A second convoy of equal size followed close behind. They had been headed toward Bruchsal when the detonation squad blew up the bypass ahead of them. Because of all the debris, the Americans headed east instead of south. No one really knew why, but it was presumed that the Americans wanted to avoid a "KESSEL SCHLACHT." The literal translation for that word is Kettle-Slaughter. I kept my thoughts to myself, but if I were an American, I'd probably want to avoid that too. A "KESSEL SCHLACHT" was the systematic encirclement and elimination of the enemy.

"Maybe there won't be any fighting after all," I said hopefully. The stranger dashed my hopes with his reply:

"No, it means the French are taking this town."

Uncle Karl sucked in his breath and let it out slowly through his teeth. Aunt Anna turned pale, and searched for her rosary.

What that meant, the man explained, was that the French would employ their Moroccan fighting force. Moroccans were infamous for their brutality.

Aunt Anna gathered what food she could find. We all carried blankets and jugs of water to the basement in preparation for the siege ahead.

Now, a few German soldiers became visible. Some of us gathered courage and stepped out into the Wuerttemberger Strasse and offered what little food and drink we could spare. We begged for a quiet surrender. The soldiers smiled. One of them looked at us and said:

"You know how it is; orders are orders."

The soldiers continued on, guns at their ready. When the first Jabos appeared overhead, the soldiers sought the safety of tumbled-down walls and shattered buildings.

Anneliese and I had returned to the house and sat in silence by the little round window between the first and second floor.

With the second strafing run of the Jabos, Uncle Karl roared at us.

"When the enemy comes over that bridge, there will be hand to hand combat and if those soldiers see movement up here, they'll shell the whole house out of existence."

For once I did not answer. I did not know anything about hand-to-hand combat, but my mind told me that it had to do with killing and I would not want to see that. Besides that, instincts told me he was right.

Ten minutes into that Easter-Sunday-early-noon the shelling started. The Third Reich was not going to die without a struggle. The battle was joined. The heavy guns lobed shell after shell our way. The poor old house shook and trembled on its foundation. Outside there were screams of agony. Aunt Anna glared at me.

"Don't even think it, remember what happened to Lot's wife when the curiosity got the best of her."

Anneliese held on to me and I held on to her. There was nothing and no one else to hold onto for support.

Late in the afternoon there was a lull in the fighting. We went upstairs briefly. Uncle Karl stood near the windows with a forbidden scowl on his face.

"No one goes anywhere near a goddamned window," he barked.

We wouldn't think of it. We didn't know what was worse, inside with a madman or outside with the shelling.

We spent that night in the basement. Time was stuck, or so it seemed. We'd be forever sitting helplessly in a basement while around us an entire world was slowly going mad.

Was it Monday or was it Tuesday. Somewhere along those days a long column of tanks rolled in. The tanks had red flags.

"They're Russians," I whispered, disobeying Uncle Karl's specific order and peeking out the window.

"They're Moroccans," the masculine voice behind me said. I turned quickly. I caught my breath. I wanted to shout, but the man standing there, held his finger to his lips to warn me to be silent. It was the Alsatian.

256

"Look at the flag on the tank. It's red, like the Russian flag."

"It's their unit flag. They're Moroccans. Now do what your Uncle tells you, if you want to survive."

I wanted to touch him to feel the back of his hand. It was like a gift from God. The Alsatian was a friend. I had a friend right there.

"Is it over?" I whispered.

"Almost," he said. He touched my head as he passed. And then I knew that he was real.

By April 5th 1945 the battle was over. At the eastern outskirts of town, the burial detail picked up the last corpses left behind. There were sixteen boys, younger than I. No one knew how many of the old men had fallen.

Only one thing good happened at this point. On the eve of April 5th, 1945, for the first time in five years, we could go to bed without fear of an impending air raid. We could speak freely about Herr Himmler. We could make jokes about Feld Marschall Goehring and his defunct Air Force. The Third Reich was now officially dead for us.

"You'll wished it weren't" Uncle Karl said.

" Why?"

"Because for the next ten days there will be no law that applies to you as a German. We will all be VOGELFREI."

That was the first time Uncle Karl and I had a conversation that didn't end in disaster. I was afraid to ask him what VOGELFREI was. I wanted to find the Alsatian, but he had disappeared as mysteriously as he came. I finally did find the other gentleman who was now living in the building. He seemed intelligent. He was also very patient. He was very secretive about his name and occupation. But he did answer my question.

257

"To be VOGELFREI means to be persona non grata. That means, without the protection of the law."

But we had laws. Surely we had laws before the Third Reich, could we not have laws after the Third Reich?

"To the victor the spoils," the stranger said. The battle was lost, the land and its people were now occupied territory. Essentially, the land, what was on it and its people, belonged, at least at this point in time, to every Moroccan soldier out there, with a pistol strapped to his side. To the victor go the spoils of war. We had no country, no law, no life, and no future. In essence, we had become Moroccan booty.

For a couple of days we remained hidden away. At night we cowered trembling under thin blankets, a woman, three children, two girls in one garret room. There was some sense of security.

That sense of security came to an end one night, when I was awakened by voices down on the street below. I slipped out of the bed and looked through the curtains, afraid to move the curtains aside. The man across the street on the second floor apartment was conversing with a soldier down below. It had something to do with the man having to attend the French Military Governor. There were a few more words and then the door to the apartment house across the street opened. The man stepped out. The soldier, who had conversed with him, raised his pistol and fired. The man screamed briefly, then collapsed to the ground. He kept calling for his wife. She rushed to the door. The soldier took aim at her and told her not to step out. It was curfew, he said and anyone stepping out while there was a curfew in effect, would be shot.

Liesel and I stepped away from the window.

258

"Hush!" Liesel whispered. We were afraid to make a sound. If the soldier below became aware of us, we could be shot, the building could be set on fire. We could be taken prisoner. We were, after all, VOGELFREI.

We began to run out of food. We were short of water. No one knew the answer. No one could leave the building.

The stories that were now brought to the building by the older men who were the first to go out in public were awful. The man across the street was not the only one to be killed. There were now the "Displaced Persons." Not all of them had been brought to the Third Reich by force. Some had come because there was abundant work and good pay. Some were camp followers, following the retreating German Army. Now all of them made up the vast number of persons that were not VOGELFREI. Displaced persons enjoyed the freedom to steal and plunder. The few homes that had survived the bombings, were now occupied by displaced persons and stripped of all valuables before they were vacated. Lilo saw the person who wore her clothes. Meta was stripped of her rings. What little any of us had left, was now plunder for a people we had never known before.

MOROCCANS

The Moroccans were basically interested in rape. Lilo told me that Maedi had been raped forty times before the French intervened. Some of the Moroccans were arrested. It was said that what few men had been left alive in the town had been forced to hold candles while the Moroccans raped their wives. No one was safe. From age seven to age seventy, if it were female and could be found, rape would occur. Men who interfered were summarily shot.

Ten days, we were told, we would be in that danger. It was before that, or shortly about that time, that someone came to the house and told us of a trainload of stuff that had been found, marooned, near the outskirts of town. It was said to contain food.

Uncle Karl could not go. Aunt Anna certainly could not go. Anneliese was too frightened and too timid to go. Heinz had just returned from where he had been in hiding. The woman placed a protective arm around her children that left Liesel and me. As far as I was concerned, there were no more Jabos. That was one danger eliminated. And looking out the window, I did not see Moroccans. There were people on the street. And if there was food available someplace, now was a good time to get it.

It was sunny out, almost warm. It felt good to be out. It felt good to have a plan, a goal, instead of sitting there, helplessly waiting for starvation and death.

We headed down the Wuerttemberger Strasse, toward the railroad yards. I did not even see the soldier. The two of them, appeared from nowhere. They were not French. Those faces were no European faces. The skin was not white. The pistol came up. It was all happening in some disjointed way. I felt the danger. Fear kept me from putting a name to it. I knew what was about to take place. The pistol was raised against my temple. The squat little soldier with the face like a pug, motioned for me to get in through the door of some abandoned house. I shook my head. I could not even make an outcry. But he insisted.

I saw the jeep with the two French officers pulling to a stop. They got out and before I knew what had happened, they had the Moroccan in handcuffs. They asked me if I was all right. My knees buckled and gave way from under me. They held me up. They took Liesel and me to the jeep. A second jeep had been summoned and the Moroccans were taken away. I did not speak French. The officers did not speak German. They packed us into the jeep and drove off. We did not look at each other. I hated to guess what was going to happen to us.

We were taken to the officers' quarters. The first person to come out of there and to meet me was the Alsatian. At the sight of him, I became incoherent. He calmed me down. He said the officers wanted to know what we were doing out on the street? I told him that we had run out of food.

French-fries, Pommes Frites; for the first time in my life I ate French Fries. We were invited to stay for lunch, Liesel and I.

We were apprehensive. Would we be asked for sexual favors in exchange for a meal? Would that be any different from being asked at the point of a gun? And would it help to tell them that I was a Catholic and sex outside the marriage bed was forbidden?

The Alsatian reassured us that we were quite safe. The Alsatian apparently served as an interpreter. He spoke fluent French. He also spoke fluent German. I really would like to have known his name, but I was afraid to ask. What he did say was that soon, almost any day now, he would be returning home. He did not tell how he came to be there in the first place; nor did I ask.

I was unable to eat much. The experience had been more than I had bargained for. We were provided with foodstuffs, K rations, the Alsatian said. He did not tell us what K rations were. We would have to find that out for ourselves.

We arrived at the front door of Wuerttemberger Strasse 7 in a jeep, escorted by two French officers. The two officers nailed a sign on the door. It read: OFF LIMITS TO ALL MILITARY PERSONNEL.

Aunt Anna's glance at me spoke volumes, but she did not ask. Uncle Karl roared something about collaborating with the enemy, and that we weren't bad enough off to have to sleep with the enemy. The officers looked at Uncle Karl and one of them made a move for his gun. All I knew to do was to rush past Uncle Karl, up the stairs, in hopes that he would follow me. A beating was preferable over a shooting. I never had a chance to thank the officers. They had only showed kindness to us. They had prevented a rape. They quite possibly had saved our lives. I felt that they deserved more than Uncle Karl's roar of defiance. Anneliese followed me up the stairs.

"Du," she said. Liesel explained to her what had happened.

"I really don't know why he has to get so mad all the time. I really didn't do anything!" That was my only defense.

I brushed away a defiant tear that made its way down my cheek. I had brought home food, and that was what I had set out to do in the first place.

262

Whether Aunt Anna believed it or not, I didn't sleep with the enemy.

"It's not about that," said Anneliese. "It's about the Werewolf Organization."

I had never heard of the Werewolf Organization, but I was tired of organization. All my life there had been one organization or another, regulating my life. Uniforms, men, boys playing at being men, and all of them making me feel inferior because I wasn't a man. Uncle Johann had said that I should have been a man, but that was God's mistake, not mine.

"Better listen to that Werewolf thing," Liesel cautioned.

Liesel was right. The Third Reich was not yet legally dead. Two organizations insisted on keeping it alive. That was why Heinz could not leave the house. Heinz would have been considered a deserter. He could have been summarily executed on the street below, just like Herr Kohl. The Werewolf and the Edelweiss Organization were in the process of resuscitating the Third Reich, or at least make an attempt at it. Printed pamphlets had made the rounds. The general public was warned not to consort with the enemy. That would be considered collaboration. Collaboration could have dire consequences. The Werewolf Organization suggested killing enemy soldiers with cunning attacks from behind, or with poison. The Edelweiss Organization suggested putting sugar in the gas tanks of enemy vehicles. Even if we had sugar, I certainly would not have wasted that precious commodity on gas tanks. The Edelweis Organization made it plain that any girl seen in the company of an enemy soldier would have her head shaved. Since membership to both organizations was extremely secret, it was impossible to know who belonged to them.

The Werewolf pamphlets also stated that any time now, the Luftwaffe would regain air superiority over the land. How, I wondered, even if they still had planes, they didn't have fuel for their engines. The German troops would return and collaborators would be killed. Leaflets from the Edelweiss Organization said the Fuehrer was alive and well and that he was working on a secret weapon that would kill the enemy and cause destruction such as the world had never seen before.

Those terrifying ten days passed. The Moroccan troops had moved toward the east and the French Occupational Forces had taken their place. It was now reasonably safe to be on the street during daylight hours. We still had a curfew; it meant that from sunset to sunrise, the streets were off limits to all Germans.

All Germans were issued I.D. cards and a meticulous search for former members of the N.S.D.A.P. was in progress. I wondered about Herr Fricker. He had been a party member. The people who had belonged to the party were now called NAZI.

Denazification was the order of the day. Displaced Persons could accuse anyone for no particular reason and whether the accused person was a Nazi or not, that person could look forward to arrest and imprisonment. Displaced persons also laid claims to what few apartment houses had been standing. We learned to avoid the streets below those apartments. One of the favorite past times of some of these people was to empty their chamber pots on the passersby below. Soap was scarce, and so was clothing. We simply could not afford to be covered by feces.

It was worse at Mentzingen. Some 1200 Displaced Persons, mostly Russian, Poles, and Slavs were encamped there. They torched the Water Castle. That castle dated back to the sixteenth century and was considered a historical monument. The Baroness of Mentzingen was the only medical doctor in the district. In an effort to protect her patients, she placed herself between the Displaced Persons and the makeshift hospital ward. She was pistol whipped and then shot. The little Dachshund, making an effort to protect his mistress, was kicked to death. Nor did the little village of Mentzingen escape their wrath. Women and female children were systematically raped.

While the excesses of the Displaced Persons were gruesome, the French, who occupied a village not far from Bruchsal, developed their own methods of torture. Whenever they felt the need for foods like butter, cream, eggs, fresh meat, and vegetables, they rounded up ten men, mostly heads of large families. If the demanded amount of groceries was not produced, the men would be shot in full view of their families. The evils visited upon us seemed to grow from day to day.

"How can they be that cruel?" I asked Aunt Anna one day. I did not converse that much with her, but sometimes she could and would tell me things I did not know.

"They're only doing what our troops did to them."

"I don't believe that," I replied. And I did not believe that. The Third Reich had always told us to be noble, helpful, and kind. True, it had made an exception for the Jews. The Jews, the Third Reich had insisted, were responsible for all the poverty and the misery in the world, because to a Jew, the only thing important was money. Jews, it was said, would walk over corpses for money. And now Aunt Anna tells me that our troops killed, raped, and plundered just like the enemy.

I had difficulty with that. I had been a child growing up when Hitler came to power. I had had no choice in the matter. What harm had I, or anyone like me, caused to anyone?

"Die Rache!" That statement, coming from Anneliese, was unique. In some ways, Anneliese was a lot smarter than I was. Vengeance, she said. Hitler had wanted vengeance for the shame and suffering visited upon the Germans by the treaty of Versailles. Apparently he got it. But that thing called VENGEANCE didn't just stop there. Now our enemies would have their vengeance. How would it end?

"Vengeance belongs to God! That is where it should be left."

Aunt Anna was right. Anneliese and I did continue our little conversation. We had figured it out as well. If women ruled the world, children would not be murdered. Men would be busy loving their wives and raising their children, instead of killing one another in a game of war and money. In the end we always came back to that patriarchy thing.

On the night of May 7th, 1945, raucous singing that issued from the street below awakened us. Liesel and I rushed to the garret window. Down below, a line of French soldiers were marching down the Wuerttemberger Strasse, arm in arm, singing the Marseilles. Something glistened in the moonlight, just ahead of them. Liesel saw it first. For me it was the first glimpse I had of a penis, twelve penises, as a

266

matter of fact, all of them engaged in urinating the number seven on the ghostly pavement. Liesel and I looked at each other and laughed out loud. We had never seen anyone urinating in public before, much less French soldiers, in unison and to the tune of their national anthem.

If the soldiers were inebriated, if they celebrated, they certainly had reasons. General Jodl had surrendered the German Wehrmacht to the Allies. Two days later, Doenitz capitulated to the Russians. Much later we would find out that Hitler had committed suicide, along with Eva Brown, Herr und Frau Goebbels, and all the little Goebbels. That was a disputed matter for some time. The Werewolf Organization made it public that Hitler's private pilot, Hannah Reitsch, had flown him to South America.

Hitler's demise had little meaning for me. Personally I felt that my education had been complete. I had seen a penis. Small, I thought, much overrated. That's what I told Liesel. She grinned.

"You haven't seen the rest of the equipment," she said. My curiosity was definitely peaked.

"There are two little ding-dongs attached to it." To Liesel, a little ding-dong was a bell clapper. No wonder men were so easily irritated. To have all of that equipment between their legs and to have to walk at the same time must be a major undertaking. It was purely an observation, precipitated by an occurrence.

The first American we saw, had pulled up his jeep down below, in front of the house, in the shadow of the willow. This time no one, including myself, had the urge to rush down and check the situation out. War, capitulation, and foreign occupation had made us cautious.

It was a solitary soldier. In the early evening he fixed his supper on a little camp stove. We could smell the bacon frying. We were not certain what he was going to do with the drippings. We knew we could definitely use them. Again we debated and again the part of fetching fell to me. Aunt Anna found a small container. I took it and rushed down the stairs with it. I was almost looking forward to meeting the first American. There had been so many firsts in my life lately that one or two more wouldn't make a difference.

Before I could get out of the door below, the soldier had walked over to the wall of the Saal and pitched the drippings in the water down below. I saw them floating away, unable to retrieve them. I came back up to the apartment empty-handed.

"Bastards," Uncle Karl grumbled, "don't they know it's a sin to waste?"

I had no answer. I was as hungry as he was. The soldier was gone by sunrise.

It was the thing that was whispered during the early days in August. A suppressive summer heat hammered the stench of decay into the pavement. It was a whispered comment: HIROSHIMA! It was the talk about a devil weapon, let loose against a city in Japan. It fell out of the sky upon an unsuspecting Hiroshima, a city made of cardboard houses, filled with women and children. It was a thing called an atomic bomb. Within minutes it had killed hundreds of thousands. It had burned human flesh to a crisp. Those who did not die wished they were dead. With cooked skin and flesh hanging from their bodies, with a sickness called radiation, they died a slow and agonizing death.

It would take two killings like that to make the Emperor surrender. So it was said. But there were those who said that the Emperor had already agreed to unconditional surrender before the bombs fell. It was also said that the bombs were dropped to impress the world. The world was impressed. Now there was peace.

SENTIMENTAL JOURNEY

For us the reign of terror that started with the French Moroccans had come to an end with the arrival of the American troops as an occupational force. Now there was no boundary between Bruchsal and Mannheim. I was starving and I was afraid of my own shadow. But the need to go home was overwhelming. I did not ask Aunt Anna this time. I simply told her that I was going home to Mannheim.

"How?" she wanted to know.

"I'll get a ride on a truck, or I'll walk," I replied. She just shrugged her shoulders.

"It's too dangerous," she said; "A girl your age on the open road in occupied territory!"

"Mary did it. And she was pregnant with Jesus!"

"Holy Mother of God, that's blasphemy!" she countered. Her eyes looked daggers. I turned away. I knew it had been the wrong thing to say even before I'd said it. But I said it just the same.

I left early the next morning. There was a truck from a nearby village headed for Schwetzingen. That was close enough to Mannheim. There were other people on that truck. Some went to Heidelberg. Some were going as far as Cologne. Most of them were refugees, attempting to return to what once was home.

I settled down on some boxes. The truck was a coal burner. One way of getting around the fuel shortage was to burn wood into charcoal. I never quite understood how it worked, but apparently it did. It was also very smelly.

The truck was loaded with foodstuffs, mostly root crops, potatoes, beets, carrots, and other things. There was no doubt that the owner dealt in the Black Market. The Black Market was illegal, but there was no police to enforce the law. Farmers became wealthy, trading potatoes, butter and cheese for gold and silver. Even if the farmer did not take his goods to the market place, the city dweller visited the farmer in a desperate attempt to keep from starving to death. It was said that the farmer could well afford to carpet the stalls of his cattle with expensive oriental rugs.

We had no gold and silver. The only jewelry I had, a small ruby ring and an aquamarine, had been taken off my hands by a displaced person at the point of a gun. Anneliese had a little gold chain with a cross. Anneliese saved that because she did not go out. She was Anneliesle, Aunt Anna's obedient child. How she felt within would not be known until she exhibited those signs of illness, the terrible stomach aches, the headaches and those symptoms indicative of ulcers. What happened to her during those awful years, would be a lifelong happenstance of pain.

I got off at Schwetzingen. The little castle was still there. It had been the summer residence of the last Kurfuerst. I recalled fondly, that last performance of the artists from the National Theater at Mannheim. It was almost like in another lifetime. I walked several miles before I was able to get a ride clear to Mannheim.

The Autobahn entered the city proper at the Hotel Mannheimer Hof. The damage to the hotel was hard to estimate. Apparently it had been fixed because, once again, uniformed persons exited. Different uniform, only the ghost of Hitler and the Waffen S.S. remained. The smell of the city had not changed that much. It still reeked of soot and smoke and something more. It was that unforgettable addition of rubbish piles, broken bricks and stones, and decayed furnishings, and still that awful odor of death.

271

The streets were clean. From a distance, the city looked like always. Then, crossing the ring and entering the city proper, there were streets upon streets, blocks upon city blocks with nothing but empty walls, windows like the empty eye sockets of a fleshless skull. It was an awesome waste land, block after block, after block.

I made my way to the old Neckar Bridge. It was still standing and traffic crossed at a brisk pace.

There were a lot of American vehicles, mostly jeeps and trucks for military personnel. Having had that previous experience with the French, I shied away from them. I preferred walking.

The old Friedrich Ebert Strasse was the Friedrich Ebert Strasse again. Nothing appeared to be changed there.

Where the two blocks of Neubauten were, Hitler's addition of family apartment houses, people avoided the sidewalk and carefully skirted the building blocks. Displaced persons occupied the apartment houses. The chamber pots, resting on the balconies, were clearly visible from below.

By the time I came within a block of Mama Roth's house I could feel those pangs of anxiety. The Kaserne, across the street from her, was still standing, but was now occupied by black soldiers. I had never seen black people before. I knew that America had Indians, but I never thought of Black Americans. They appeared to be well dressed, well fed, and certainly well mannered.

It was before I reached the Friedrich Ebert Strasse 64 that I came across the Litfass Saeule. It was an advertisement pillar once used to advertise theater performances. At first I had given it a casual glance. Then the picture became the grotesque imitation of

272

death. Above it in bold black letters was written DACHAU. Although the picture repelled me, I needed to see the writing. That was when I found out for the first about the existence of the concentration camps and what had happened at Dachau. What was there, in those pictures, was not acceptable, could not have happened and if it did happen, should not have happened. But pictures don't lie.

I rushed to the house at Friedrich Ebert Strasse 64 and walked up that cool granite flight of stairs. I breathed a sigh of relief when I saw the name was still there. I rang the doorbell. The moment of waiting was almost endless. Then the door opened, and there she was. She had not changed I could still see the same old wonderful large eyes. That slow smile spreading across her lips and her arms stretched out in welcome. My knees shook. My body trembled and my voice would hardly give credence to my words.

"It's been a long time," she said. But my mind was still with those pictures on that Litfass Saule.

"Did you know anything about Dachau?"

I kept bombarding her with questions. She had a small smile and replied: "Isn't it customary to say hello first?"

I sat down in the kitchen. The same old kitchen where I had confronted my first fear, the shadow on the wall, and where I had conquered that fear with the help of a wooden spoon.

"There is so much going around in my head, I just don't know what to say!"

She nodded. I suppose we were both happy to see that we were still alive.

Mama Roth had been a widow for some time, but she had managed to survive. She had rented out a room to some displaced couple. She said they were from Holland and they were nice to her, although she was sure they dealt in the black market. Their name was Jupp and Kory. They helped with food supplies so that she would not go hungry.

I told her about Bruchsal. I told her about Uncle Karl.

"It must be hard on him," she said. "The First World War took his mind and the second took his pride."

I had never thought of it that way. But she was right. The bullet fragment in his brain would be there until the day he died. He would have pain, and because he would have pain, he would have rage.

Frau Roth prepared a light snack of black bread, butter, and salami. Pommes Frites with the French had been a banquet. Black bread, butter, and salami with Frau Roth in the house of my childhood was like a banquet in paradise. When I asked her how that kind of treat was possible, she said:

"Jupp and Kory. They're Displaced Persons. He said he spied for the R.A.F. and she worked someplace. When the war was over, they were considered Displaced Persons, victims of a forced labor policy. Now they enjoy special privileges. Jupp has a friend who does very well in the Black Market. Jupp has a wooden leg. He smuggles diamonds and priceless jewelry stolen from God-knows-where, in the hollow of his leg."

Although she did not approve of dishonesty, she was a widow bent on survival. Frau Roth said the biggest income for the D.P.s came from trading alcohol for cigarettes at the barracks across the street.

274

AUSCHWITZ

Eventually the talk returned to the pictures on the Litfass Saule. It took some time for her to make me understand that there were adults who knew about it. She said she knew about it. What she did not know about, she remarked, were the ovens.

"What ovens?" By this time I concentrated on her every movement.

"It was sort of like a crematorium, except it had showerheads, except there was gas instead of water."

"You mean those people were killed with gas? For what?"

"No one really knows. Some say it was Himmler's concept of the final solution!"

"Final solution for what?"

"Final solution for getting rid of the Jews."

"Women and children?"

"Women and children."

If I had any feelings left for my nationality, for my country, for my homeland; If I had any pride left in being German, now I would have to lose that as well. It was one of two things: I could believe the Litfass Saeule, the pictures, and Frau Roth, and if that were so, I could no longer consider that which once was German of moral value, of human value, or I could disbelieve and at least be left with love for my country. If there was nothing left worth believing in, worth hanging onto, what was there left to live for?

It was early afternoon when I left. I told her that I would return, but I did not know when. She said she would be looking forward to that, and she meant it. She had tears in her eyes.

I returned to the city and made my way to H.7. It was almost like a little gift from God. The blocks G and H had not been destroyed. The Ghetto was still complete. G.6.13 was still standing. I looked at it for a long time and then I went to the Malli's apartment. That was still standing as well. I rang the doorbell and Maria came to the door. Frau Malli was happy to see me. Annel and Maria were there. Herr Malli was not. By this time I was afraid to ask anyone about the presence or absence of a person. Maria and Annel grabbed their coats and we went for a walk. We went to the Luisen Park, to the Planetarium. There we sat at the stone bench and talked about all the things that had happened. We talked about the friends that had died, about the people who were missing, and we talked about the Litfass Saeule and the awful pictures. We knew that if the pictures were true, we would be a generation damned for all eternity.

"Why didn't anyone tell us?"

"Tell us? And what if we had said something at the H.J. meeting, or at school? We could have been in those camps as well. Our parents could have been in those camps. Would you have wanted to be responsible for your mother's death?"

I looked at Maria. I heard her say those words. And I remembered Aunt Anna's words at my mother's funeral. Maybe I was responsible for my mother's death, but would I want to be responsible for my mother's internment in a concentration camp? That was another question. And there was an even bigger question: Just who was responsible? Was it Himmler, that Praying Mantid? Did Hitler know about it. Did Hess know about it and if he did, why did he fly to England?

We were eighteen, almost nineteen, skinny from living this side of starvation too long. We had seen horrors and cheated death countless times. We had forgotten how to sing, how to laugh, how to dance. We had been deprived of our childhood, cheated of our youth by a government we did not elect.

It was late afternoon, almost evening. We returned to the city. I stayed with the Mallis that night. Frau Malli had made some sort of vegetable soup. It filled the stomach. We sat up late that night and talked about the past and the present and the future.

"There really is no future," Maria said.

"How so?"

"You can work in the Blocks, cleaning bricks, but you have to be careful not to hit an unexploded device. Worse yet, you might still find one of the persons killed last year. Or you can work for the Americans. That pays better and you get extra food, but the Werewolf Organization will be after you. You can be raped or have your head shaved or get killed or all three."

I thought about what she said for a long time. She was right. There was little future. From what I understood, Mannheim suffered 80% devastation. Every church, every museum, every apartment house every block almost within the ring was bombed out. Mannheim had no access to food and shelter. Once the city housed 300,000 people. One third of its population survived the war.

Once the city had large apartment houses to live in, churches to attend, concert halls, museums, the theater and the castle, the public bathhouses, the Schwimmbad. Now only one fifth of its buildings remained and strangers who spoke a foreign tongue occupied most of those buildings. Mannheim had again 300,000 people; it just lacked the wherewithal to feed them and to house them. Mannheim had become a city of homeless people.

"Are you coming back?" Maria asked.

"Am I coming back? Of course I'm coming back, at least for a little while," I replied.

With evening descending, we returned to the Malli's apartment.

I was eighteen years old. I had no professional training for earning a living. I had no money. I had little more than the clothes I wore. I certainly did not have connections to people who could help me. But I did have Mama Roth. One thing was certain; I would not remain in Bruchsal.

I stayed at the Mallis that night. I woke up screaming in the middle of the night. Frau Malli came to calm me down. I was drenched in sweat.

"Nightmares," I said.

She nodded her head. Who didn't have them? We all sat around until the break of dawn, talking about the plight of the average person, talking about Dachau and the concentration camps. It was too hard to comprehend that such a thing could have happened without anyone knowing.

"There were people who knew, but they were afraid to talk about it because of the Gestapo."

I felt like such a fool. I didn't really believe there was such a thing as the Gestapo.

"That's why Hannelore's mother hanged herself. She was sure that Hannelore had talked about things said in strictest confidence. Hannelore's father was arrested."

"I thought he was arrested because he molested a child?"

Frau Malli shook her head. That was a cover story, she said. She thought it was political and that it had something to do with Herr and Frau Rettig.

"But didn't they take Hannelore after her mother's death?" That was all I intended to say about that. What came into my mind about the whole affair was best left unsaid.

In the early morning hours I said my good-byes. I told Maria that I would return. I also told her that I would see my foster mother again.

Frau Roth was happy to see me. She had breakfast for me. Hot Chocolate, I could not believe it.

"Hot Chocolate?"

Mama Roth smiled. Jupp and Kory were good providers. Kory was pregnant she said, but she was sure that they would leave once Jupp had made his fortune on the black market.

"How would a person go about to get permission to live in the city?" I asked.

The answer came quickly and without forethought. "You'd have to bribe the officials?"

"With what?"

"Candy and cigarettes."

That, I knew, would be a big problem. But Mama Roth simply smiled. That, she said was no problem for Jupp and Kory. And if I wanted to, I could move in with Mama Roth.

She wanted me back. She was getting on in years. She was alone in the world and she had no children of her own. I understood what she had in mind.

We talked to early noon. Herr Jupp came and told us that if I wanted a ride back to Bruchsal, there was a truck that was going as far as Bretten. Bretten was not that far from Aunt Anna's house. That was within walking distance. I promised to return and she said she would help me to get established. She was certain I would have no problems finding a job.

"If you think I'm going to clean bricks, forget that." For once in my lifetime, I was not going to buckle under to someone else's plan. Mama Roth shook her head.

"That's not what I had in mind," she answered. I looked at her puzzled.

"There is work available in the American sector at Feudenheim."

"Doing what?"

"They have a P.X. out there where they sell stuff to the soldiers," said Jupp.

"What's a P.X.?"

"It's like a super store. They hire girls who speak some English. Attractive girls."

I didn't know about attractive. I was as skinny as a rail. But I did speak some English.

"What about the Werewolf Organization?"

"I wouldn't worry about that," said Jupp, "We have friends."

It was difficult to see Mama Roth dealing so calmly with circumstances that were less than honorable. After Jupp and Kory had gone to their room and before they were taking me to the truck that was leaving, I had a moment to be alone with her.

"They sound like gangsters," I cautioned. She just smiled and shrugged her shoulders.

"What's the difference? The world is full of them. Before the war ended they sat in offices. Now there is a new kind of gangster emerging. If you want to come back to Mannheim, if you want to survive, you'll have to learn to cope with that."

I embraced her, told her I was definitely coming back and walked with Jupp and Kory to the truck.

The man behind the steering wheel did not speak German well. He said he was Russian. I went white-faced and wide-eyed. He laughed a deep rumbling laugh. He said I need not be afraid, he was a good Russian. I was afraid to talk. I sat there beside him. If I'd had a rosary, the beads would be turning through my hand. I was silently praying. The God who kept me alive through all the things that had happened, surely did not intend to hand me over to a Russian.

In his broken German he told me that he had been brought to Germany to work. He showed me scars on his back, and pointed out the scar across his face.

"Nazi did that," he explained. The story he told me was not pretty. I told him of the Russians that killed the Baroness.

On the road to Bretten I was educated about the practice of forced labor. The Third Reich may have been dead, but its deeds were far from gone. Russians had died in forced labor camps. Poles had died in forced labor camps. He said he did not know if any of his people had survived the war.

"Very few of mine did," I told him. We knew that we had a common pain. We lived on a continent where people were forced to kill each other at least every other decade. He had a bottle of strong drink. He offered me a sip. I was afraid to turn it down. By the time we got to Bretten, he decided to take me all the way home to make sure I was safe. We pulled up in front of Wuerttembergerstrasse 7 singing the Volga Boatmen Song.

"Noch einmal, da da da da da" I sang in German, he sang in Russian. He helped me off the truck and gave me a small package of what appeared to be food stuffs.

"I believe you're slightly inebriated," said Aunt Anna and rushed me up the stairs before Uncle Karl could see me. Maybe I was slightly inebriated. But I had just returned from a remarkable journey. I had discovered that The Third Reich had brutally killed people simply because they were not German. I had discovered that The Third Reich had taken people and forced them to work in places far away from home. And now I was stuck asking myself the same old question over and over again. Was there anything honorable about that Third Reich? And exactly how long would I stand accused, simply because I was a German and I grew up in The Third Reich.

I gave the package to my aunt.

"Chocolate!" she said. And there was a pack of American cigarettes. Uncle Karl had no difficulty accepting them.

I had little to say to Aunt Anna. But when I had the opportunity I talked to Anneliese.

"I'm thinking of going back to Mannheim," I said, "but first I want to talk to Uncle Johann."

"You're leaving again?"

I nodded my head. There was no way I could tell her what I had in mind without first talking to Uncle Johann.

EMIGRANT-AUSWANDERER

It was not an easy visit to Neibsheim. Uncle Johann was not in a talkative mood. Nor was he an easy listener. I had persuaded him to go to the Clay Digs with me. I wanted some time alone with him. What I had to say would not be easy.

Neibsheim, the village, had changed. Uncle Johann said it would change even more. The village that I knew and loved would be out of existence by the next decade.

"That sort of makes it easier," I said. He looked at me expectantly.

"I won't be here before the next decade rolls around." He read my mind. Before I could tell him what I planned, he'd said it: "Auswanderer, you're going to leave this country, aren't you?"

I was afraid of his rage. Most of the men in this clan had a terrible temper. But he did not burst into a rage. "I always told your mother she didn't go far enough!"

"Uncle, how many wars did grandmother endure? Three? And you endured two? And I just finished my first war. Well, I don't plan to stay here, in this country, on this continent and wait for another batch of discontented old men to start another war. My children, if I have any, aren't going to be butchered by a - what was it you called it - a Patriarchy?"

His mouth popped open. I thought for a moment I was due to be backhanded. But he made no move. He just sat there. When he talked it was with a soft voice.

"Remember when you and Lioba and Friedl played here and found those bones? I never told you all of it. But those were the bones of early clansmen. No women, just men. I guess they didn't bury women.

Women were just so much chattel. The men buried here were warriors. They were buried with their weapons. Maybe this thing called Patriarchy has been carried to extremes. You know, there is no doubt that you may be right. But do you think that running away is going to change that? Will it solve that problem?"

We were engaged in a game of intellectual chess. He had honored me with the role of opponent. He was right. Running away would not solve the problem.

"I didn't cause the problem that exists, and I'll be damned if I solve it. I only know that I am not going to see my children grow up in a country that kills its women and children every decade or two." I could not say much more, I choked down the tears.

"How will you leave and where will you go?"

"I don't know."

I had no way of knowing anything except that my mind was made up. I was going away, as far as I could get from this continent.

"I'm going to put an ocean between me, what's mine, and this land."

"I always said, you should have been a man."

He agreed to keep this discussion silent. I had no way of knowing how I would set any kind of plan into action. But I had given myself a goal and a deadline.

I had lunch at the farmstead. Aunt Martha wanted to know why I came. I looked at her and said:

"I just wanted to say good-bye." It was not a lie.

"Where are you going?"

"I'm thinking of returning to Mannheim."

Well yes, she thought, that was quite a ways from the village. I could not say good-bye to my grandmother. Her eyes were clouded over. She had cried too many tears. She was asking God for a speedy release from her body. If she recognized me, she did not say so.

Nor did I see anyone else in the village. When the Angelus rang I stepped out of the door. Uncle Johann stood there, cap in hand. His lips whispered the ancient prayer: "Der Engel des Herrn brachte Maria die Botschaft —"

Ask me God, I said to myself, I just might turn you down. Was that just one more aspect of patriarchy to ask a very young girl to bear the godchild, only to see him crucified in his prime? But God did not answer. After the prayer, I literally shook the dust of the village from my shoes and slowly set out for Bruchsal.

By the time I had returned to Bruchsal I had my plan set. I would not allow an argument with Aunt Anna. All she needed to know was that I would temporarily accept Mama Roth's generous offer to stay with her. If possible, I would seek employment at Mannheim. I would keep her informed. With a place to stay, and possible employment, Aunt Anna would not need to worry about me. I would have to be careful. I would have to be submissive. I would have to make promises I did not intend to keep. One thing was certain. I would never again live in Bruchsal. That I kept to myself as well.

DENAZIFICATION

Leaving Bruchsal was easy; saying good-bye to Anneliese was not. We had spent our first two decades on earth, sometimes together, sometimes apart, but always with caring and sharing, always with unconditional love. We should have been sisters, but as it were, we arrived at a different time and had different mothers. Our mothers were sisters. But Aunt Anna and my mother were never as close as Anneliese and I. I lied to her when I told her that I was coming back. It was easier that way. I just couldn't stand to see her cry. When she saw me packing my little Poesie Book she knew I was not coming back. My little remembrance book with all the little poems from all the girlfriends and the teachers and some of the boyfriends remained with me for my entire life. In the end it was good-bye. I did not tell her what that good-bye really meant. I was not yet twenty-one and I was uncertain if the old laws still applied. Did I have a guardian or was I really free?

Establishing residence at Mannheim was a monumental task. It could not have been accomplished without the assistance of Jupp and Kory and their gangster friend Harry.

"These middle-aged little Napoleons who ensconce themselves behind their big desks. Do you know what an official stamp goes for these days, on the black market?" Harry apparently knew or he would not have asked. "Five cigarettes, that's what it goes for. And you can get an entire set of papers, complete with ration tickets for half a carton. And now this crummy little prince of ink wants a pair of nylons?"

"That's what he said," I answered. "He said he didn't smoke but his girlfriend would like a pair of nylons."

"That's not a bad fee for a Strich Dame." Jupp threw that in for good measure.

I was learning more lessons. I found out that a Strich Dame was a high-class prostitute. And I found out what nylons were. I did not know that silk stockings could be made from anything but silk, and to be that sheer! I admired the pair of silk stockings Kory had given me. Kory and I had developed a friendship. Tall, blond, big-boned, with a high forehead and blue eyes, she was typically Nordic. Kory was from Holland. No one seemed to know where Harry came from. What we did know was that Harry carried a pistol. Kory whispered something about Harry being a Kingpin of the underworld.

"Administrators, Paper Shufflers, what's the difference." Mama Roth wanted to get this whole thing over with. And I lacked one more stamp from being officially once more a Mannemer, a citizen of the city of Mannheim. I had made the mistake of asking the official what kind of bribe it would take. Mama had stopped me and completed the sentence with "GRATUITY."

"Why don't you go with her at that next try," Jupp said to Harry. Harry looked at me.

"That's not a bad idea," he said. I wasn't sure. Mama was a bit weary.

"Supposing he goes for the police?" Kory wanted to know.

Harry shook his head. He knew the police department very well. According to Harry, they were as eager for the "GRATUITY" as the housing department.

There were others at the office when we arrived. There were American soldiers and their girl friends. There were displaced persons who did not need to bribe, and one girl my age who simply rolled up her sleeve and showed a small tattoo on her forearm. The official paled. He shook just a little, accepted her papers and disappeared. The girl turned to me and smiled.

"You really made him nervous," I said. She laughed. "They don't like to see any survivors from the camps. He knows I can get him fired if he doesn't get me what I want."

I had never seen a survivor from the camps before. I had only recently found out about the camps. Harry was quick to take advantage of the situation. By the time the official had returned, Harry was in a deep conversation with the girl. Just as quickly, Harry placed an arm around my shoulders as he addressed her:

"So nice to see you again. Maybe we can get together over a glass of wine." I had no problem chiming in. Talent in performing for an audience could came in handy even without a stage.

The girl, with the number tattooed on her arm, scooped up the papers and walked out the door. We were next in line. Harry glared at the man, pushed me in front of the desk and said:

"I believe you forgot to place a stamp on this document the last time we were here."

"So I did, so I did!" replied the official. We didn't even have to pay for the stamp and the "GRATUITY" was mine, all mine. I had earned my first pair of nylons. And it had been so simple.

I wore them the next time I went to see Maria Malli.

"They make your legs look like a million marks," she said. I was slowly getting accustomed to the those burned out ruins and learning to pick my way around the danger zones.

Maria had a surprise for me. We slipped into jackets. The temperature was still very cool. We walked down the Planks. Some of the houses were still standing. Maria stopped in front of one of the houses and rang the doorbell. The door opened and we went up the stairs. There she stood, with a smile on her face.

"Caught you by surprise, didn't we?"

I did not know that Elinore Gruenewald was still alive. The last time we had seen each other was in 1943 before my mother's death. There are times when God smiles on man and the universe grants a favor. I could only hold on to her hand. I could not talk.

We were off to the observatory. But were unable to gain entrance. The air raid had made the little structure unsafe. We walked beyond the castle grounds to the Rhine River.

On the way back we stopped at a little ice cream place on the Breite Strasse. TESSITORE, the sign said. "Immaculate," my lips shouted. There was Titi Tessitore, the lady of the ice cream parlor. And now there were five of us. We had survived. We did not have the ration tickets for the ice cream, but Titi took care of that. We were seated in the little alcove by the street. I could see S.1.7 from where I was seated.

"The people who live there are from Latvia," Titi said. There was no need to go there. I could see the place from where I was and I was leery of chamber pots from the second floor.

By the time I walked home I became aware that I was not walking alone. I stopped at a department store window, trying to catch a glance of the person who followed me. It was not that easy. I was a long way from the Friedrich Ebert Strasse, but I had to go on. I wore nylons, I had a residential permit, and I had friends that were not German. I worked for the American Sector in the P.X.

I hurried along as best I could. Then, just within a block from where I lived, the stranger hailed me. I turned around, ready to put up a fight when the man laughed.

"You do not remember a Noch Einmal, and da dum da." It was the Russian. I felt such a relief I almost hugged him. He walked me home the rest of the way. I told him that I had been afraid and he agreed with me. From that time on I made sure that I was not alone on a lonely stretch of street.

WARBRIDE

If getting the residency permit had been like pulling hen's teeth, the papers I needed only a year later were even more difficult to get. I had met an American soldier and he had proposed marriage. I was going to be a "WAR BRIDE." I was going to America. I had not informed the clan about it, although I felt that I needed to make an appearance at the village with my husband.

It was not an easy thing. The whole matter had come full circle. I saw those hateful stares. They had a name for people like me. They called us "ARMY WHORES." As far as the German people were concerned, those of us who were leaving the land as wives of American soldiers, had sold ourselves to the devil. It was not uncommon for someone to spit in front of me. The obscene remarks were cutting. The paper shufflers were no more willing than anyone else to see us go. We were collaborators; traitors to the Fatherland. Frau Roth had not anticipated this move. She would not speak to me. I could not make her understand why I had to leave. Annel and Maria Malli tried to be cheerful about it. Elinore was devastated.

"It's wrong," she said. "It's all for the wrong reason, it's all wrong. You don't know what you're getting into!"

"I know what I'm getting out of," I replied.

My husband was from a place in Missouri, called the Ozarks. America offered freedom and opportunity. I had spent my childhood and my youth having to do whatever I was told to do. I had no choice. I did not have a choice during my brief encounter with the thousand-year Reich. And after it was all over with I was still shackled to fears of

291

reprisals by the underground. I still existed on a starvation diet and I still had no opportunity for a professional life.

If there was one good-bye I dreaded, it was the one that would take place at Victoria Strasse 7. Herr Hoelzlin had survived the war. Times were difficult for him, but the theater had managed to find a place until a new theater could be built.

I stood in front of that house, wondering if I would not be better off leaving well enough alone.

From the moment I rang the bell, 'til he opened the door, was like an eternity. He welcomed me in with open arms. He was a widower now. The ring was on my finger. I was a married person. He had the maidservant bring in tea. His eyes were so terribly penetrating. I did not have to tell him what I was about to do. He understood.

"It was such a hard young life for you," he said.

"Do you see this as a betrayal of my country?" I asked. He shook his head. He did not see it that way. He thought I should have given it more time.

"Things don't get back to normal after such a war," he said.

In a way he was right. But I wasn't staying. I only had one lifetime.

"If you had known that I was alone, would you have stayed?"

That was the one question I was not prepared to answer. He had meant so much to me. And he had been forever unobtainable.

"It really doesn't matter now, I'm leaving shortly. I don't know what's ahead. But there is freedom, I understand."

"Do you think you can handle freedom?"

It was too late to think about that.

"My mother's people were serfs at one time, a people tied to the land, sold by the Bishop, conscripted by the knight, betrayed by the king. Do you suppose freedom can be worse?"

"What will you do when you get there?"

"Live, one day at a time."

"Promise you'll write?"

"Promise".

It would be one promise I intended to keep. I would also keep my marriage vow. America offered freedom and opportunity and I would take advantage of that without compromising my own personal values.

There remained then the farewell from the village. I had not intended to return to the village, but my husband was entitled to know where I came from.

The village was not open and not friendly. The village had lost others before me who couldn't stand whatever it was that I couldn't stand.

Uncle Johann extended a hand in welcome to my husband. Uncle Johann seemed a giant and my husband was visibly affected by the mere size and timbre of the man. The town crier, on the other hand, was not that overpowering. I explained his job.

"He stands on the street corners and cries out the news."

Alva thought I was kidding, till he saw it for himself.

The town crier was a generous man. Second cousin to my mother, he insisted that we honor his house with a visit. Alva agreed. After the town crier had completed his evening chores, we met him and walked with him to his farmstead. Alva was a bit uneasy. The man looked every bit the reprobate, but he was friendly, and bade us to be seated.

293

As the head of the household, the town crier took his place at the head of the table. Conversation drifted back and forth. The town crier reached for a big cutlery knife. He sharpened it very carefully. Alva watched uneasily. Then the man reached across the table toward my husband. Alva went white with terror. I failed to understand that. The town crier reached up above Alva's head, opened the little door to the smoking chimney and pulled out a partially carved ham. He showed the ham to Alva and with pride pronounced the only word he knew in English.

"Okay?"

Alva laughed with a sense of relief. He had seen quite a few training films and when that big knife came toward him, he was certain he was not going to emerge from the village alive.

"Okay," Alva replied, and shook hands with him.

We had been guests of honor at the town crier's house and yet had not been welcome at the farmstead. The clan considered my marriage an act of treason. We were staying at the shoemaker's house, and we were the guest of Friedl and Lioba's mother. My mother's furniture had been kept there for safe keeping during the war. Aunt Antonia stayed there temporarily. Lioba's mother was not that fond of Aunt Antonia, but she was willing to put up with the situation until other arrangements could be made.

'Other Arrangements' came about much more quickly than Liaba's family had anticipated.

I intended to visit Grandmother at the homestead. But when I mentioned that Liaba looked at me and asked: "Don't you know?"

"Don't I know what? "

"Grandmother died."

It was very clear to me now. I was no longer a member of the clan. Uncle Johann had met us outside the homestead. Had met my husband as he had promised. But Uncle Johann would not see me again. Nor would any of my aunts. I was now, in more ways than one PERSONA NON GRATA.

"You can't really blame them can you? Look at Bruchsal. Look at Mannheim." What Friedl was saying was that the clan blamed America and, in a way, each American for the devastating air war. My husband didn't drop a bomb any more than I voted for Hitler. Why blame people who had no active part in whatever killing was promoted by whatever nation? I looked at Liaba's mother.

"Do you really want Aunt Antonia out of here?"

She said yes. And so it would be. What the clan had in mind for me, I too would have in mind for the clan. The Outcast would also cast out.

Aunt Antonia arrived at Lioba's house the night before we left. I was ready. I had an anger that had been accumulated ever since my mother's funeral. Now I would answer the clan.

"Was there any reason why I was not informed about Grandmother's death?" I asked.

"You were in Mannheim!" Aunt Antonia replied.

"You knew where I could be reached. You had my address."

She had no answer. For me the words came tumbling out quick, hot, and angry. It was my furniture, my place, and my money. It would now be off limits to anyone, except my stepfather, should he be still alive.

Aunt Antonia mumbled something about being prepared to take the consequences. I had been prepared for taking consequences by the clan, The

295

Third Reich, the Catholic Church just to name a few.
And if family and clan saw me as an outcast, then
family and clan could take consequences as well.

OUTCAST

After the argument was over, after she had left, we sat at the kitchen table. Now the tears came unbidden. My husband did not know how to comfort me. He had no understanding of the life I had known prior to becoming his wife. Lioba and Friedl and I sat there, clutching each other's hands. This wasn't about Aunt Antonia. This was about a whole world that came tumbling down on my head. Lioba and Friedl understood that well.

"Remember the Clay Digs," Lioba said.

I would always remember the Clay Digs. It had been whispered that one of Caesar's eagles was found there. But if the standard was carried to the village after the battle in the forest of Teutoburg, the person who found it would carefully conceal it 'til it was safe to barter with it.

We did not remain in the village very long. Alva was not comfortable in a place so far removed from his base. For him it was alien territory.

"Can you imagine? They never told me that she died." I told Mama Roth about the things that had transpired in the village. She just shrugged her shoulders.

"You should have known that this would happen the moment you came to live here. And when you married the American, that only made it worse."

She was right of course. Not only the clan, but most of the people I came in contact with, felt the same way. The amount of paperwork required to leave the country was staggering. There were papers to prove that I had not been a Nazi. I could have been a Nazi and one pack of cigarettes could have denazified me. There were physical examinations to

297

prove that I was free of communicable diseases. There were those references from people who had known me for a long time. Mama Roth would not write one. She did not approve of my leaving and if she could prevent it, she would. There was that reference from the church. I had not been to church for a while and I did put off seeing a priest. But I went back to the St. Sebastian Church, where I had made my first communion. The priest there was new, and approachable. He inquired about my relationship with my husband. He encouraged me to talk about my impending departure. I felt at ease with him. I was reluctant at first. But soon the words slipped right across my tongue.

" I just don't think I could ever live here and just wait while some person in government dreams up another excuse for another war."

"America has had its wars."

"America has freedom. People vote and people decide."

We talked for a long time. He felt compelled to warn me that freedom was not an easy thing to accept.

"Freedom only works when you're willing to assume responsibility for your own actions." I agreed with him on that point. He also talked about that freedom of religion.

"In America they have many types of religion and all kinds of Christian Churches," he told me.

I had no problems with that. As far as I was concerned, there was only one and that was the Catholic Church. And while I did not see my own faith endangered, I certainly felt that the way the church carried out its God-ordained task left a lot to be desired. The priest smiled.

298

"We're human, you know. We make mistakes. People forget that sometimes."

He was right. I almost regretted having to leave. He was a kind and gentle priest. There was nothing hell-fire-and-damnation about him. In the end he wrote the reference.

Dealing with the Police Presidium was not that easy. That official was not interested in a bribe. He simply did not wish to cooperate. When he finally conceded to do so, he did it with all the dislike he was capable of. He pointed out to me that from this moment on, I was a person without a country. To underline the way he felt, he brought out my certificate of German Citizenship. He tore it in half before he handed it to me. He said that as a German, I no longer existed. I took that certificate and carefully stashed it away with my other papers. I would not lose that. How could one country be so wonderful and its people become so despicable. I did not say it. I was fearful of that bureaucrat. I wanted to spit against his door after I left his office. But I knew that my family would never approve of that. And though I knew my family disowned me, I was still the person they had created.

It was in the fall of 1948 that we arrived at the coast. It was my first sight of the ocean. It was my first sight of the big ships.

"There she is," Alva said. Her name was painted on the bow. It was the ELDON H JOHNSON. The moment I walked up that gangplank, the moment I felt the swaying motion of the ship beneath me, that moment would place an end to all that I had known. I stopped for one brief moment. Was it really wrong to leave? I looked at my husband. He just smiled reassuringly and placed his arm around my shoulder.

Whatever lay ahead of me could not be worse than all the things that lay behind. And I was right to choose a country for the birth of my children, where freedom was a way of life and such matters as peace and war were decided by a government elected by the people.

America was not a disappointment. Life was not always easy. I did not remain a person without a country very long. I earned my citizenship with the help of American friends. The judge who officiated told me that I should always love the country of my birth and that this feeling for my native soil would not interfere with my loyalty to this land, this America.

Uncle Johann was right as well. There are times when I'm homesick. And when I'm homesick, I reach within myself. I remember the village, the gooseherd, the village church, the Angelus and the people reverently praying. I can almost smell the hay in the barn and hear the cattle lowing in the stalls. And I remember the Clay Digs.

I shall always remember Mannheim, as it once had been, with the Linden trees in full bloom and the Buckeye trees with their blossom candelabras all along the Neckar River. And I will see the castle at Heidelberg in my mind's eye. After all, being there is only a thought away.

I knew love of art there. I knew love of intellect and love of nature. I had been taught all these things. That's what makes it so hard to reconcile that this is also the country that drank the blood of fifty-seven million victims. From my perspective all the sacrifices of the Incas, the Mayas, and the Aztecs pale in comparison with that one sacrifice. Russia lost twenty million people. Of those twenty million people, seven million were civilians. Many died in Stalin's Siberian Labor camps. Germany lost 6.8

million. Of those 2.5 million were refugees and 400,000 died as a direct result of air raids. Poland, a small country as it is, lost 4.3 million and of those 4.2 million were civilians. There is no getting around the fact that with the war on Poland, Hitler established a precedent for unconditional warfare from the air, on helpless women and children. Yugoslavia lost 1.7 million. France lost 600,000 thousand, half of those were civilians. England lost 390,000, Rumania 380,000, Czechoslovakia 370,000, Italy 330,00, USA 230,000, Netherlands 210,000, Hungary 140,000, Belgium 90,000, and Denmark 14,000. It is said that those who were guilty never paid for their crimes. All vengeance, all hatred fell on those whose only fault it was to have been born a German, living in the Third Reich. Members of Hitler's elite and his Nationalsozialistische-Deutsche-Arbeiter Partei cashed in their chips, took the money, and left the country. The infamy of such killing fields as Dachau, Auschwitz, Dresden, Berlin, Hiroshima, and Nagasaki will remain with us long after we have ceased to exist. The question is, will those awful memories be sufficient to keep the world from World War III?

HOMECOMING

True to the tradition implanted in me as a child, I took my daughter to the village. We were Anneliese's guests and we made that pilgrimage according to her timetable.

This time we were required to go to all the houses of the people of our clan. The clan, it appeared, had forgiven me. The clan loved my blonde, blue-eyed daughter.

True to tradition we rode the train to Gundelsheim and walked through the forest to Neibsheim. We stopped at the lower village first, although I would have loved to have seen Uncle Johann first.

True to tradition we went to Mass. And nothing there had changed. The deacon still wore his red habit. Children were still at the front, boys to the right, girls to the left. Men still had the pews on the right side; women at the left.

What was not according to tradition was my cousin Anneliese.

"I'm not going to sit with a bunch of smelly old women," she said and went right on to the men's pews. She stopped behind a little bald headed old man.

"That's Uncle Johann," she whispered. It took me awhile to get over the shock. But then I was as unconventional as she was. I bent forward, kissed his bald spot and whispered:

"Hello Uncle Johann."

A tremor went through the old man. But he never flinched. He never turned. He did not acknowledge me until Mass was over. God was first and foremost. After I could get out of the crowd of people around us, I made my way over to Uncle Johann. His eyes

302

still ablaze, bright blue, undimmed by age, his strong voice quavering just a little under the stress of emotions. He looked at me, raised his walking stick and said:

"Gib Deine Seele zu der Scholle nicht!" He said.

"What did he say?" Barbara asked. It was most difficult to translate. But I knew and understood what he said.

"Do not give your soul to the earth." He had given himself to the land. In the end the land was sold because there was no heir. The clan would die out with him. All the young men had died in the war. The stalls were empty of cattle. Hard life had crippled and shrunk his body.

He would not permit an embrace, but he permitted me to take his arm. Together we walked to the farmstead. Aunt Martha, almost bent double by osteoporosis, a toothless grin on her face, walked ahead of us.

Uncle Johann stopped at the entrance. He raised himself as tall as he could and shouted: "Weib Abba!"

Aunt Martha hurried to place food and drink on the table. Then she ushered us into the house.

My daughter looked in my eyes and said: "He wouldn't order me around like that."

It was then I knew I had made the right decision so many years ago.

AFTERWARD BY EDITOR

In late 2015, Elsa Hazell, my grandmother, passed away at home among loved ones and family, bringing to a close the journey she began in this book. Following her death, her son Alva Jr. sought to republish her first self-published book, *And Then There Were None.* I volunteered to edit this book.

I grew up seeing copies of this book, and my grandmother's other books, around our house. Even after the book was originally released in 1999, I did not sit down and read it cover-to-cover. As an adolescent and young adult, I had my own concerns and did not wish to read about anything too serious, especially if my education did not require it. I remember finding the original book and thumbing through it, reading passages and recognizing the content as my family's history. Many of these stories were passed down to me verbally, in some form, and a few I heard from Grandma herself. I met my German relatives and their descendents. I generally knew about my grandmother's history and her adventures. However, I did not know the details.

After my grandmother's death and the second publishing of her second book, my father located an original transcript of *And Then There Were None* and sent it to me. When I looked over it, I quickly realized that I would have to read the book to make the formatting consistent for the second publication. My primary goal was to arrange the format in such a way that the reader could become immersed easily. I did not want the spacing, quotations, or organization to detract from the storytelling. I attempted to keep everything as true to the original phrasing as possible.

While reading this book, I quickly began to realize that it was going to be an emotional experience for me. The text starts out with my grandmother as a child. She introduces a variety of friends, family members, and guardians. As the book progresses, many of these people are lost to the War. For most readers, these people do not exist as humans, but as characters in a book. For me, these people are my history.

Yet I also found several aspects of my grandmother's life conspicuously absent. My grandmother journeyed to the United States with my uncle, Wolfgang, when he was still very small. Growing up, I believed him to be a child of love from one of her romantic interests. My grandmother was glamorous, charismatic, and quite intelligent. As this book demonstrates, she was also spirited and rebellious. It was easy for me to believe that my Uncle Wolf was the result of a romantic union from before my grandmother married my grandfather. As an adult, my family informed me that my grandmother was raped by a German solider. To this day, I still prefer my version. My grandmother took the truth to her grave, as she did Herr Ruebenacker's secret. Her second published history begins on the boat from Germany with Wolfgang.

This story also lacks an epilogue. My grandmother's adventures began in Germany, but her life continued to unfold in waves of both joy and strife in the states. In America, she pursued her education and obtained a Master's degree in education. She taught special education for years. Even after she retired, her ex-students would recognize her in public and introduce their families.

She had an insatiable appetite for nature that permeated every aspect of her life. She had a greenhouse attached to her house with 8-foot tropical trees that would remain green and vibrant, even with snow on the ground outside. She always had pets around, ranging from the perennial dogs and cats to monkeys, seahorses, and hermit crabs that roamed loose in her home. My father recalled a tame turtle living in the house when he was young; the creature would come out in the morning for bacon with fruit and disappear back into unknown regions of my grandmother's personal castle. Elsa rehabilitated wildlife, something I have remembered vividly from the time I was a child. She raised orphaned raccoons, squirrels, skunks, and a fox in complex, human-sized structures built by my grandfather. Even into her later years, I would visit and bring her dinner. She would go into the kitchen and cook an elaborate meal anyway. When I asked, she would explain that the dog must eat too, and it never failed to surprise me when she placed the entire dish on the floor.

My grandmother had an affinity for rocks and artifacts. She would bring back hundred-pound stones in her modest sedan, sometimes from hundreds of miles away, and place them in the yard. Her shelves were decorated with many books, crystals, sea shells, and souvenirs from all over the world. She would give these out freely to those whomever shared her interests. Each came with a story, and they all held greater value than any amount of money. One year she found an alligator on the side of the road in Louisiana. It was dead, having been hit by a vehicle. She brought this home with her and had it stuffed. This large, preserved beast graced her large bookcase for most of my life and, last I knew, is still there.

My grandmother's legacy has also greatly influenced me. She started my fossil and mineral collection, a hobby I still gladly pursue as an adult. She gave me my first saltwater aquarium when I was about nine, and to this day I have no less than a dozen aquariums in my house. I continued to have a special relationship with my grandmother until her death. I would bring her food and small treasures, and she would share with me her experiences. She always encouraged my endeavors with praise and gifts.

It is my hope that my grandmother can continue to influence and encourage others through her written works. It continually amazes me that she survived the War. Despite trauma and surrounded by death, she maintained hope and love of her homeland. She came to the United States and met poverty with ingenuity and spirit. I am thankful that I had the honor of knowing her and that, through this book, you might be able to know her as well.

BIBLIOGRAPHY

Arnscheidt, Grit. et al. Festung, Fuersten, Freie
Buerger. Heidelberg: Brausdruck, 1995.

Huber, Peter. Vor 50 Jahren. Bruchsal: Dorr
G.M.B.H..1996

Jacob, Gustav. Mannheim. Duesseldorf: Droste 1971.

Klein. Diethard, H. et al. Mannheim Ein Lesebuch.
Husum: Husum Druck. 1988.

Pleticha, Erich. Deutsche Geschichte. Volume XI.
Guetersloh: Bertelsmann, 1984.

www.ingramcontent.com/pod-product-compliance
Lightning Source LLC
Chambersburg PA
CBHW051815090426
42736CB00011B/1483